Reputation:
A Network Interpretation

Reputation:
A Network
Interpretation

Kenneth H. Craik

OXFORD
UNIVERSITY PRESS
2009

OXFORD
UNIVERSITY PRESS

Oxford University Press, Inc., publishes works that further
Oxford University's objective of excellence
in research, scholarship, and education.

Oxford   New York
Auckland   Cape Town   Dar es Salaam   Hong Kong   Karachi
Kuala Lumpur   Madrid   Melbourne   Mexico City   Nairobi
New Delhi   Shanghai   Taipei   Toronto

With offices in
Argentina   Austria   Brazil   Chile   Czech Republic   France   Greece
Guatemala   Hungary   Italy   Japan   Poland   Portugal   Singapore
South Korea   Switzerland   Thailand   Turkey   Ukraine   Vietnam

Published by Oxford University Press, Inc.
198 Madison Avenue, New York, New York 10016
www.oup.com

Oxford is a registered trademark of Oxford University Press

Library of Congress Cataloging-in-Publication Data

Craik, Kenneth H.
Reputation: a network interpretation / Kenneth H. Craik.
   p. cm.
Includes bibliographical references and index.
ISBN 978-0-19-533092-2
1. Social perception. 2. Public opinion. 3. Social networks. I. Title.
HM1041.C73 2009
303.3'801—dc22   2008011231

9 8 7 6 5 4 3 2 1
Printed in the United States of America
on acid-free paper

For Jan and fifty wonderful years

Preface

My route to this book on reputation began with my experiences as director of personality assessment programs and has radiated out from them.

From Assessment Centers to Reputational Networks

Over the years I have come to realize that the attraction to my special field of personality theory and assessment has derived from my fascination with the ways we observe each other's everyday conduct and attempt to reach distinctive characterizations of each other.

In personality assessment center programs I have managed at our Institute of Personality and Social Research on the campus of the University of California in Berkeley, ten or twelve staff members observe and interact with ten or twelve participants (e.g., architects, MBA students) over a three-day weekend of activities, such as interviews, leaderless group discussions, role improvisations, and team charades, as well as at meals and social hours. On Monday morning, staff members independently record their impressions of each participant in the form of character sketches and personality trait ratings.

In this way, we create a temporary community of observers for our participants, and on Monday morning we compile our reputation-like impressions and evaluations of them. But naturally occurring reputation emerges from a much different real-world and lifelong network of other individuals who know the person. Thus, when I began my investigations, I looked into the research by anthropologists and sociologists on social networks. I did so with the firm expectation that I would be able to demonstrate that, with regard to our reputation, we each live our lives within a small village-like social setting. And yes, indeed, even within highly populated urban settings, the evidence points to typical social network sizes in the hundreds or thousands, rather than tens of thousands or more.

Yet there is another side to the story. To my surprise, recent developments in network theory suggest that our reputational networks are better characterized as typically provincial but potentially global or boundless. For this and other reasons, I have had to expand the notion of "social network" to a new and broader concept of "reputational network."

From Independent Observer Descriptions to Chat and Gossip

In order to calculate statistically the degree of agreement among staff members in their descriptions of each assessment center participant, it is necessary to enforce the strict rule of no discussions among staff members regarding the participants during an assessment center program. Such discussion must wait until after their individual Monday morning descriptive recordings are completed.

It is tempting to think that in social life individuals also form their impressions, beliefs, and evaluations of a person independently, based entirely upon their own personal observations and interactions with the person. But, of course, that is not the case; we delight in chatting and gossiping about other persons.

As an assessment center manager, I have come to realize how difficult it is, especially for junior staff, to adhere to this rule and to acknowledge the artificial condition it creates. Contexts in which such discourse is ruled out are rare. The temptation is strong to share and discuss seemingly important or merely telling tidbits of information about specific participants. The discursive facet of reputation deals with this ongoing discourse about specific persons.

From Assessment Centers to the Libel Court of London

The pervasive presence of hearsay communication within a reputational network raises the prospect that error and falsehood about the person will enter and flow along unknown routes throughout it. During the times I have lived in London, I became fascinated by the heavy newspaper coverage of libel cases held in the Royal Courts of Justice at the head of Fleet Street. In certain technical ways, action for libel and slander is easier to bring by plaintiffs in England than it is in the United States.

I reasoned that the age-old legal process for defending individual reputations must hold lessons for a student of reputation. I began reviewing libel cases in the legal journals at the Supreme Court Library there, looking in on libel cases in process in the courtrooms and reading the standard, and very hefty, law textbooks, such as *Carter-Ruck on Libel and Slander*, as well as lively commentary on specific cases, such as David Hooper's *Reputations Under Fire*. After all, here was a repository of thoughtful argument and reflection on the fate of reputations in real-life contexts. I discovered that network concepts and issues pervade the assumptions and framework of actions for defamation in the English common-law tradition. I later set about empirical research on the characteristics of the disreputable acts at the heart of each of 184 successful libel cases.

From Personality to Posthumous Reputation

From the outset, I had vowed to examine the matter of posthumous reputation, if only because the phenomenon establishes an intrinsic distinction between personality and reputation. Personality treats the individual as an agent of self-reflexive and integrated action. Reputation is comprised of what is generally said and believed about the person; its locus is in the person's reputational network. With death, the former ceases but the latter need not do so. In fact, I was eventually surprised to find that some of the most novel implications of a network interpretation of reputation yield a better understanding of posthumous reputation.

The lifetime reputational network encompasses the surviving network members generated during the person's own lifetime, which includes the chorus of survivors and the keepers of the flame. The transitional posthumous reputational network comprises the posthumous surviving lifetime members plus the overlapping new posthumous members including those recruited through an evolving biographical network. Ultimately, the biographical network will spin off and prevail as the major locus of the person's posthumous reputational network, along perhaps with a continuing remembrance within the oral tradition of the families of the person and of the person's associates.

In my explorations of these interconnected facets of reputation, I have become convinced that reputational analysis has a sufficiently broad and unexamined agenda to constitute a distinct new field of inquiry. My first draft chapter dealt with the size of social networks (now Chapter 1) and my second summarized the process and structure of actions for defamation (now Chapter 8). The other chapters have grown out of my steady articulation of the network model of reputation.

From this network interpretation of reputation, we have two rallying cries. First, a reputation is a phenomenon sharply distinct from a person. The reputational network of a person begins to form prior to birth and continues for briefer or longer durations beyond death. Reputation is in the social environment, not in the head of the person. Reputation is in the heads of other persons and in their everyday chat and discourse. Reputations can affect persons; persons can affect reputations. Epistemologically, from reputation we can come to know something about a person; from the person we can come to know something about a reputation. Nevertheless, a reputation and a person are distinct realities, ontologically.

To make this point crisply, Part I of this book is devoted to reputation. We keep the person as a possible agent of reputation under wraps until Part II.

Second, reputations exist only within reputational networks. The notion of reputational networks organizes this book. Because the reputational network is an original conceptual contribution, Part I will necessarily be less familiar to the reader. It will be interesting but in ways different from Part II, which deals with such topics as managing, defending, and rehabilitating reputation, which are more familiar, accessible, and immediately engaging. My initial tactic is to acknowledge this difference up front and invite and challenge you, the reader, to join me in thinking in a different and innovative way about reputation. The challenge for us is to grasp a new perspective on reputation—one that might be at odds with preconceptions—and to discover how it leads us to a comprehensive integration of reputation's many aspects. Even so, this approach will allow us, at relevant points, to look ahead to some of those more accessible and immediately engaging topics that will be addressed more fully in Part II.

In the course of our analysis of reputation, we will move from medieval Lucchese courtrooms in Tuscany to the libel court of contemporary London, from the social networks of residents of Florida to the publicity agencies of Hollywood celebrities, from George Washington to Virginia Woolf. Reputation is a fascinating phenomenon, and I hope this book will do it justice.

Acknowledgments

My focus on reputation began twenty years ago. At that time, venues for presenting my initial notions on the topic were afforded me by Rob Farr in the Department of Social Psychology at the London School of Economics and Political Science and by the late Michael Argyle at the Department of Experimental Psychology at the University of Oxford. Further efforts were supported by a 1988–1989 James McKeen Cattell Fund Sabbatical Leave Award.

I am grateful for the assistance of the staff of the London Library, the Supreme Court Library of the Royal Civil Court, the Social Science Library of the London School of Economics and Political Science, and the libraries of the University of California at Berkeley.

I am much obliged to Robert W. Levenson, director, and my colleagues at the Institute of Personality and Social Research for their support. Jennifer Quan and Elizabeth Peele helped to produce usable figures for the book. Thanks to Amy Craik and Ken Craik for help with the computer. Lori Handelman and Jennifer Rappaport, my editors at Oxford University Press, have provided wonderful assistance and enthusiastic encouragement.

I am indebted to colleagues who have discussed reputation with me or who have read and commented on early writings related to this book. They include the late Theodore R. Sarbin, Robert Hogan, Anne Tsai, Dennis B. Bromley, Nicholas Emler, Daniel J. Ozer, John G. Darley, Geraldine Moane, Carolyn Phinney, Robert R. McCrae, Avril Thorne, Richard W. Robins, Thomas Priestley, David M. Buss, Aaron P. Ware, Michael Shopshire, Gerald A. Mendelsohn, and William McKinley Runyan. For reading and commenting on draft chapters of this book, I thank Simine Vazire, Randall C. Young, Samuel D. Gosling, Brian R. Little, Maria Logli Allison, Eliot R. Smith, Robert C. Post, and David Lowenthal. I have been encouraged to continue to pursue this topic by my many useful conversations with Maria Logli Allison and David Lowenthal.

I take full and sole responsibility, of course, for the errors, inaccuracies, and wrongheaded notions that remain in this book.

Thanks to Luigi Boccherini, Tomaso Albinoni, Marin Marais, Maurice Andre, Thelonious Monk, and the Modern Jazz Quartet for a facilitating musical environment.

Thanks to Jan and to Amy, Emily, Jen, John, Ken, and Lynn for a warm and supportive family environment. I am happy to have this book to dedicate to Jan.

Contents

Introduction

Reputations Within Networks

This book argues that a network interpretation of reputation advances our understanding of an essential and inescapable feature of social life and integrates many of its varied facets.

Reputation is not located on or in a person, like a left elbow or a knack for languages. Reputation is a dispersed phenomenon that is to be found in the beliefs and assertions of an extensive number of other individuals. Having a reputation has to do with an external, extended, and distributed entity, rather more like owning a vineyard or apple orchard than having a limb or a gift for languages. Reputation is part of the social environment but uniquely referenced to a specific person. Discussions concerning reputation are often vague with regard to who are those others holding beliefs or making assertions about a person and thereby contributing to that person's reputation, with reference perhaps to "people in general" or "society at large." But in principle, those others are specifiable, finite in number, and unique to each person.

A network model of reputation generates conceptual innovations that have systematic implications for such diverse disciplines as network theory and social network analysis, gossip research, person perception and cognition, social representation research, personality theory and assessment, publicity and public relations, libel law, biographical studies, and cultural history.

For purposes of reputation analysis, we must explicate the person's relation to every other individual, as shown in Table Intro.1.

Cell A encompasses the person's social network, those who know the person and are known by the person. Cell B is also centrally relevant to reputation with regard to prevailing common knowledge, encompassing that perhaps surprisingly large number of individuals who know the person but are not known by the person. A less relevant asymmetry is depicted by cell C, constituted by those individuals the person does know but who do not know the person. These individuals do not contribute to the person's reputation even though the person plays a minor role in their reputation as fan, voter, informant, or other observer and commentator on public lives and celebrities. Finally, cell D reminds us that even with modern telecommunication, we do not know nor are we known by billions of other individuals.

Over the course of social participation and acquaintance, each of us generates a lifelong reputational network that is not exactly like that of anyone else.

Table Intro.1 Reputational Network

		Other knows person	
		Yes	No
	Yes	Social network members A	Local and public figures C
Person knows other			
	No	Unseen audience B	Everybody else D

Overview

In the first three chapters of Part I we will direct our attention to three major themes for the study of a person's reputation that provide conceptual continuity throughout the book.

First, we will consider the membership of a person's reputational network, that is, those other individuals who in some minimal sense know or recognize the person and thus are in a position to form impressions, beliefs, and evaluations concerning the person and to express and discuss them with others (Chapter 1).

As our second theme, we will sketch out the ongoing social communication process through which news, observations, and impressions about an individual circulate along that person's reputational network via chat, gossip, and more formal means (Chapter 2).

Our third theme will deal with the ways in which each member of a person's reputational network gathers and cumulates impressions, beliefs, and evaluations about that specifically identifiable person. This network of cognitive nodes, or *person bins*, constitutes the distributive facet of reputation (Chapter 3).

These theoretical elements generate two major aspects of reputation: the discursive facet, dealing with actively flowing information, and the distributive facet, dealing with latent stored information about the person. They constitute the two forms in which the common knowledge of the specific person is socially represented (Chapter 4).

The final chapter of Part I addresses a central feature in most meanings of reputation—the content claims about attributes of the person. The truth of these claims entails two issues: the accuracy of the claims as representative of what is actually being said and believed about the person, in contrast to the validity of the claims themselves as checked against other sources of knowledge about the person (Chapter 5).

Thus, Part I focuses upon our network interpretation of reputation. In Part II, we broaden our perspective to encompass topics dealing with the relation of person and reputation.

Chapter 6 considers the person as both agent and resultant of reputation. For example, a thorough analysis of reputation management demands attention to its pragmatics. In doing so, we will examine the craft wisdom to be found in the professional realm of reputation management that is increasingly available to public figures, celebrities, and corporations.

In Chapter 7, we will explore the mutual relevance of reputation and personality, two important constructs that appear to address the same question: What kind of person is this individual? A primary claim of our network interpretation is that the reputation of a person resides within the social system. At the same time, constructs such as the self-concept and social image and tactics of reputational management can be formulated as reputation-relevant elements of the personality system.

In Chapter 8, we will mobilize our network interpretation to analyze in detail a classic venue for taking action in defense of one's reputation—the libel courts. A network structure is implicit in key elements of the rationale and structure of common-law actions for defamation.

Finally, our theoretical framework generates not just one but three reputational networks for each person: the lifetime network, the posthumous network, and between them for several decades their overlapping coexistence as a transitional network (Chapter 9).

In the Conclusion, I will argue that reputation is not simply a central topic for the study of social life. Rather, it holds the potential to sustain an interdisciplinary field of inquiry in its own right. We will explore those prospects guided by our network interpretation of reputation.

PART I

Reputational Networks

I

Where Do We Look for Reputation?

A Person's Lifelong and Distinctive
Reputational Network

Every Person's Own Small Village

In order to keep some hold on the notion of reputation and to prevent it
from floating away into a stratosphere of vague generalities, we must securely
tie a specific person's reputation to that individual's own particular network
of other persons. The nature of a person's lifelong personal community bears
upon the parameters and characteristics of the person's reputation.

Identification Within a Person's Lifelong Reputational Network

At the end of an individual's life, that person has been acquainted with or
known by not everybody else in the world but a finite number of other persons. Those other persons have observed and otherwise acquired information
about the individual, have formed various beliefs and evaluations on that
basis, and have probably chatted with many others regarding their impressions

of the person. Somehow, out of these observations, impressions, and discussions, the reputation of a specific individual emerges.

Recognition Identity

For the purpose of exploring reputations, the issue of identity can be approached in a pragmatic fashion. Other persons must be able to recognize that the fellow who helped the old gentleman cross the street is the same chap who volunteered to assist in the charity drive and who also loaned you some power tools. Furthermore, when two or more others gather to chat, they must be able to identify clearly the specific nonpresent person they are discussing. Facial image and name typically suffice for establishing what we will call "recognition identity."

Other, more complex notions of identity will become pertinent later in our analysis. For example, each person has a wealth of social attributes that are relevant for characterizing what has been termed a person's "social identity" (Abrams & Hogg, 1990). Finally, each person develops a self-conscious, "insider" notion of who he or she is, which is referred to as an individual's "personal identity" (Cheek, 1988).

Recognition identity is a central concept when anthropologists and sociologists examine individual social networks. Other persons typically count as members of a person's social network if they can be expected to identify the individual by face or name. Later, we will learn that research on gossip sessions shows that a preliminary step in the sequence is to be sure everybody is talking about the same person. Once that is settled, the gossipers can "let loose." Furthermore, in bringing legal action for libel or slander, it must be demonstrated at the outset that the allegedly defamatory assertions refer specifically to the plaintiff and not somebody else (Milmo & Rogers, 1998; Sack & Baron, 1994).

In small intact villages, face and name are surefire indicators of a person's distinctive identity. In large, modern, mobile societies, the matter has become increasingly problematic. Personal signatures, facial photographic representations, and various identification (ID) numbers have become widely accepted surrogates for the direct presence of the person. The conveniences afforded by this practice must be counterbalanced against the risk of *identity theft*, in which actions are taken fraudulently "in the name" of the person, such as money withdrawals from bank accounts, consumer purchases, Internet communications, and other social actions that may impinge upon and distort a person's reputation, as well as being harmful to one's financial well-being.

Reputational Network Parameters: Size and Patterning

Social network research suggests that persons live their lives within their own unique and relatively small villages, whether these personal communities are spatially concentrated or widely dispersed (Webber, 1970; Wellman, Carrington, & Hall, 1988). Because social network analysis deals with others who are known to the person, the target person has typically served as the main source of information in delineating social network membership for research purposes.

Estimating the Size of Individual Social Networks

Social network research offers only a handful of empirical studies that estimate the size of ordinary persons' social networks. Some authorities on the social network research literature (e.g., Marsden, 2005) tend to cite relatively conservative estimates, such as the figure of 290 reported by McCarty, Killworth, Bernard, Johnson, & Shelley (2001). Others, such as McCue (2002), take account of more ambitious and varied modes of elicitation which yield substantially higher estimates of average social network size that hover around 1,700; these estimates include 2,025 (Freeman & Thompson, 1989; Killworth, Johnsen, Bernard, Shelley, & McCarty, 1990), 1,702 (Killworth et al., 1990), 1,391 (Bernard et al., 1990), and 2,130 (see Guervich, 1961), with a wide range (e.g., from 122 to 5,053 in Guervich, 1961). In his pioneering study of two villages in Malta, Boissevain (1974) cited average sizes of 638 in Cecil and 1,753 in Pietro.

An example of an ambitious approach is illustrated by the Network Suite, an illustrative computer-based elicitation procedure (Bernard et al., 1990) that entails four modules aimed at aiding a person in the challenging task of evoking as much as possible about her or his entire social network. Module 1 deals with intimate member nominations, asking you to list all individuals with whom you discuss important matters. Module 2 entails 11 probes eliciting nominations with regard to social support (e.g., from whom could you borrow money?) and social roles (e.g., coworkers, in-laws). Module 3, the reversed small world technique, presents a standard list of 500 names of individuals along with their purported worldwide locations and occupations; the task is to nominate members of one's own social network who would be an effective first intermediary for conveying a message to each target individual. Module 4, the telephone directory prompter, presents a list of 305 names drawn randomly from a large-city telephone directory; the task is to list any and all specific individuals you have ever known with each last name listed. The number of nominees is scaled up or prorated to the total of names listed in the directory.

Given the difficulties of bringing to mind every individual a person has known over a lifetime, the resulting findings on network size are likely to be underestimates. Note also that modules 1 and 2 are name generators, evoking specific affectional and social support members, while modules 3 and 4 seek simply to estimate directly the total size of the social network.

An enumeration gap can be seen in the results of these procedures: for example, the intimate members yielded by module 1 account for only one-half of 1% of the global size estimate of module 4; the percentages for module 2 and module 3 against module 4 are only 3% and 10%, respectively. Thus, the central core represents a small component of social networks and, as we shall see, presumably even less of reputational networks.

Much of social network research has focused upon the small central realm, with results tending to show that an active and secure core of members offering affectional and social support enhances personal well-being (Campbell & Lee, 1991; Fischer, 1982; van der Poel, 1993). But for the purposes of reputational analysis, which deals with the flow of information about a person rather than the sources of social support available to the person, the remaining 90% of the social network requires comparable research attention. Furthermore, the size of membership in the cell B sector of the reputational network must also be estimated and, to the extent possible, delineated (see Table Intro.1).

Estimating the Size of a Person's Reputational Network

Thus far, we have focused upon the first tier of the person's reputational network, that is, the social network component. Since reputation consists of the impressions, beliefs, and evaluations of all those who know the person, the research agenda of reputational analysis must face the task of exploring the ripple effect that generates the membership of the outer tiers of a person's reputational network (e.g., friends of friends, friends of acquaintances of friends). Estimating the size of tier 2 or 3 from tier 1 requires additional information on the density and clustering patterns of tier 1 (Newman, 2003).

In the Introduction, we used Table Intro.1 to depict a person's relation to every other individual. Recall that cell A signifies the person's social network (the other knows the person, the person knows the other). Cell B fills out the membership of the reputational network (the other knows the person, the person does not know the other). A less relevant component, cell C, is constituted of those others the person knows but who do not know the person (e.g., public figures). Finally, cell D is comprised of the billions of others who do not know the person and are not known by the person.

At first glance, Table Intro.1 may appear to be painfully obvious, but its implications will become evident as we proceed.

The categories represented by cells A and B indicate an essential structural feature of reputational networks: levels of awareness. The members of cell A are known to the person and constitute the first tier of a person's reputational network.

Cell B members include unattended observers and bystanders from the person's typical lived day, such as regulars in an espresso café, bus drivers on the daily commute route, and others who may form only a part of the hazy social background for the person but who may be asymmetrically much more closely attentive to that person.

Other cell B members may be drawn from friends, coworkers, or relatives of the person's direct acquaintances who may, over the supper table, be the ongoing recipients of a cumulative storehouse of social facts, anecdotes, and act descriptions of this person they have never met and, thus, become hearsay-only members of the person's reputational network. Furthermore, any of these network members may in turn pass on information about the person to happenstance acquaintances (e.g., strangers on a train, back-fence neighbors).

Over the course of social participation and acquaintance, each of us generates a lifelong reputational network that is not exactly like that of anyone else.

Thus, as Table Intro.1 indicates, those others within cell B represent reputational network members who may observe and discuss the person without the person knowing them or even being aware of their existence.

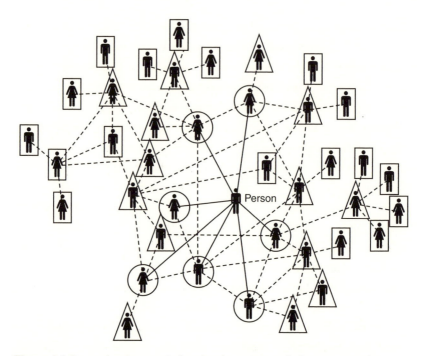

Figure 1.1 Reputational network showing three tiers: *circle*, first tier; *triangle*, second tier; *rectangle*, third tier.

Figure 1.1 is derived from a figure developed by Duncan J. Watts to illustrate facets of social networks, in his volume *Six Degrees: The Science of a Connected Age* (2003). In our version, Figure 1.1 shows that cell B members can be considered to form a second tier, who are once removed from the person's direct acquaintance, a third tier twice removed, and so on.

In future research of this kind, two supplementary name generator tactics can be employed using the person as the source of network member nominations. First, we have seen that social network research has tended to focus upon social support and the inner core of members with positive or at least neutral relations to the person. One tactic is to urge the person to identify possible competitors, rivals, or even enemies. A second tactic concerns the often unattended background attributes of a person's social environment. For example, the person might be asked to identify typical behavior settings of his or her daily routine and to focus more closely upon identifying other regulars typically found there as candidates for status as peripheral reputational network members.

A more ambitious elicitation strategy would shift the emphasis to the social network membership, including peripheral members. In this process, members of the first tier would be asked to confirm that they know the person by face and/or name. They would then be asked to identify any relatives, friends, neighbors, and other acquaintances and passing strangers to whom they have talked about the person. These second-tier nominees would then be contacted to confirm that they have talked about the person with one or more individuals, although they may not know the person directly. They would then be asked to identify other individuals they have in turn talked to about the person. This process would continue in a snowball fashion (Newman, 2003).

We can now appreciate why this procedure is even more challenging than identifying and enumerating the cell A social network component. But it must be explored as fully as is logistically possible in order to articulate and analyze a comprehensive network interpretation of reputation.

Occasionally, the police are forced to make use of resource-intensive snowballing procedures of this kind, for example, when a person has gone missing and foul play is suspected. One of the largest missing person inquiries in recent British history dealt with the disappearance of Suzy Lamplugh, a 25-year-old estate agent at noontime on July 28, 1986, from her office in the Fulham section of central London. In thoroughly reconstructing her extensive social network, investigators came to realize that this task was made difficult because Suzy had kept several subsets of her many acquaintances unaware of each other (Stephen, 1988). Sadly, neither this effort nor other clues resulted in her discovery, either alive or dead. After a recent two-year reinvestigation, police concluded they had insufficient evidence to charge their prime suspect, now serving a life sentence for another murder (Hopkins, 2002). If this man is indeed her murderer, he had probably been a complete stranger to Suzy Lamplugh and not a prior member of her extensive social network.

From Small Village to Small World

The formal pattern of interconnectedness within networks can range from low to high density. At one extreme, none of those who know the person knows each other; at the other extreme, all who know the person also know each other. The density estimates reported in social network research are calculated as the proportion of observed linkages among members over the total of all possible linkages and tend to range between 8 and 36% (Pool & Kochen, 1978; van der Poel, 1993). However, the network elicitation methods employed appear to tilt them toward overestimates of density.

In any event, the typical structural pattern of networks can be further described as a set of clustered interconnections. That is, most persons have subsets of acquaintances who know one another, while some persons may have acquaintances who are mostly strangers to each other. In an isolated mountain village, for example, perhaps all the other individuals who know a given person also know each other. Under these conditions of highly dense social networks, information about the person is likely to spread quite rapidly and comprehensively. Furthermore, because everyone is acquainted with everyone else, the likelihood of a consensual portrait of the person emerging may be relatively higher than in case of low-density or clustered social networks.

Consider the comparison with modern urban life, where the degree of segmentation among a person's social network has steadily increased. In a village funeral, those attending know not only the deceased but probably each other. In striking contrast, those present at an urban funeral may know only a handful of others from a shared social context (e.g., some from the family, some from the neighborhood, some from the work setting, some from the bowling team, some from voluntary organizations, etc.) (Bowman, 1959; Craik, 1985; Webber, 1970). Statistical techniques can be usefully mobilized to identify subclusters or cliques of this kind within a social network.

Change and continuity in social networks across the life span have received only sporadic research attention (Fischer, Jackson, Stueve, Gerson, & Jones, 1977; Suitor, Wellman, & Morgan, 1997). Most studies of personal networks have measured such attributes as size, density, composition, and duration and then related these characteristics to such potential influences as gender, socioeconomic status, degree of urbanization, and life-cycle stage (van der Poel, 1993). For the time being, we can rest content in drawing upon social network analysis to contrast it with our more expanded notion of reputational analysis and to highlight the two most important network features for understanding social communication about specific persons, namely, network size and density.

In his classic contribution to the analysis of network structure, Granovetter (1973) examined the functions of strong and weak ties between a person and the other members of her or his social network. The *strength of ties* refers to the extent to which the person and a network member spend time together, share activities, offer emotional support, confide intimately with each other, and exchange reciprocal services and resources. Strong ties entail several of these attributes; weak ties feature few of them or are limited to mutual recognition and acknowledgment.

Granovetter (1973) reasoned that strong ties constitute the building blocks for a highly dense social network structure. If the person maintains strong ties with members B and C, then B and C are likely to be acquainted with each other, perhaps to the extent of sharing moderate to strong ties with each other. The multiple beneficial functions of strong ties are evident in providing personal and social support. At the same time, basic logistical constraints are likely to limit the number of strong ties that can be developed and sustained within a person's social network.

From a comparative point of view, what functions might weak ties serve? Granovetter (1973) identifies weak ties as serving as potential bridges for the flow of information and influence to a wider realm than that represented by the dense clustering of strong ties. A member with weak ties to the person is likely to sustain few additional ties to that person's network. Nevertheless, that member will offer the person a bridge to that member's own social network. Thus, via this member, a weak tie will afford a wider array of distinctive sources of information and influence. In contrast, the information and influence that come to a person by means of members with strong ties are likely to be redundant and, in that sense, provincial.

In illustrating his argument, Granovetter drew upon his empirical studies of the social process of getting a job (Granovetter, 1974). In New England in the 1970s, before the advent of job search websites, information about job openings was sought through personal contacts. In an analysis of the ties between recent job changers and their effective informants or contact persons, he found support for his structural thesis: "those to whom we are weakly tied are more likely to move in circles different from our own and will thus have access to information different from that which we receive otherwise" (Granovetter, 1973, p. 1371). More generally, he viewed weak bridging ties as "channels through which ideas, influences and information socially distant" may reach a person (Granovetter, 1973, pp. 1370–1371).

As reputation analysts, we can immediately see an important reverse corollary. The flow of information about the person that is communicated by members with strong ties is likely to stay local and to circulate narrowly within core clusters of the social network. In contrast, information about the person communicated by members with weak ties is likely to be communicated more broadly, forming reputational bridges to more remote networks, indeed, even to those unfamiliar to the person. Weak ties that serve as bridges in this way augment the person's unseen audience.

In his 1973 article, Granovetter cited the small world phenomenon identified by Milgram (1967) as another context for testing his argument concerning the function of weak ties. Milgram had shifted inquiry from the small villages of typical individuals to the overarching global networks that might or might not link all six billion of us. From this perspective we might readily consider ourselves to reside in an immense, dispersed, remote, and bewildering world.

Milgram's studies suggested that any two persons on the globe can be connected—for example, for the purpose of sending a message from one to the other—by means of a surprisingly limited number of intervening direct acquaintance contacts.

This bridging function plays a central role in the so-called small world phenomenon articulated and demonstrated by Milgram (1967; Korte & Milgram, 1970; Kleinfeld, 2002). The assertion was that any two persons on the globe are connected within six degrees of separation. In Milgram's directed search task, a sample of initial senders was instructed to forward a message packet to the acquaintance most likely to move the packet toward an ultimate recipient; the second sender does the same until the packet reaches the recipient. For example, in one sample of senders, a total of 24% of messages reached the target recipient, using a mean of 5.7 intermediaries; in a second sample, 31% of the chains were successful using a mean of 5.4 intermediaries (Travers & Milgram, 1969).

Formally, Watts (2003) and other network theorists have shown through graph theory that a few random connections within a set of tightly interconnected clusters of points dramatically reduce the length of pathways for information transmission. Analysis of computer simulations of social networks tends to show a formal pattern of clustered density with bridging shortcuts to other clustered densities (Watts, 2003; Watts & Strogatz, 1998). Thus, graph theory makes the small world phenomenon plausible. However, tests of empirical confirmation have proven to be difficult. Kleinfeld (2002) found that surprisingly few direct replications of the small world phenomenon have been reported. In an ongoing ambitious Internet study, entailing a world-wide set of eighteen target recipients and samples of senders in 150 countries, the completion rate was running at less than 1% (Watts, 2003, pp. 134–135). The samples of initial volunteer senders were committed, but apparently apathy was taking a severe toll on secondary and subsequent senders. Nevertheless, compared to incomplete chains, successful chains disproportionately entailed professional and work ties rather than friendship and familial links, thus supporting a stronger role for "weak ties" (Dodd, Muhamad, & Watts, 2003).

Implications for Reputational Network Analysis

Even when successful, the senders need not and typically are not aware of the full chain of links in the pathway to the ultimate receiver. Rather, the senders draw upon local knowledge without awareness of the entire successful chain (Killworth & Bernard, 1978; Kleinberg, 2000). In this regard, the term "small world" is misleading, in that the initial sender need not be directly linked to the ultimate recipient or to other senders in the chain. Between the initial sender and the ultimate recipient are not simply a handful of individuals but the all-important bridges linking networks to successive networks.

The pathway need not be retraceable or recoverable. Thus, for example, a false and defamatory assertion may travel quickly or slowly across the globe but in ways that cannot be subsequently identified for purposes of reputation correction and rehabilitation. Other individuals can send reputational information about a person far beyond the person's own local and known network. Cascades of information about the person may also flow through the contemporary international media due to the person's association with an attention-getting news story. In summary, although a person's reputation may seem to reside in one or more local village-like clustered densities within everyday life, a boundless potential for an expanded cell B component of the person's reputational network also exists.

Life-Span Dynamics of Reputational Networks

A person's reputational network is assumed to take the form of clustered densities with bridging overlaps to other networks and with varying zones of awareness on the part of the person. The lifelong generation of a reputational network is a process over which the person has varying levels of initiative and choice.

Few longitudinal studies of personal networks have been reported. Burt (2000) cites only eighteen out of 365 articles published in *Social Networks*, and only a handful address issues of change and decay in network ties. The estimated pattern is that only 5% of nominated work ties, 32% of nominated non-kin social ties, and 47% of nominated family ties survive over four years. Bridge ties that connect two otherwise unlinked clusters, which play a distinctive role in transmitting nonredundant information, decay quickly; in a large organization, bridge ties showed a bit more than 1% survival after four years (Burt, 2002). In Burt's analyses, decay does not signify disappearance; for example, it can refer to whether a banker cites others as having frequent and substantial business contacts during a previous year. With regard to reputational networks, colleagues who have received less attention and fewer social initiatives from a banker may nevertheless have continued to maintain a cognitive person bin for that banker (see Chapter 3).

The broad outlines of this dynamic lifelong process can be discerned in Anthony Powell's renowned twelve-volume novel *A Dance to the Music of Time*. The novel follows its narrator Nicholas Jenkins through much of his life and social circle in twentieth-century England, from childhood into his sixties, introducing over 400 of his acquaintances along the way (Powell, 1951–1975; Spurling, 1977).

The sequence of social contexts from which Jenkins' lifelong, idiographic network is generated includes his childhood home and neighborhood, his early schools, his college, his colleagues in publishing, his wife's family and friends, his military posts during World War II, and his return to the London world of publishing. With regard to a network's members in general, initially of course most are older, then after Jenkins reaches midlife the drift is that most are younger. But siblings, playmates, school acquaintances, work peers, and other generational cohort members remain the same age as Jenkins—first young, then old. In childhood, parents and parental acquaintances continue to be older and then decrease in number. Indeed, deaths and funerals become a fairly steady form of event and social occasion. Finally, within Jenkins' own family, his offspring and their associates are younger and increase in number.

His network members are spatially and temporally varied. Some are fairly constant presences; some disappear and permanently drop from view. Some reappear in more or less predictable ways (e.g., at weddings and reunion dinners). Others reappear at seemingly surprising and certainly unanticipated occasions (e.g., at protest parades, art exhibits, or conferences).

Powell reminds us that many of our reputational network members seem beyond our choice or control (e.g., friends of friends, other guests at a dinner party). Accompanying every new acquaintance whom we may actively and selectively seek out comes her or his own social network, into which communications about ourselves may soon readily flow, thereby expanding our reputational network in ways that will remain indeterminant from our own vantage point and perhaps beyond our awareness (see also van der Poel, 1993, pp. 47–48). Certain figures in Jenkins' network turn up repeatedly in unlikely contexts, quite independently of his or the other individual's volition, preference, or plan. Although various acquaintances may rarely or never reappear, they remain holders of beliefs, evaluations, and impressions of Jenkins. In this sense, a person's reputational network is cumulative and dispersed even though some rather large portion remains "inactive," perhaps increasingly and selectively so with age (Carstensen, 1992; Lang, 2000). The spreading process may entail only intermittent encounters, but the rippling effect is incremental over the life course with regard to continuing and scattered communication among others about the person.

Powell's novel embodies the sense that social life takes place within an endlessly surprising and tightly interconnected social world. He stresses the seemingly haphazard but perhaps patterned appearance and reappearance of acquaintances and even acquaintances of acquaintances. As one commentator notes, "When lives cross in time, when we meet a stranger on the Munich express who turns out to be the uncle of a neighbor in Ohio, we feel a kind of unseen power at large in the world. The probabilities are against such encounters, yet all people seem to express them, and repeatedly" (Brennan, 1974, p. 130). And, of course, the meeting on the train offers an occasion for the two strangers to chat and update each other about their acquaintance in Ohio, within whose reputational network they share membership.

One's parental family is a given, of course, beyond choice. But Powell makes clear that accompanying every new acquaintance we may actively and selectively seek out and maintain comes her or his own social network, into which communications about ourselves may circulate, thereby expanding our reputational networks in ways that will remain uncertain and fortuitous from our own vantage point. And these new social networks become interlinked with others in quite extensive snowballing fashion (van der Poel, 1993, pp. 47–48). Indeed, these mundane interlinkages have come to constitute the conceptual building blocks, within contemporary social science, for "ground–up" microanalyses of social structure and community (Fischer, 1982; Wellman et al., 1988). Change in a reputational network may come through new initiatives on the person's part (e.g., taking up a new hobby or work project, with its attendant new set of acquaintances) (Watts, 2003). But new third-tier hearsay network members may also accrue when one of that individual's direct acquaintances takes up a new hobby or work project. In that way, a person's reputational network can be expanded via decisions made by others and entirely outside the knowledge or control of the person. Thus, over the life course, the dynamic evolution of one's reputational network is a process of constrained choice and murky awareness.

Fame and Celebrity

We have seen that the typical social networks of ordinary persons probably number a few thousand, with moderately dense structure at the center and with the core twenty or so individuals linked among themselves in 30%–40% of all possible ties. However, estimates of social network size vary widely among individuals. In one of the first studies (Pool & Kochen, 1978), the estimates for just a 100-day contact period ranged from 72 to 1,404 different others. As a working assumption, let us estimate an average lifelong social network (cell A) of 2,000 others and an average cell B of 2,000 others, for a total average reputational network size of 4,000 others.

One obvious constraint on the size of social networks is the cognitive limit on how many other individuals a given person can validly claim to know, even at the minimal level of recognition identification. Research in social cognition has not addressed the scope of this capacity to maintain recognition of specific other individuals, including direct acquaintances, historical person-ages, public figures, and celebrities (see cells A and C, Table I.1).

In any event, the maximum number of individuals a person can know is wildly exceeded by the number of others who might claim to know that person, especially in light of modern modes of mass communication. Huge asymmetrical reputational networks are the hallmark of fame, celebrity, and notoriety (see cell B, Table Intro.1).

In any event, fame is more than simply social network size. One concep-tion of fame is offered by the novelist and essayist Milan Kundera (2006, p. 40): "Let us try to sharpen the terminology: a man becomes famous when the number of people who know him is markedly greater than the number he knows. . . . Fame is a disequilibrium."

In our framework, then, the size of cell B (in Table Intro.1) must exceed that of the social network (cell A).

We have no good research to guide us in estimating how many oth-ers may know a person whom the person does not reciprocally know. We have seen that given the everyday phenomenon of communications among friends of friends and acquaintances of acquaintances, the size of an ordinary person's total reputational network can be many times the size of the social network.

In the case of public figures and celebrities, the augmentation accompa-nying this disequilibrium in asymmetrical relations may be enormous. Alex-ander III of Macedonia, known as Alexander the Great, was without doubt one of the first very widely known individuals, as indicated by the spread throughout his extensive empire of coinage with his actual or purported facial image or name (Braudy, 1986; Hammond, 1980; Fredricksmeyer, 2000; Throx-ell, 1997). While his own efforts to enhance his posthumous fame favorably by selecting his own historians had mixed results (Bamm, 1968), he clearly evidenced a very contemporary "ambition to stand out from the crowd, to be known to those not known to one, to make an impact on time" (Gamson, 1994, p. 16). Indeed, "for the worldwide scale of his grappling with the prob-lems of fame and his constant awareness of the relation between accomplish-ment and publicity, Alexander deserves to be called the first famous person" (Braudy, 1986, p. 32). In later chapters we will return to the publicity industry and to the many strategies available for the self-conscious production and management of reputational networks.

Nowadays, any one of us might become as well-known as Alexander the Great was, through the mass media's potential to create unsought celebrity. A person can become the recipient of unbidden worldwide fame inadvertently because of some indirect association with notorious events, such as a hostage situation. We will see in later chapters how unsought status as a public figure can lead to severe restrictions on one's ability to bring defamation action and legally defend one's reputation. Of course, it can also result in various forms of commercial gain, through publications and product endorsements.

Seeking Fame Through the Internet: The Friendster Era and Beyond

Over the past decade, what had once been a tedious task for research partici-pants attempting to elicit and inventory all the members of their social net-works (e.g., via the Network Suite) has been transformed into the absorbing, self-motivated personal use of new online social networking Internet sites, such as Friendster (2002), Facebook (2004), and MySpace (2004).

Facebook offers a relevant example. Harvard University has long had the practice of issuing a student directory to undergraduates that contains photographs and personal information about all of their classmates, locally referred to as the "facebook." In 2004, a team of undergraduates undertook the project of placing this material on an Internet site, initially under the name Thefacebook (which in the fall of 2005 became Facebook). Facebook was subsequently expanded to other undergraduate colleges and by the spring of 2006 had over seven and a half million registered users. MySpace, which has open, unrestricted membership, had seventy-five million users as of May 2006 (Cassidy, 2006).

Facebook allows nimble and savvy users to map and build their own Internet social networks. It allows users to post a profile (including photo-graph and personal information) and a search box to call up and link to other users' profiles and to monitor counts of when their profile has been viewed by others. By altering privacy settings, users can control whether portions of their profile are accessible to friends only, to other undergraduates, or to everybody at the university. They can track other network information, such as how many "friends" they share with other friends. Situated in a specific college, Facebook sites are thereby anchored in a shared location and community of professors, classes, and so forth. Noncollege members are restricted to only those others from whom the user has obtained permission to register and list them.

One might anticipate that these social network sites would facilitate our quest for estimates of the total size and other parameters of individual social networks. But based upon the reports from observers of the Internet social network scene, the motivations of users are aimed at other purposes and outcomes.

Some users seek to achieve efficiency in keeping in touch with their friends. Researchers have found that Facebook users keep in touch with a wider network of casual acquaintances than those who do not use it (Ellison & Lampe, 2006).

Some users seek self-expression and self-promotion within the college community. Users appear to be highly self-conscious about what they might be conveying about themselves through such facets of their profile as their interest in specific music or books. At the same time, this form of self-fashioning is a central project in their creation of an Internet social network. Others are geared to self-promotion and have a competitive stance toward assembling very large Internet social networks, for example, bragging about having compiled over 800 "friends" (Cassidy, 2006).

Some users have the instrumental goal of pragmatically increasing their potential resources for social support and social capital. In this case, the aim is not simply to list a large number of "friends" but to assemble them as potential sources of social support in the real world. Thus, the upshot is that users seldom make the full delineation of their real-world social networks a self-generated personal project.

Internet Social Networks and Real-World Social Networks

In the real world, recognition identity is the gathering point for a person's social network. The pre-Internet Harvard directory, through its photographs and personal information, provided an institutionally credible form of face and name identity. The early versions of Facebook sought to continue this real-world anchor. The more open and accessible social networking sites, such as MySpace, forgo this anchor and thereby generate an ingredient of dissimulation and self-fashioning and shift the focus from utilitarian purposes to entertainment.

The Ephemeral Nature of Internet Social Networks

The Internet representation of one's social network can encompass individuals never met, while seemingly significant members of one's offline social network, such as parents, may not make it. An informative research project would compare the kind of specific social support that can be called upon through members of a person's real-world social network and that is available from members of Internet-oriented social networks. Real-world social networks have an abiding quality. A person can attend to them or not, but the everyday cast of characters they know and who know them persists and cannot be disappeared with the click of a delete button.

In contrast, a user's Facebook site is not a social network but rather a representation of one. It is created by the user and can be abandoned, neither maintained nor updated. Depending upon the purposes of the user, the online Internet social network can engage with the real-world offline social network. For example, it can be used as a tool for maintaining social relationships, reestablishing former relationships, developing new relationships, and, in general, keeping in touch with friends and acquaintances (Ellison & Lampe, 2006).

On the other hand, the Internet social network can be a more distinctly imaginative product, affording explorations of personal identity and image making and dealing with Internet relationships that are never intended to be extended to real-world encounters or ties with its cast of "friends."

Clearly, being in control of one's Internet social network is far from the same as being in control of one's real-world social network. And, of course, for the Internet social network user, the membership of reputational network members who know the person but are not known by the person remains as opaque as it is for all the rest of us in the real world.

Finally, the sense of control of one's Facebook or MySpace site may be illusory in important ways. The designers and operators of Internet social networking sites have their own agendas; for example, their policies can control access to individual sites by marketing companies, potential employers, law enforcement officials, and sexual predators. Users vary widely in their awareness of their multiple audiences, and researchers are distressed by the ways in which constant change in these Internet systems hinders systematic research (Ellison & Lampe, 2006).

In Chapter 6, we will return to an examination of how the use of Internet social networking constitutes one of many ways in which persons seek to convey their self-image to others and to manage their reputational network.

2

Social Communication About Specific Persons

Information Flow

If you were to hike along a country path near power lines strung on towers, you might hear the hum of electricity flowing along the transmission network. In a similar fashion, the lively hum of chat heard within towns and villages and neighborhoods embodies the transmission of social communication, much of it dealing with the doings and expressions of specific persons.

If you lived across the street from a hairdresser's shop in an Italian village in the summertime, you would hear a steady hum of chat. In Italian, the onomatopoeic verb for "chat" or "gossip" is *chiacchierare*. Even without understanding spoken Italian, you will nevertheless realize that much of this discourse is about various specific persons in the community. If you stroll through a Tuscan town and pass by the stone benchwork alongside the clock tower, you will hear a similar hum, generated this time mostly by menfolk who gather there. And all along the town streets during the afternoon *passeggiata*, you will hear families and friends encountering each other and you will surely enjoy the pleasure of moving around and through the comfortable hum of humanity that they generate.

The Emotional Tones of Chat

These auditory aspects are noteworthy because they highlight the atmospheric and enveloping nature of social chat, which is ongoing and pervasive. We are dimly aware of much more mundane discourse than we can ever individually attend to and take in—some of it surrounds us but much more takes place just beyond our hearing. What we can hark to are its differing emotional tones.

Our general repertoire of emotional terms has been shown to fall into a pattern described by the dimensions of activity and evaluation (see Figure 8.2 in Russell & Snodgrass, 1987, p. 250). Within this conceptual framework, our reference to "the hum" might very well characterize the bulk of social chat, which is by and large relaxed and appreciative. A more active but still positive form of chat is conveyed by our contemporary focus on "the buzz," which relates to the rustle of a more excited, urgent, and intrigued form of attention to specific persons. In contrast, "the noise" is a term employed by Gross (2001) to refer to the din of slanderous and discordant words associated with active but also negative forms of chat. Finally, "the murmur" of grumbling, suspicious, and complaining discourse is encompassed within the passive but negative emotional domain. Thus, our discourse about specific other persons takes place with such varied atmospherics as the hum, the buzz, the noise, and the murmur. But my own impression is that, by and large, the prevailing tone of chat about other persons is the hum.

Information Flow Within Reputational Networks

A favorite general exemplar among network theorists is the electric power grid, for example, the one stretching across the United States and Canada. Network analysis contributes to an understanding of crises caused by failures to maintain optimal flow through its many linkages (Watts, 2003). Social communication about specific persons flows through reputational networks comprised of other individuals who know them. Thus, information about a person circulates much as electricity streams through the grids of electric power networks. In the former, communication media link the members as nodes within the reputational network, while in the latter, transmission lines in an electric power grid link its nodes in the form of power stations and substations.

A person's reputational network differs in important ways from the physical transmission on grid. One striking difference is that the electric power grid affords transmission but not storage of electricity (Watts, 2003, p. 22). In contrast, as information about a specific person comes along the lines to particular reputational network members, it may be not only passed on to certain other members via everyday chat but also stored cognitively by each member within a "person bin" (see Chapter 3).

Reputational Information Flow

The network interpretation of reputation entails a finite number of other individuals who directly or indirectly know the person by face or name and who are more or less in communication with each other about the deeds and utterances of that person. In principle, the entire network of its members and their

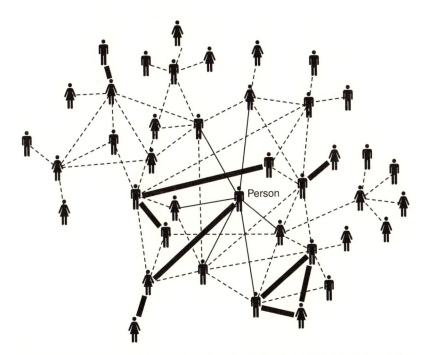

Figure 2.1 Reputational network showing information flow: *thick link*, activated; *thin link*, not activated.

linkages can be mapped. At any given moment, one can imagine these links lighting up red on a display board when communication about the person happens to occur among any two or more network members.

While seemingly far-fetched in implementation, the possible capacity to delineate a person's dynamic reputational network and to monitor communications along it serves the heuristic purpose of conveying the ontological nature of reputation and its functioning. The advancing technologies of surveillance available to the U.S. National Security Agency and other institutions for trolling telephonic and Internet communications makes the pervasive monitoring of communications about a specific person ever more plausible (O'Harrow, 2005). In everyday social life, we are surrounded by and awash in chat and gossip, much of it about specific persons. This running discourse about a person bears directly upon the notion that reputation points in part to what is generally being said about a person (Figure 2.1).

Media and Occasions

Spontaneous communications about a specific person within a reputational network are episodic, intermittent, fleeting, seldom recorded, and scattered across diverse kinds of occasions. Yet through this ongoing discourse the eyes and minds of other individuals complement our own direct observations of and interactions with specific individuals, as well as our own recollections of them.

From an evolutionary perspective, reputational networks constitute an important cultural invention for keeping in touch with the adaptive human landscape. From the small social group living arrangements characteristic of the Pleistocene era onward, humans have selected to attend closely to the doings of other individuals whose actions may affect their survival and reproductive fitness (Barkow, 1992; Buss, 1991). Within human evolution, the availability of reliable third-party information about specific persons freed us from total reliance upon our own direct observations and afforded the feasibility of larger social groups (Dunbar, 2004; Emler, 2001).

Social scientists view ongoing communitywide discourse about specific persons as a valuable source of updated intelligence, useful for making decisions about such matters as whom to go to for advice, to assign as night sentry for the village, to undertake a difficult negotiation, and to lend money, hire, wed, elect to office, or report to the police (Borkenau, 1990; Foster, 2004; Kenny, 1994; Hogan, 1996).

The media and occasions that afford opportunities for chat about a specific person are varied. The occasions when red links glow on a person's reputational network board include special social events, such as annual conferences, family holiday gatherings, the July 4 block party, and the school reunion, as well as more mundane behavior settings, such as the grocery store, the post office, the pub, the hairdresser's, and the barber shop (Altman, Brown, Staples, & Werner, 1992; Wicker, 1992). A common knowledge impetus toward validity in disseminating information about specific persons is counterbalanced by the surrounding positive spin of bolstering friends (Argyle, 1984; Goode, 1978) and the negative spin of denigrating rivals (Bailey, 1971; Buss, & Dedden, 1990). Within the flow of information about a person, errors may occur and blatant falsehoods may be intentionally introduced and circulated.

Informal oral communications nowadays are not only face-to-face but also via cell phones and the Internet. At least within the context of defamation law, written defamation (*libel*), with its greater durability, is considered more serious than spoken defamation (*slander*) (Carter-Ruck & Walker, 1985). Despite the imagery of "chat rooms," Internet defamation possesses greater permanency than may be apparent and is being treated in the courts as libel rather than slander (Collins, 2001).

Keeping in Touch with the Human Landscape

Of course, the ongoing chat is not focused exclusively upon any one person; a chat session typically ranges across the news and doings concerning several acquaintances. And some of it deals with general current events, sports, politics, and so forth. However, studies of the content of everyday conversations indicate that much, and probably most, of it has to do with specific persons in a way that intermeshes and distributes information flows along many reputational networks in seemingly haphazard fashion (Emler, 2001; Foster, 2004).

What is the point of all of this chat? From an evolutionary point of view, other persons constitute a crucial component of our adaptive landscape (Buss, 1991; Emler, 2001; Hogan, 1982). Primarily, the focus would be upon information concerning potential mates, sexual rivals, kin, and other allies and competitors. Thus, casual conversations could convey consequential information. Eventually, the psychological mechanisms that evolved for the acquisition of social information about others have come to yield their own gratification and entertainment potential and to be extended to strangers, celebrities, and even fictional characters (Barkow, 1992; Schickle, 1985).

Thus, everyday chat generates a constant flow of possibly important intelligence (in the espionage sense of the term) about the human landscape. Our surveillance is seemingly casual but also persistent and collective. We keep in touch with the human landscape much as a general constantly reconnoiters the enemy lines, an explorer continually sends scouts ahead, and a farmer repeatedly checks the condition of crops, fences, and fields.

Chat as a Team Effort in the Informal Surveillance of Others

Each of us maintains knowledge of other individuals through a variety of sources, some direct and some from hearsay. One source, perhaps overrated in some respects, is direct interaction with or observation of others in everyday social life. In his commentary on the pursuit of glory, Montaigne (1960) emphasized the importance but also the accidental and selective nature of observation: "An infinity of fine actions must be lost without a witness before one appears to advantage. A man is not always at the top of the breach or at the head of an army in sight of his general, as on a stage" (p. 328). Rather, he "is taken by surprise between the hedge and the ditch" (p. 328), and thus, his sacrifice goes unrecognized and unheralded.

A related source of knowledge of others is the capacity to bring to mind recollections of the acts and expressions of others gained on earlier occasions. However, our opportunities to observe the conduct of each and every member of our social circle are severely limited by time, circumstances, and even decorum.

To compensate for these restrictions on our direct observation of others, we rely upon key supplemental sources of information about them, primarily in the form of information exchanges with individuals who have also been in a position to gain direct or indirect knowledge about them. Indeed, only in such rare and distinctive communities as certain monasteries, where members take a vow of silence, do individuals restrict themselves primarily to their own direct observations of others.

On the contrary, human communities are composed of *chiacchieroni*—awash with chat about the doings of other persons. Such hearsay reports afford community members with an impressive amplification of surveillance capacities, giving access to contexts of observation within which they were not themselves present or, due to reasons of propriety or due to simple logistics, could not have been present.

Seldom do any two or more persons regularly spend 24 hours per day within each other's gaze. Indeed, much more typical are the instances in which direct observation of an acquaintance is episodic, quite fleeting, highly selective, and often separated by considerable periods of time across the life span. Nevertheless, through the ongoing flows of chat, the eyes and minds of other community members are mobilized to complement our own direct observations of and interactions with others, as well as our recollections of them.

Thus, reputational information is a team effort on the surveillance side. The social invention of chat sustains an ongoing and ever-changing pool of aggregated information about specific community members. From this vantage point, the reputation of a person resides as much in this ongoing discourse about specific persons as it does in the minds of individual community members.

Occasions for Acquiring and Exchanging Information About Other Persons

Various factors sustain the likelihood of encounters with specific persons that afford the opportunity for direct interaction and observation of them, as well as encounters with other individuals that facilitate the exchange of hearsay information about them.

Constrained Choice in Observing and Being Observed

Little scientific attention has been devoted to examining the determinants of direct encounters between individuals in everyday social life. These factors would include, for example, shared presence at various behavior settings and social occasions (e.g., an annual conference, a holiday family gathering).

Shared daily routines in moving through behavior settings also bring individuals together for causal conversation (e.g., at the grocery store, the post office, the pub). The structure of the social calendar of community members also gathers certain of them together (e.g., at the neighborhood Fourth of July block party, the school reunion).

In some instances, the parties to an encounter are directly selected. For example, certain specific dyadic initiatives are generated within ongoing relationships, such as when an accountant sets up a meeting with a business client. In other cases, the constellation of participants is a function of the specific choice of some, but not all, parties to the encounter. For example, when one person invites several others to a dinner party, each guest has directly chosen to interact with the host or hostess but not necessarily with the others to be encountered during the course of the evening. Finally, when a person chooses to enter a public behavior setting for a specific purpose, such as the grocery store or post office, the array of others encountered there is more or less a matter of happenstance.

Thus, we see that a broad continuum of personal choice prevails in the membership and constitution of a person's reputational network. Individual selection may be largely at play in the development of friendships from among schoolmates, coworkers, and acquaintances in social life generally. However, many other schoolmates, coworkers, and acquaintances also willy-nilly form a major component of a person's reputational network that constitutes membership outcomes not reflecting personal choice.

The same holds true even in the more or less free flow of social life, where new members of a person's reputational network accrue from the mutual social acquaintances of individuals explicitly sought out for interaction. For, after all, these sought-after acquaintances bring along their own idiographic social networks, some members of which are likely to become members of one's own reputational network. Thus, a rich system of potential observers and occasions for observation is generated.

From Planned to Unanticipated: The Occasions for Chat About Other Persons

A second important classification of occasions has to do with opportunities to chat and exchange hearsay information about specific other persons.

Some occasions for social communication about others are explicitly intended and systematically designed, planned, and scheduled. These contexts can be counted upon to gather together many members of overlapping reputational networks; they include school reunions, conferences, and birthday and anniversary celebrations (Altman et al., 1992). Such occasions permit the exchange of hearsay information concerning mutual acquaintances (i.e., those present but out of hearing range as well as those absent).

Another category of less tightly scheduled but fairly frequent occasions must be considered. These intermittent contexts include social dinners, dances and parties, weddings, funerals, art exhibits, and so forth.

A third category of occasions often makes social life intriguing. These are the completely unplanned and unanticipated encounters with old acquaintances. They include meetings along the street, encounters at public events such as a protest rally, and "small world" encounters in far away places, as when former Californian neighbors come across each other on a little ferry landing along the northern Italian coast.

Finally, a more mundane category encompasses the intimate, routine, and quotidian encounters of close acquaintances in flats, automobiles, schools, and workplaces.

While we have turned our focus upon the ways participants in these encounters exchange information about third parties, we must also bear in mind that the chat sessions themselves grant mutual opportunities of direct observation of each other. Thus, the chat sessions themselves provide new grist for future hearsay information and reports. The flow of intelligence about specific persons is multilayered and never-ending.

Communicating About Others: The Validity Versus Bias Tension

We have asserted that ongoing communitywide discourse about specific persons is a valuable source of updated intelligence, useful for making decisions about them. These purposes place a premium on the validity of the information flows about specific persons.

Validity of information about persons does not mean nonevaluative information, however. The information commonly exchanged about specific persons is an appraisal as well as a description; indeed, these functions tend to be overwhelmingly intertwined. Over 95% of thousands of terms available in the English language to describe persons are evaluative rather than neutral in valence (e.g., boastful, kind, sneaky, fearful, curious) (Buss, 1991; Peabody, 1984). Thus, we can rephrase the community's interest as residing in the accuracy of the evaluative descriptions of specific persons that emerge from the exchange of information about them. The belief that the person assigned to duty as a village sentry is indeed conscientious should itself be well-founded, dependable, and predictive (Borkenau, 1990; Emler, 2001; Hogan, 1982, 1996).

At the same time, the evolutionary perspective as well as common experience suggest that social life is characterized by competition and rivalry as well as coalitions and cooperative endeavors (Barkow, 1992; Cosmides & Tooby, 1992). Thus, the impetus toward validity in disseminating information and impressions concerning specific other persons is counterbalanced by the surrounding favorable spin of supportive friends (Argyle, 1984; Goode, 1978) and the unfavorable spin of competitors and enemies (Bailey, 1971; Buss & Dedden, 1990).

These countervailing interests in fostering a lively but tendentious discourse about specific persons, on the one hand, and sustaining a modicum of validity in the flow of information, on the other, can be seen in the English common law tradition regarding defamation and occasions of qualified privilege.

Thus, our social structure affords a myriad of occasions for communication about a specific person. The two illustrative examples of privileged occasions and gossip sessions are derived from the contexts of defamation law and social science research, respectively.

Occasions of Qualified Privilege

The English common law tradition embodies an individual right to protection of reputation and access to means for seeking remedy when public assertions are circulated that may harm reputation. The common law acknowledges a tension between this individual right and a second fundamental societal interest. In the latter view, important benefits accrue to the social welfare through unfettered communication about specific persons for a variety of purposes.

As a consequence, communications arising out of these specified occasions are sheltered to varying degrees from actions for defamation (Carter-Ruck & Walker, 1985). In occasions of qualified privilege, one participant is deemed to have a moral, social, or legal duty to communicate about a specific third person with another individual, who in turn is deemed to enjoy a moral, social, or legal right to receive the information.

For example, a merchant sailor might report to a ship's owner that he believes the captain is an alcoholic and has put the ship and its sailors at risk. The sailor may turn out to be in error. Nevertheless, his duty to convey his belief, even if later shown to be false, and the ship owner's right to the information can be entered in defense in an action for defamation brought by the captain. Other occasions of this kind are varied: for example, a relative or advisor providing information about the other participant's potential suitor or mate, a former employer or teacher providing a letter of reference, or participants considering a potential business associate. Qualified privilege constitutes a defense against legal actions for libel and slander even if the derogatory assertion was false or could not be shown to be true (Milmo & Rogers, 1998).

Note that the defense of qualified privilege does not refer to the content of the communication or the types of assertions made about the third party. Instead, it refers to the nature of the occasion as defined by the duty of one participant to communicate information about the third party and the right or reciprocal interest of the receiver of the message. Finally, strict discretion is required with regard to the spread of this discourse and the array of additional individuals, if any at all, with a need to know and to whom the information might also be further circulated.

Gossip Sessions

Gossip sessions entail two or more individuals exchanging information—typically derogatory—about a third person who is not present or at least not within hearing of the communication.

The communication of derogatory information about a person to others carries a number of risks. First, even if the attributions about the person are true and valid, it appears to be the case that in general negative assertions about a person's conduct carry more weight and are more consequential than positive assertions. In Chapter 3, we will turn to research that supports the prevalence of this form of "negativity bias." Without presuming general knowledge of such scientific studies, we can infer that individuals in everyday social life recognize the unfavorable consequences for the person that may ensue from dissemination of such negative, even if accurate, accounts of conduct. Second, the social contexts of gossip sessions differ from those meriting the legal status of occasions of qualified privilege. In the latter case, reciprocal duties and rights are at issue and the exchange of information is focused and constrained by the situated parameters of the communication. In the instance of gossip sessions, the situation is typically characterized as more idle and purposeless, in which the negative information is treated with more casual regard for its accuracy and is exchanged in part simply to pass it on and sometimes for its entertainment value. Another risk entailed in gossiping is that through misperception, misinterpretation, or willful falsehood the negative information being circulated is untrue. Of course, we should not presume widespread knowledge of defamation law, including the likelihood that such false assertions are not only unsheltered by qualified privilege but also subject to the rumor repetition rule. As we shall discover in Chapter 8, libel law holds that a person who simply repeats a false and defamatory assertion about the plaintiff carries as much liability as the originator of the assertion. Perhaps gossipers dimly grasp some sense of these risks. Indeed, part of the pleasure of gossiping is the titillation and sense of transgression that can accompany it.

Bergmann (1993) has characterized gossip as an indiscretion in that it runs the risk of harm to the gossipers as well as to the person gossiped about. Furthermore, the information is often of the sort that the person is attempting to keep relatively private, if not secret. The gossipers are to some extent thwarting that aim of the person gossiped about. For these reasons, Bergmann points to certain discreet boundaries of gossip, in that participants may explicitly or implicitly signify those individuals who might handle the further circulation of the information and the way they would wish it to be dealt with (e.g., to whom else within the person's reputational network the news about the person as well as accounts of the gossip session itself are to be circulated).

Although some discretion may be taken in gossip sessions, their dynamics tend to be relentlessly negative in direction.

The Structure of Gossip Sessions

In the territory beyond the conscientious contexts of privileged occasions lies the less disciplined realm of everyday chat and gossip, where discourse is often deemed to be frivolous and indiscreet. For example, lunchtime conversations among adolescents at a school cafeteria are often occasions for gossip sessions, which Eder and Enke (1991, p. 496) defined as episodes in which a positive or negative evaluation of someone not present was followed by at least one further response by another student. Their participant observational research revealed that gossip sessions are structured as, and tend to follow, a sequential pattern. For example, an initial negative assertion is typically factual, that is, a bit of news about a specific absent person's conduct. Indeed, explicit clarifications sometimes occur to ascertain the particular identity of the target person. If an initial negative attribution to the person is not followed by a more positive or at least neutral countering assertion, then a snowballing of additional negative recollections, anecdotes, or comments tends to follow.

In everyday social life, however, the realm of discourse concerning specific other persons appears to be more encompassing than the distinctively structured gossip sessions described by Eder and Enke.

Person Chat and Gossip

We can no longer ignore the distinction between chat and gossip that has already crept into our discussion. Imagine a big old barn of a pub in the rolling countryside southeast of Sligo, Ireland. Groups of family and friends are gathered about many large round tables. Other acquaintances mill about, wandering from table to table or simply passing through to a table. A fellow stops at our table and asks whether anyone has seen Sean lately—a mutual acquaintance of several of those present. "Ah, he's off to the horse races down in Galway," is said to smiles of acknowledgment and recognition, followed by a string of presumably prototypical racetrack anecdotes about Sean, all publicly communicated within the hum of a warm and much amused social atmosphere. These exchanges might be called gossip by some social scientists, generated out of a "gossip session," but it seems too public rather than secretive, too kindly rather than derogatory. Now if, at one section of the table, three participants quietly huddled and exchanged conjecture and purported news on what other more scandalous things Sean might be up to in Galway, then perhaps we have bona fide gossip. Researchers on gossip have been unable to come to any firm agreement about whether both of these incidents or only the second meets the definition of gossip (Goodman & Ben Ze'ev, 1994; Young, 2001). The temptation is to attempt to broaden the meaning of gossip and employ it as a general term, encompassing both positive and negative forms of person chat; but we will resist this temptation.

In our conceptual framework, we have already drawn a distinction between the positive and negative affective tones of certain kinds of chat. We assume that most chat is positive in tone—the lively buzz and comfortable hum of appreciative chat that is sympathetic, good-natured, curious, and even praising. But some chat is derogatory—cruel, mean-spirited, and fault-finding—ensuing in worried murmur or excited noise. Thus, we can think of gossip sessions as generating the negative manifestations of chat.

Students of gossip have yet to reach consensus about whether positive or relatively nonevaluative news about specific persons should be subsumed under a broadened conception of gossip or whether a more encompassing category, such as chat or talk, should subsume gossip (Bloom, 2004; Fenster & Small, 2003a). We will adhere to the latter position.

Among the many contexts for social communications about specific persons, probably only a small percentage consists of privileged occasions or gossip sessions in a strict sense of those terms. Studies of naturally occurring conversations suggest that about 50% deal with person chat or "the doings of others" and only 10%–20% concern negative attributions. Thus, much, if not most, chat about specific persons is positive rather than negative in implication (Emler, 2001; Foster, 2004; Young, 2001). Indeed, Westacott (2000) has argued with regard to ethical analysis that while some forms of gossip are morally unacceptable, talk and specifically gossip very often have more to be said for them than against them.

What little empirical research has been reported has tended to focus upon the communicators, targets, and recipients along with their relationships. For example, within a college living group, those who tend to be receivers of gossip or person chat are rated by the group as having more social status and being better liked than those who tend to be targets of gossip (Young, 2001).

What we must aspire to delineate and understand better through this line of research is the overall operation of the person chat or gossip system, in which we all play multiple roles, as gossip transmitters, gossip receivers, and targets of gossip. And by participating in the gossip system, we put ourselves in a position to listen and learn about how others conduct themselves and live their lives and how our acquaintances tend to evaluate the full range of everyday conduct (Baumeister, Zhang, & Vohs, 2004).

But the network interpretation of reputation reminds us that we must also focus especially upon the target of gossip and upon the communicated message's content, context, and consequences within that target person's reputational network (Foster, 2004). Of course, as targets of gossip, we are absent from the scene, although we may be dimly aware of what is being said about us. In general, evaluative information about a person seems to circulate freely among friends but tends to be withheld from the person being evaluated. "It is as if the social norms were devised to keep people from learning too much about what others think of them" (Blomberg, 1972, p. 161).

Person Chat at a Distance

We have found that person chat is a major vehicle for the circulation of information about identified persons throughout reputational networks. The odd and seemingly pointless phenomenon of the newspaper gossip column reminds us that our trade in small talk about other persons is not limited to individuals we know by direct acquaintance. The category of persons known to us but who do not know us, ranging from local public officials to global celebrities, is not only large but also surprisingly engaging (see cell C of Table Intro.1).

Within the fragmented world of contemporary social life, communication about celebrities provides us with shared pseudoacquaintances (Gamson, 1994; Schickel, 1985). Indeed, we often know more about celebrities than we do about our neighbors and coworkers. For some individuals, social communication about celebrities offers a surrogate social circle, affording a context for exercising our person chat skills and for the satisfaction of curiosity, interpretation, and fantasy (Barkow, 1992). Consideration of celebrity lives supplies a supplemental arena for affirming moral values and a repertoire of possible models for one's own self-fashioning (McAdams, 1993). In addition, celebrities and other public figures often have recourse to actions for defamation. These trials offer useful and often vivid public examination of the risks and dangers of social communication about specific persons (Hooper, 1984, 2000).

Conclusion

We have now sketched out the ongoing social communication process through which news, observations, and impressions circulate along a person's reputational network via chat, gossip, and more formal means. Crisp specifications can be delineated for certain settings of information exchange about specific persons, such as privileged occasions and gossip sessions. However, they must be identified as occurring within a much larger realm of person chat. And a central function of this flow of information about specific persons is the sharing in a form of common knowledge about them.

The constrained occasions of qualified privilege are sheltered from actions for defamation on the rationale that society as a whole gains by certain forms of unfettered communication about specific persons. Yet many social scientists would argue that the full range of more idle and seemingly disorganized chatter about others tends also to serve similar useful informational functions (Buss, 1991; Borkenau, 1990; Hogan, 1982; Kenny, 1994).

Thus, the adaptive functions of the flow of information about specific persons tend to bridge and unite the conscientious contexts of qualified privilege with the looser contexts of person chat. Having fewer constraints, the latter serve the purpose of conveying information about specific persons more widely as well as less selectively. Since a community may not be able to determine what information about what persons might eventually prove useful for various subsequent purposes, it may be best to push for maximum circulation and minimum editing.

3

Person Bins—Assembling Information According to Specific Persons

Information Storage

We have seen that each person lives within a delimited and idiographic reputational network or personal community. We have also reviewed the many ways that social communication about everyday conduct flows through such networks.

Now we must fuse these two perspectives in order to further our understanding of that interesting human invention, the conceptual tool of primary interest to us, namely, the reputation of specific persons.

If information flow were strictly like energy flow within electric power grids, then the information and discourse we discussed in the last chapter would immediately run its course and leave no residue. A person's reputation would exist only when the reputational network linkages were lit red. News about a person's conduct, achievements, or dishonors would disappear when not an active topic of chat or discourse. Reputation would be even more fragmented and ephemeral than it actually is.

Instead, the members of a person's reputational network serve as nodes that store as well as transmit impressions, evaluations, and specific news concerning the person. This storage is dynamic, not static, as research on person cognition and social cognition has demonstrated. Nevertheless, it is specifically localized at the human nodes throughout a specific person's reputational network.

Person Bins

Information and discourse about a person do not simply continue to flow along the reputational network. Instead, each member serves as a gathering, cumulating, and to varying degrees integrating agent and, thus, as one of many cognitive repositories located throughout the person's reputational network.

We will now turn to the ways in which each member of a person's reputational network gathers and cumulates impressions, beliefs, and evaluations about that specifically identifiable person. This array of cognitive nodes, or person bins, generated by a person's reputational network members constitutes the distributive facet of reputation.

Of course, each of us is a member of multiple reputational networks. If we retained information about our observed everyday events and utterances only in some abstract form, then we would be useless as reputational informants. We must cognitively tag our impressions, beliefs, and evaluations according to individual identities. These individualized mental files are what I will term *person bins*.

Figure 3.1 is our third version of Watts' (2003) depiction of a person's network. The nodes represented in Figure 3.1 vary in size to suggest a range in members' representation of the person, from minimal recognition identity to an abundantly informed portrait. Note that the mere existence of a node consisting of only minimal recognition identity still provides a potential routing, receiving, and storage unit for new and fresh information about the person. The evaluative salience of the information can range from highly positive to strongly negative, with the more typical shades of gray falling between these extremes.

The flow and storage of information about a specific person can be likened to a team effort in informal and largely unself-conscious surveillance, in which observations and information from many members of the reputational network are circulated, pooled, and discussed. It is worth belaboring the

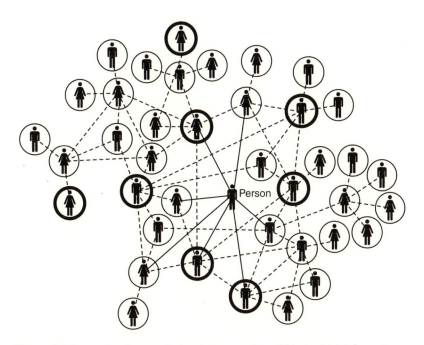

Figure 3.1 Reputational network showing person bins: *thick ring*, high information volume; *thin ring*, low information volume.

point that information is not simply conveyed along the network linkages but is retained in varying ways by each network member, functioning as an agent gathering and compiling this everyday social intelligence.

If a previously obscure person, through a strange disappearance or notorious act, suddenly becomes a CNN-level target of a nationwide search, then we can expect that quite a few individuals from all phases of the person's life will come forward, giving accounts of her or him as a car-pool commuter or a teenage lifeguard. We maintain a surprisingly large number of person bins on peripheral as well as central members of our own network.

What goes into these person bins? We will see that retained reputational information tends to be partial and selective, as well as pervasively evaluative. We will encounter the negativity bias, in which negative assertions about a person tend to be confirmed with less evidence than positive assertions and require more evidence to be disconfirmed.

Before turning to these topics, we might note how our concept of the cognitive person bin bears upon the term "storage bin" found in the research literature on social cognition and person memory (Wyer & Srull, 1980;

Wyer & Carlston, 1994). Both terms refer to the storage and retrieval of information about specific persons. However, the concept of "storage bin" is situated within approaches to the internal analysis of how that information is internally represented and processed. Beyond its locus upon a particular person as its key referent, this line of inquiry examines, for example, whether person memory is organized by acts or by traits, by description or by evaluation, or by prototypes (Wyer & Gordon, 1984). In contrast, our use of the term "cognitive person bin" is in the general context of its external relations of observations and information flow among members of the person's reputational network. As the network interpretation of reputation becomes fully articulated, the mutual relations of these two concepts will become clearer.

Reputational Information Storage

The members of a person's reputational network individually serve as initiators and transmitters of information about the person but also as nodes for the selective storage of that information.

Information about ordinary human conduct can be sorted and transmitted in a variety of ways (Barker, 1968; Ozer, 1986). At the end of a day, directly through our own observations or indirectly through chat, small talk, gossip, and the mass media, we have each encountered an ample and mixed bag of anecdotes, episodes, and accounts of human experience and action.

These accounts of human action might be grouped, categorized, and disseminated in a variety of ways, for example, (*1*) according to the types of conduct (e.g., playing soccer, speaking in public), (*2*) according to the situations in which they occurred (e.g., instances of math class conduct, aboard airplane conduct), (*3*) according to the time of the activities (e.g., siesta conduct, weekend conduct), or (*4*) according to the source of the information concerning other persons' conduct (e.g., gossip from Luigi, stories from Martha).

But central to reputation is the method of bundling information about everyday conduct according to the person who generated the conduct or is otherwise associated with it. Recall that we have set the most minimal of criteria for membership in a person's reputational network, namely, the bits of knowledge that signify recognition identity (i.e., regarding face and name).

That identity bin then becomes the focal point for the accumulation of additional information about that same person via observation and hearsay.

Thus, recognition identity, by face or name, becomes the cognitive bin in which information about that person is stored. Consider the following two examples.

Female African lions show individual differences in how they respond to challenges to their pride's territory. Lead lions move toward the forefront in confrontations with potential intruders, while laggards tend to trail behind. Furthermore, the lead females recognize that certain companions are laggards and consequently the lead lions "behave more cautiously in their presence" (Heinsohn & Packer, 1994, pp. 1260–1262). That is, they show the capacity to tag previous laggard conduct to specific pride mates and subsequently act upon this reputational information.

A second example deals with attention to reciprocal interactions. In direct reciprocity, A helps B and B in turn helps A. In indirect reciprocity, A has been observed by C or others to help B and subsequently A receives help from C or others. Indirect reciprocity differs from direct reciprocity in that the donor of the help receives the return not from the initial beneficiary but from another individual. A society of nonhuman animals lacking language is dependent upon directly experienced or vicariously observed reciprocity. With language, humans can expand the scope of indirect reciprocity; the observers, the donor A, and the recipient B can inform others via chat (Ohtsuki & Iwasa, 2004; Pollock & Dugatkin, 1992).

Theoretical and empirical analyses of indirect reciprocity stress "the importance of monitoring not only partners in continuing interactions but also all individuals within the social network. Indirect reciprocity requires information storage and transfer as well as strategic thinking and has a pivotal role in the evolution of collaboration and communication" (Nowak & Sigmund, 2005, p. 1291). Thus, within our own species, the capacity to tag and communicate information about the conduct of others to specific persons is the core ingredient to any network conception of reputation. Within human reputational networks, information not only flows from member to member but is stored in cognitive person bins as well as transmitted onward to others.

A person's reputation derives in some fashion from information circulating and stored within a reputational network. This information is dispersed in a very partial and scattered manner. Taking a bird's eye view of a person's reputational network, we can readily imagine the flow of information sporadically circulating along it via chat, gossip, and privileged occasion. Some of the information goes to certain members and some to others, entering the various bins tagged to that person. Some of the recipient members may be long-term acquaintances but possess only a relatively narrow range of prior information (e.g., a neighbor, a shopkeeper), while others may be short-term acquaintances but more broadly informed (e.g., within the context of a summer vacation fling or sessions of brief psychotherapy).

Of course, each of these network members maintains many more person bins, one for each of the hundreds or thousands of individuals he or she claims to know at least by face or name. Given that we have estimated the size of an average social network at 2,000 with an augmented size for reputational networks, any member of a particular person's reputational network can be expected to maintain in excess of 4,000 person bins, one of them tagged to our target person. Furthermore, recognizing the role of cell C in Table Intro.1, an additional set of person bins will reference individuals known to a person, such as public and historical figures, celebrities, and characters in novels and plays. Thus, in everyday life, each individual can mobilize an impressive quantity of cognitive person bins with specific recognition identities.

Human person bins are formed on the basis of direct interaction and observation as well as from the flow of information within the network to which a member has had access. These cognitive person bins encompass and, to a greater or lesser extent, integrate each network member's impressions, beliefs, and evaluations regarding that specific person, gained over a period of acquaintance and observation. In addition, a distinctively meta-level set of measures must encompass each network member's beliefs about the parameters of a given person's reputational network itself (e.g., its size, its general positive versus negative valence).

Reputational Information: Partial and Selective

Each member of a person's reputational network presumably has some minimal contribution of observations and impressions to offer toward a collective summary account of a person's lifelong conduct. But due to a host of ecological and logistical factors, each member's vantage point is necessarily partial. Furthermore, severe hindrances typically prevent the gathering of all available networkwide information into a continually updated summary portrait of the person.

Over the life course, a person wanders through social life, provoking and persuading, charming, astonishing, impressing, and appalling her or his idiographic community of other individuals. No one other individual is privy to all of a given person's conduct. Observations are made and communicated by various individuals in a hit-or-miss fashion. Even if another person did serve as a kind of constant presence, that "clone observer" would be subject to inescapable fluctuations of attention, cognitive constraints, and memory limitations.

To the extent that a person's conduct has been observed and attended to by others, even these particular observations and impressions remain fragmented and dispersed throughout the reputational network; many may never be communicated from one member to any or many others. As a person's reputational network expands and embodies the kind of low-density interconnections typical of modern life, the opportunities and circumstances for gathering and integrating community information about a person diminish.

Although we cannot approximate a God's eye record of a person's lifelong utterances and doings, the analysis of one day's worth of conduct is quite a bit more feasible. If we had such records, we could examine what aspects of the information generated by a person during the course of a day are noted by others, assigned to that person's bin, and recollected and communicated at various points later on.

As a research program, "lived day analysis" is in an early stage of its quite slow development (Craik, 2000b, 2007). A half-century ago, Barker and Wright (1951) published *One Boy's Day*, a detailed account of the minute-by-minute conduct of 7-year old Raymond Birch during the course of a single day in Oskaloosa, Kansas. An eight-person relay team of researchers working in thirty-minute sequences set out to record their verbal descriptions and impressions of the lad's observable activities from the time he appeared at breakfast in his home at 7:30 A.M. until his bedtime at 8:32 P.M. Their descriptive account required 422 pages of *One Boy's Day*. More recently, my associates and I have explored the use of small video camcorders and miniature microphones to track and record the lived day of persons in a way that captures the visual environment and interactions that were lacking in the Barker and Wright approach.

Both of these efforts are primarily devoted to grappling with the immediate problems entailed in attempting to capture a comprehensive quotidian portrait of the person's conduct. Once these methods are established, we will be able to address our reputational question: What aspects of a person's lived day are noted by others, and to what extent are these observations and impressions communicated to third parties? Clearly, we have a long way to go in achieving systematic research on these issues.

However, we do have *Ulysses*, James Joyce's (1961) masterpiece of twentieth-century fiction, which offers an account of a day in the life of Leopold Bloom—June 16, 1904—in Dublin, Ireland. Using innovative narrative techniques, Joyce affords us accounts of some events in Leopold's lived day as seen by his young friend Stephen Dedalus, his wife Molly, and other Dubliners to be found at the Ormond Hotel's dining room and bar, at the office of the *Evening Telegraph* newspaper, at Barney Kiernan's pub, and at other settings encountered by Bloom in the course of his wanderings about the city on that day.

To learn how observations by others are disseminated through a person's reputational network, we must examine what aspects of all that a person does on a given day are noted by other individuals at all, recollected, and then conveyed to others. To put the question another way, what kind of account of a given person's lived day might be gathered only on the basis of interviews the following day with the cast of characters whom the person had encountered during the day under study?

Take, for example, Leopold Bloom as he walked along Westland Row about midmorning on June 16 and encountered Bantam Lyons, who asked to borrow Bloom's newspaper to check on the horse race listings. Instead, Bloom actually gives his newspaper to Lyons, saying that he was just about to "throw it away" in any case. Lyons misinterprets this comment as a betting tip: a horse named Throwaway is running that day in the Ascot Gold Cup. Shortly after 5 p.m., Bloom is conversing with a group at Barney Kiernan's pub. During the chat, Lenehan brings in the news that the 20-to-1 Throwaway has indeed won the Gold Cup race. This means nothing to Bloom, who has no interest in betting, but it does mean quite a lot to some of the others present who had put their money on the favorite, Sceptre. Bloom goes off on an errand to the nearby courthouse. In his absence, Lenehan, apparently having heard from Bantam Lyons, spreads the mistaken idea about Bloom's supposed betting tip. The group discussion continues in some outrage that Bloom has furtively gone off to collect his winnings, too mean-spirited to stand them a round of drinks in celebration before going off (Blamires, 1988; Joyce, 1961).

Here is a set of events whose misinterpretation circulates around Bloom, without his awareness but with some damage to the way he is perceived by others. The account highlights the question about what social communications are generated by a person's lived day, how that information is dispersed and circulates among various onlookers, and then how it is conveyed further through the person's reputational network.

The Lived Day of a Person: On a Treadmill to Oblivion?

Fred Allen, the great radio comedian, entitled a volume of his memoirs *Treadmill to Oblivion* (Allen, 1954). In commenting on what he considered the ephemeral nature of his art, Allen lamented, "When a radio comedian's program is finally finished, it slinks down memory lane into the limbo of yesterday's happy hours. All that a comedian has to show for his years of work and aggravation is the echo of forgotten laughter" (p. 240). A historical geographer, Hugh Prince (1978), voicing a similar lament, noted that his own scholarly efforts "to record and interpret the past may delay but cannot prevent the past receding into oblivion" (pp. 36–37).

Of the total amount of potential information generated by a person's lived day, just a relatively small proportion seems to be socially noted. That meager amount of information is dispersed among members of the person's community, and much of it is unlikely ever to be reintegrated. First, at the moment-to-moment level, many stretches of a person's lived day may seem quite uninformative, including such mundane activities as walking from one's residence through campus to a classroom. Despite the considerable effort that must be devoted to gathering video records of the lived days of persons, as my research team initially viewed them, we paradoxically found ourselves tempted at many points to press the fast forward button on our video recorder. At this initial impressionistic level, many stretches of a person's lived day seemed quite uninformative in comparison to others—thus, the appearance of what we termed the "fast forward impulse" (Craik, 2000b).

Is it the case then that, rather than being characterized as a steady, even flow of information, a person's lived day is punctuated by a relatively few revealing or consequential episodes (Craik, 1993a; Gould, 1995)? A person's interactants and onlookers may focus upon these attention-getting but rather rare events, in a bias that tends to make persons and their daily lives more interesting and intriguing than they really are (Craik, 2000b).

When a day is done, what is the likely fate of such highly selected remnants? How rapidly and in what patterns will the information of a day's actions and events recede from the person's reputational network and into oblivion? Weeks and years hence, what aspects might still be retrievable from some of the person bins of the network members? Under what circumstances and for what purposes might this occur (Connerton, 1989; Middleton & Edwards, 1990)?

Reputational Information About a Person: Fragmented and Scattered

To gain a useful perspective on the information naturally generated by a person's daily conduct, we must consider varied points of view: a God's eye view, the person's own view, and the view of the members of her or his reputational community.

The God's eye view is admittedly a heuristic device. The notion of an omniscient, continually attending observer and recorder of a person's life-long conduct can be found in the popular song about Santa coming to town: "He sees you when you're sleeping; he knows when you're awake; he knows if you've been bad or good. . . ." The person's conduct in this respect can be considered to be an ongoing sequence of historical events. Implicitly, reconstructing this historical record is one aim of biographers and autobiographers—but one that is quickly acknowledged to be unattainable (Craik, 1996b; Lowenthal, 1985, 1996).

The person as agent of action seems to occupy an advantaged position as the constantly present observer of the actions generated. Nevertheless, a comprehensive and inclusive view of one's own lifelong doings is withheld from us, due to fluctuating states of consciousness and attention as well as the limits of memory (Rubin, 1988).

In Jean Anouilh's (1967) play *Traveler Without Luggage*, an unidentified World War I soldier seemingly suffering from amnesia is taken from his hospital to the estate of his possible family. He learns from the recollections of household members that he was cruel to animals, had cheated on an important examination, had crippled his boyhood friend by pushing him down a flight of stairs, had bilked an old family friend out of funds, had had an affair with his sister-in-law while his older brother was off to the war, and was not on speaking terms with his mother when he himself had left for the war front. Alarmed and repelled, our hero exclaims "for a man without a memory an entire past is too much to take on one's back at one go" (p. 159). A central message of Anouilh's play is that, amnesia or not, the soldier's past had continued to exist socially in recollected observations by family members and servants, who will now expect him to accept or accommodate their accounts with his own.

Indeed, we emerge as infants into our preexisting reputational community. Conversations around collections of family photographs offer one kind of occasion when parents communicate their own memories and impressions from their offsprings' early childhoods (Middleton & Edwards, 1990). Shortly after her birth, my two and a half–pound, early-arriving granddaughter was consensually reported by the nurses of the neonatal intensive care unit to be "feisty." When she left the unit for home, healthy and nearly five pounds, another nurse apparently independently noted how "feisty" she was. Thus, the beginnings of a reputation.

But as a person's reputational network expands and embodies the kind of low-density interconnections typical of modern life, the opportunities and circumstances for gathering and integrating community information about a person decline. These possible occasions include security clearances, testimonial dinners, and eulogies.

Reputational Information About a Person: Evaluatively Charged

The information about persons that travels along the transmission lines among members of their reputational network and is stored in their person bins is not only partial and selective, fragmented and scattered but also positively or negatively charged. Most trait adjectives used in everyday language to characterize persons and their conduct are evaluatively positive or negative rather than neutral (Hampson, Goldberg, & John, 1987; Peabody, 1984).

Positive and negative trait concepts have been shown to display different properties with regard to inferences observers make when confirming or disconfirming their attributions to specific persons (Rothbart & Park, 1986). As the favorability of traits decreases, the number of prototypical acts required to confirm a trait as descriptive of a person also decreases, while the number of positive acts required to disconfirm undesirable trait attributions increases. The findings by this classic 1986 study that unfavorable traits appear to be easier to acquire and harder to lose have recently been replicated (Tausch, Kenworthy, & Hewstone, 2007).

The negativity bias in forming and maintaining impressions of other persons refers to a general pattern of research results indicating that, compared to favorable traits, unfavorable traits appear to be easier to acquire (i.e., requiring fewer confirming unfavorable acts) while also harder to lose (i.e., requiring a greater number of disconfirming favorable acts) (Birmbaum, 1973; Lupfer, Weeks, & Dupuis, 2000; Skowronski & Carlston, 1989, 1992).

For example, Birmbaum (1973) reported that adding a single immoral act to a sequence or trend of otherwise uniformly moral acts attributed to a person produced a sharp decrease in how commendable (versus reprehensible) the agent of the acts was rated. However, the reverse did not occur. This finding suggested to Birmbaum that "a person may be judged by his worst bad deed" (p. 399). The highly moral acts included "Rescuing a family from a burning house" and "Donating a kidney to a child who needed an organ transplant." The highly immoral acts included "Putting razor blades in children's apples on Hallowe'en" and "Torturing prisoners of war to extract information."

Recent research has indicated that the negativity bias appears to be moderated by the degree of consistency featured in the act trends at issue (Lupfer et al., 2000; Skowronski & Carlston, 1989, 1992). Drawing from a pool of act descriptions exemplifying a set of traits deemed moral versus immoral (e.g., humble versus arrogant, honest versus dishonest), Lupfer et al. (2000) asked judges to make predictions about a person's future conduct based upon these varying act trends offered as descriptive of the individual's conduct to date. For example, a set of three acts illustrating moral conduct is presented and the judge is then asked to decide whether the person when asked by his sister for help on a personal problem either (*1*) helped right away (caring) or (*2*) said he did not have time (uncaring). Judges were found to form their predictions as congruent with general past conduct. And when presented with an additional act trend, judges revised their predictions in response to both inconsistent favorable and unfavorable act trends. Nevertheless, the negativity bias still prevailed: "Learning that actors previously thought to be of good character had subsequently committed immoral acts caused respondents to reverse their initial predictions more completely than did learning that actors thought to be of bad character had then displayed one or more moral acts" (p. 1362).

The negativity bias and its consequences offer one rationale, and perhaps a source, for the development of defamation law and the individual right to protect reputation from false and defamatory assertions. This bias is a manifestation of the disproportionate impact of negative attributions. The network interpretation of reputation adds the recognition that once false-negative attributions are circulated, efforts to trace or track them in order to correct the falsehood become extremely difficult. We will return to this issue in our review of defamation law in Chapter 8.

Traits, Sins, and Crimes as Categories of Everyday Acts

We have noted already that the everyday acts of a person can be categorized into various trait categories. That is, certain situated acts can be considered as prototypic of certain personality traits; for example, "taking charge after the accident" can be judged to exemplify the trait category for "dominant" (Buss & Craik, 1983a, 1985; Shopshire & Craik, 1996). When we describe a person as "dominant," we are making a summarizing assertion about a relatively high incidence of prototypically dominant acts in the individual's everyday conduct over a period of observation (Buss & Craik, 1983b, 1984; Craik, 1997; Hampshire, 1953; Wiggins, 1997). The thousands of trait-like terms to be found in ordinary English (Allport & Odbert, 1936) have been structured usefully into five classifications: extraversion, agreeableness, conscientiousness, neuroticism, and openness (John & Srivastava, 1999).

Although we seem to have the capacity to make fine discriminations between relative levels of the social desirability of both acts and traits, it clearly does not follow that we—and especially other people—manage to abstain from conduct that is widely and consensually judged to be negative and undesirable. Otherwise, what would be the use or function of such disreputable trait terms as "cowardly," "cruel," or "negligent"?

In addition, specific sins and crimes can be conceptualized as specific acts or categories of acts (Katz, 1997; Moore, 1993; Aquinas, 1952; Brown, 1948). Indeed, Moore (1993) asserts that "In today's highly regulated, industrialized society, a criminal code typically prohibits approximately 7000 types of actions" (p. 1). These prohibited acts are categorized in various ways. For example, the *Model Penal Code* is an illustrative system upon which most U.S. state legislatures draw in drafting new criminal statutes (Katz, 1997, p. 35).

The main distinction of this classificatory system is between felonies and misdemeanors, which is intended to differentiate "between serious and minor offenses" (American Law Institute, 1985, Part I, Volume 1, p. 70). Felonies are further subclassified as first-degree (e.g., acts of murder, robbery), second-degree (e.g., acts of aggravated assault, arson), and third-degree (e.g., acts of negligent homicide, bribery of public officials) (American Law Institute, 1985, Part I, Volume 3, pp. 38–40).

The domain of sinful acts has also been categorized. Within Roman Catholic theology, preparation for the sacrament of penance entails the confession of sinful acts. In the confessional booth, churchgoers report the types and frequencies of specific sins they have committed (Brown, 1948). Several categorical distinctions among sins have been drawn, including mortal versus venial sins and spiritual versus carnal sins (Aquinas, 1952; Coriden, Green, & Heintschel, 1985). Mortal, or grave, sins are considered to be sins against God's law and must be confessed in order to avoid the death of the soul and exclusion from the kingdom of God. They include idolatry, adultery, and avarice. In contrast, confession of venial, or daily (i.e., *peccata quotidiana*), sins is merely recommended; however, their remission does serve the health of the soul (Coriden et al., 1985, p. 695). A kind of parallel can be seen here with the distinction between felonies and misdemeanors in the criminal code.

Although enjoying stronger standing in literature than in theology, the well-known set of seven deadly sins also offers some taxonomic guidance (Bloomfield, 1952; Lyman, 1979; Schimmel, 1992). This system of cardinal

Table 3.1 Alternative Systems for Categorizing Acts

Domain	Category System	Higher-Order Taxonomy	Example
Personality	Traits	Five-factor model	Conscientiousness (high to low)
Morality	Sins	Seven deadly sins	Sloth
Legal system	Crimes	Model penal code	Misdemeanor

sins, traceable to pre-Christian and Egyptian sources, includes pride, glut-tony, lust, anger, greed, envy, and sloth. Although the term "deadly" may derive in part from the notion of mortal sins, the two systems do not fully overlap (Bloomfield, 1952).

Table 3.1 presents the basic elements of these three alternative systems for categorizing everyday acts of persons as exemplars of specific traits, crimes, and sins as well as their higher-order domains of the five-factor model of trait terms, the seven deadly sins, and the classifications of the criminal code. The systems of sins and crimes focus entirely upon unfavorable acts, while the trait taxonomy offers a much broader coverage of everyday human conduct.

Disreputable Acts

In the present analysis, the dispositional characterization of disreputable acts will be employed both to illuminate the nature of reputation and, at the same time, to highlight the often neglected "dark side" of the five-factor domains of trait concepts (John & Srivastava, 1999).

When juries decide in favor of the plaintiff in cases of libel and slander, they are usually holding that the defendant's assertion about the act of the plaintiff at issue was likely to be harmful to reputation "in the 'meaning' of the words in their ordinary sense" (Milmo & Rogers, 1998). Thus, a review of successful actions for defamation furnishes us with a pool of disreputable acts, certified by the deliberations of a common jury (or judge in cases tried without a jury).

The category of disreputable acts evokes the construct of reputation and those attributions of conduct that are seen to endanger a person's reputation. Furthermore, through the common law tradition on libel and slander, judges and juries, in actions for defamation, must make specific and informative judgments regarding the kinds of attributions of conduct that can be expected to harm an individual's reputation. To explore this matter, I have examined a pool of disreputable acts, based upon the specific core acts at issue in successful actions for defamation. Typically in these cases, the core acts were judged to be harmful to reputation (Craik & Gosling, 2001).

In this way, an empirical analysis of disreputable acts serves as a window on what kinds of acts attributed to persons within the process of everyday social communication can make the person's reputation vulnerable. Specifically, analyzing how a sample of disreputable acts is categorized among the major five-factor domains of trait concepts will serve to delineate the dispositional nature of conduct that is believed to put an individual's reputation in harm's way (Craik & Gosling, 2001).

Dispositional Analysis of Core Acts in Defamation Case Summaries

Records of successful defamation cases are not easy to find, for no official central repository is maintained. However, one of the two major British texts on defamation law does provide a comprehensive set of brief summaries for 182 successful cases from 1951 through 1985 (Carter-Ruck & Walker, 1985; Carter-Ruck, 1990), to which case 183 was added from a newspaper account. Thus, these cases provide a pool of acts whose attribution to an individual is likely to damage that person's reputation. The fact that these assertions of conduct were deemed in many defamation cases not to be true regarding the plaintiff is irrelevant to our purposes in these analyses.

Prototypicality Judgments

What are the dispositional characteristics of certified disreputable acts? To examine this question, a panel of six raters with prior knowledge of the "Big Five" dimensions of personality descriptors received additional reading and training exercises based upon John (1990) and Saucier and Goldberg (1996). They then independently rated the core act description at issue in each defamation case summary on how prototypic it is of each of the Big Five dimensions. Rather than assume bipolarity, we had ten dimensions rated: high Extraversion, low Extraversion, high Agreeableness, low Agreeableness, high

Conscientiousness, low Conscientiousness, high Neuroticism, low Neuroticism, high Openness, and low Openness. Thus, the raters independently judged the prototypicality of the core acts with regard to each of these ten five-factor model (FFM) domains. Judgments were recorded on a seven-point rating scale, with instructions adapted from Buss and Craik (1983a, 1984). The order of subsets of cases was counterbalanced among the six raters.

Table 3.2 offers an overview of the FFM findings with regard to disreputable acts. Of the sixty-three disreputable acts that received strong prototypicality judgments (above 6.0 on the seven-point scale), thirty are situated within the low Agreeableness domain, 18 within low Conscientiousness, and 14 within high Extraversion. Prototypicality judgments above 5.0 (including those above 6.0) place ninety-two disreputable acts within low Agreeableness, seventy-four within high Extraversion, and fifty-nine within low Conscientiousness. For high prototypicality judgments, little engagement is demonstrated beyond these three FFM poles. Furthermore, a paucity of high prototypicality ratings is shown for the Neuroticism and Openness domains.

Disreputable Acts: High Extraversion

The disreputable acts characterized by high Extraversion typically entail conduct in public places by those who tend to lead public lives. It is not simply the high incidence of entertainers, celebrities, nightclub owners, and columnists as agents or facilitators of this conduct. Rather, the specific acts tend to be "over the top" in being boisterous, carefree, spirited, loud-mouthed, or flamboyant. Furthermore, even within popular expectations concerning

Table 3.2 Distribution of Highly Prototypical Disreputable Acts

Mean Prototypicality Rating	Five-Factor Model Domains Frequency Distribution				
	High E	High A	High C	High N	High O
Above 6.0	14	0	0	0	0
Above 5.0	74	1	6	9	1
Above 5.0	2	92	59	0	8
Above 6.0	0	30	18	0	1
	Low E	Low A	Low C	Low N	Low O

Table 3.3 Disreputable Acts: Illustrative Cases for Characterizing Dispositions

Trait Domain	Prototypicality Rating
High Extraversion libel cases	As an actor, his wild nightlife led to his forgetting his lines, thereby holding up the filming (case 121: 6.83) At a restaurant, she drunkenly spilled wine on other patrons and got into an argument with one of them (case 154: 6.67)
Low Agreeableness libel cases	He provided funds for a plot to kill a male model (case 141: 6.83) He was involved in performing 17,000 "experimental" operations without anesthetics at a Nazi concentration camp (case 067: 6.83)
Low Conscientiousness libel cases	As a boxer, he was fat and out of training for a major boxing match (case 034: 6.67) He was engaged in the development of a housing estate that was untidy and dangerous (case 076: 6.67)

public figures, this conduct edges toward the impetuous, unrestrained, sexy, or exhibitionistic. In summary, this array of disreputable conduct represents, at a minimum, extraversion's loud and showy side (see Table 3.3 for illustrative act descriptions).

Disreputable Acts: Low Agreeableness

The disreputable acts characterized by low Agreeableness entail forms of conduct that are cold-hearted, harsh, bigoted, brutal, and destructive. The criminality of this set of acts encompasses murder, assassination, war crimes, rape, blackmail, robbery, and swindling. The conduct often represents a ruthless, bullying, and predatory misuse of authority by police officers, physicians, teachers, employers, and business agents. This domain of cold-hearted and cruel acts is all too familiar in contemporary life but less often encountered in reports of personality research.

Disreputable Acts: Low Conscientiousness

The disreputable acts characterized by low Conscientiousness entail modes of conduct that are negligent, undisciplined, or irresponsible. The acts typically represent a failure to meet the standards of an individual's occupation, trade, or profession through conduct that is reckless, ineffective, lax, or unreliable. Often, the conduct places at risk public health and safety, public monies, or the welfare of professional clients.

In future research, an analysis of the overlap of prototypicality judgments of the same act descriptions for both the seven deadly sins and the FFM domains might be undertaken. Note, for example, that several disreputable acts prototypic of high Extraversion are evocative of the deadly sins of lust and gluttony (which encompasses excessive drinking as well as eating). Furthermore, trait terms that exemplify FFM Extraversion allude to the deadly sin of pride (e.g., proud, show-off) (John & Srivastava, 1999; Saucier & Goldberg, 1998). The disreputable acts prototypic of FFM low Agreeableness as well as trait term markers appear to resonate with the seven deadly sins of anger (e.g., antagonistic, belligerent), greed (e.g., greedy, selfish), and envy (e.g., egotistical, jealous). Finally, the disreputable acts prototypic of low Conscientiousness encompass those that point to the deadly sin of sloth, as do several trait markers (e.g., lazy, negligent).

Conclusion

We have noted that a network model consisting only of linkage and flows of information yields a rather odd and unsatisfying formulation of reputation. Similarly, a prenetwork model entailing only nodes would also fail to do an adequate conceptual job for us. It is possible to imagine a community of adults taking a vow of silence and a commitment not to communicate with each other about others. Then the nodes would store only results of their direct interaction with each other. However, such an isolated-observer model covers an extremely rare situation and cannot further our understanding of the developmental and life-span nature of the reputational process. We will return to these issues in the next chapter. The distinctive dual facets of discursive reputation and distributive reputation must be recognized but within a unified model.

4

Buzz and Bins

The Discursive and Distributive Facets of Reputation

The theoretical elements of our network interpretation generate two major aspects of reputation: the discursive facet dealing with actively flowing information and the distributive facet dealing with latent stored information about the person. They constitute the two forms in which the common knowledge of the specific person is socially represented.

This distinction between reputational information flow and storage generates two modes of reputational network analysis. The discursive facet of reputation requires the analysis of spontaneous occasions of chat, gossip, and talk about a specific person, drawing upon methods from the fields of social linguistics and communication studies. The distributive facet of reputation employs elicitation methods and the systematic sampling of reputational network members, drawing upon techniques from the fields of survey research and personality assessment.

Reputation as Fama

In its ordinary meaning, reputation, with its reference to what is generally said or believed about a person, constitutes a particular form of common knowledge.

During the twelfth and thirteenth centuries in southern Europe, the term *fama* referred to a semantically rich and important cultural construct. For example, within the courts in the walled town of Lucca in 1188, one legal issue was the personal status of a man named Betto. Betto argued that *"publica fama"* supported his claim that he was an independent peasant proprietor and free tenant and not in service or vassalage to the local cathedral and its monks.

Fama referred in this context to what was generally said, what was common knowledge about community events or actions. In other contexts, it could refer to reputation, to what was generally said about specific persons. In a primarily oral culture with few written documents, individuals such as Betto could bring witnesses to testify to the fama regarding his socioeconomic status, to what people generally said about it, and according to what in the modern context would be considered merely hearsay testimony (Wickham, 2003). Unfortunately, testimony suggested that Betto was widely known to engage regularly in the semiservile actions of cutting stone and wood for the cathedral. Although he maintained that he did so merely as a favor, not as a sign of his dependent status, Betto lost his case (Wickham, 2003, p. 18).

Historians of medieval Europe have been examining such legal cases because witnesses were sometimes asked by judges to give their own understanding of fama. For example, the question might be as follows: What is fama? "It's what people say is good about someone" or "Fama is that which is generally said among people about any business or fact." Or the question might be as follows: Where is the fama? "It is in the street Bertrand lives on, among his neighbors." Or the question might be as follows: How many people make the fama? "Three, four, or even more than four make the fama" or "Ten, twenty, thirty, forty people say these things" (Fenster & Small, 2003a, p. 3).

In criminal court cases, witnesses were restricted to testifying about direct knowledge. But in civil cases dealing with personal status and rights, property, contracts, debts, and various disputes, fama played a key role: "What the public environment accepted as true was, indeed, to an extent valid in law as well" (Wickham, 2003, p. 19). Furthermore, testimony was taken about the common knowledge concerning not just the matter at hand but also the participants in the action: "Though there was fama about debts, quittances, and the ownership of goods and property, the fama or renown of people—plaintiffs, defendants, and witnesses—was probably of greatest interest to jurists and users of the courts alike" (Fenster & Small, 2003, p. 3).

A shortcoming of the appeal to the common talk and knowledge is found, of course, when consensus is lacking as two or more different interest groups, families, or factions generated alternative renderings of the common knowledge. Betto's version lost the case due to a conflicting and more persuasive account of fama.

Reputation as Social Representation

The notion that mere talk is important and can embody the common knowledge of the community has diminished somewhat with the advent of literacy, printed documents, and other media and the rise of experts claiming more sophisticated kinds of knowledge. The theory of social representation holds that talk and common knowledge nevertheless continue to play a central and pervasive role in contemporary culture (Farr & Moscovici, 1984; Moscovici, 1984b). Moscovici and his associates have introduced a systematic examination of social knowledge that embodies the spirit of fama (Moscovici, 1984a, 1984b).

Reputation can be readily viewed as more or less informal, nonexpert social knowledge concerning a specific person. Thus, reputation can be subsumed within the conceptual framework of social representations (Bromley, 1993; Emler & Ohana, 1993).

Social Representation and Common Knowledge

A prototypic image for the act of acquiring knowledge entails an isolated individual consulting an encyclopedia. The theory of social representations holds that, on the contrary, most of our understanding of the world does not consist of that kind of expert knowledge of a topic possessed by the authors of entries in an encyclopedia nor is most of our knowledge communicated to us by the mode of systematic presentation found in an encyclopedia, textbook, or lecture.

On the contrary, the knowledge of the world possessed and developed by members of a community is derived from a multitude of forms of informal everyday communication and discourse, including family discussions, newspapers, conversations with coworkers, television programs, explorations of the Internet, mundane exchanges with friends and neighbors, as well as perhaps a bit of the more systematic treatments found in books and classes on various topics. Out of this ongoing communication and discourse emerges everyday knowledge and commonsense understandings of that community's world. The content of that knowledge is comprised of social representations that allow members to answer such questions as follows: What is this new phenomenon of biotechnology? or What were the character and influence of Abraham Lincoln? or What are the requirements of the recently adopted zoning plan for our city?

In contrast to expert knowledge, everyday knowledge is more fragmented in coverage, more uneven in the reliability of its sources, and more selective in its dissemination. Nevertheless, the formation and shifting nature of social representations of entities and processes constitute the informal and dynamic understanding that most of us have available to comprehend most of our world.

The analysis of social representation has attracted the attention of social scientists in the fields of anthropology, linguistics, psychology, and sociology (Breakwell & Canter, 1993; Doise, Clemence, & Lorenzi-Cioldi, 1993; Deaux & Philogene, 2001; Farr & Moscovici, 1984). Within this research tradition, at least two methodological guilds exist, which reflect long-standing tensions in the history of attitude research (Bauer & Gaskell, 1999; Gaskell, 2001).

Implications of Social Representation Analysis

By locating the reputations of specific persons within the framework offered by the theory of social representations, we can appreciate the kind of knowledge that is carried by reputations. That knowledge is informal, mundane, commonsense knowledge. As we shall see in later chapters, it can be contrasted, for example, with the kind of expert, scientifically based knowledge claims about persons advanced by such fields of inquiry as personality psychology and social psychology.

Furthermore, we can appreciate the tremendously crowded arena of commonsense knowledge within which the reputations of specific persons must coexist. Think of the incredible number of distinct objects and ideas filling our minds and those of our contemporaries. Consider, for example, that every entry in a comprehensive dictionary or encyclopedia also exists as a potential individual social representation. The reputation of each person exists within this crowded multitude of social representations, nested and escorted within its reputational network and having to squeeze its way throughout the person's life course and posthumously thereafter. This dual analysis generates the two facets that our network formulation has already identified: information flow and information storage. The discursive component of reputation captures the flow of social communications within the networks of specific persons. The distributive component of reputation encompasses the cognitive person bins that reputational network members develop to tag and store impressions, beliefs, and evaluations of specific persons.

Analysis of Discursive and Distributive Reputation

One tradition in the analysis of social representation focuses upon the naturally occurring discussions found around the family dinner table and tends to employ techniques of discourse analysis such as narrative textual analysis (e.g., Billig, 1993; McKinlay, Potter, & Wetherell, 1993). The other tradition examines the distributed nature of social representations, eliciting standard and systematically sampled responses evoked from individuals and then employing multivariate statistical analyses in examining the structure of aggregated findings (Doise et al., 1993; Fife-Schaw, 1993). This dual approach will reappear in our analysis of complementary formulations of reputation.

Analysis of the discursive facet of reputation requires a communication model asserting that reputation consists of what has been spontaneously said about a person or is currently being said. This model highlights the flow of information along the communication lines of the reputational network. The discursive model hews close to everyday social life, capturing the socially manifested aspects of reputation in naturally occurring settings. Thus, the discursive facet entails the active exchange of information about a person in a process of offering, accepting, and negotiating impressions, beliefs, and evaluations of the person.

Analysis of the distributive facet of reputation requires an evoked aggregate model, asserting that reputation consists of the collective impressions, beliefs, and evaluations formed and held about the person by individual reputational network members, whether or not they have ever heretofore been spontaneously expressed or communicated to others. This model highlights the nodal elements comprised of network members and the substantive content of their relevant person bins.

The distributive facet refers to a probabilistic or latent environment of pre-existing person bins arrayed among the members of a person's reputational network. These person bins function as a source of information to convey to other reputational network members a basis for forming predictions concerning the person's future conduct and a set of expectations each reputational network member holds concerning ongoing encounters with that person. The reputation that is often said to precede the person refers to this facet of reputation.

Thus, the likelihood of the person taking the social initiative can serve as the focus of a prediction about the person's future conduct, as information to be conveyed to other reputational network members, and as an expectation with regard to the nature of a reputational network member's subsequent encounters with the person.

Assessing and depicting the structure and content of a person's reputational network entail two methodological approaches. The research strategies appropriate for analysis of the discursive facet of reputation require a different set of techniques compared to the analysis of the distributive facet. The former enlists expertise in social linguistics and communication analysis, while the latter bears more on sampling methods in survey research and multivariate statistical analyses.

Meanings of Reputation Within Reputational Network Analysis

A useful conceptual framework should yield a clearer, more articulated understanding of reputation. After all, we need not remain burdened with the imprecise and fragmented notions of reputation discovered in the usage of ordinary language. We have earned the privilege to advance new and more systematic formulations. We will discover that our analysis reveals multiple sensible facets of reputation. The richness of the term in everyday usage does indeed hint at such conceptual complexity.

Two Models of Reputation

How does our conceptual formulation respond to what we will call the "reputation question"? What is this specific person's reputation? Figures 2.1 and 3.1 offer a simplified depiction of a person's reputational network and its main elements. The circles depict the various members of the network. Remember, however, that a full diagram would typically entail a few thousand circles. The lines indicate the communication connections between members; the thick lines indicate current and active information flow between members. Recall also that network members not only receive, initiate, and redirect information but also selectively store it in specific person bins.

To organize the argument that follows, we will anticipate our conclusions. Reputational network analysis generates two distinctive, complementary, and self-sustaining formulations of reputation: the spontaneous communications model and the evoked aggregate model. At a later point we will review a third option: the belief system model.

Model 1. Discursive Reputation: The Spontaneous Communication Model of Reputation

The spontaneous communication model asserts that a person's reputation consists of what has been said or is currently being said about the person. With regard to Figure 2.1, this model highlights the flow of information along the communication lines. The model is linked to everyday life, capturing the socially manifested aspects of reputation. It is anchored in naturally occurring social events. In this sense, we find that a comprehensive formulation of a person's reputation within the spontaneous communication model entails an omniscient God's eye perspective on everything that has ever been discussed about the person.

Model 2. Distributed Reputation: The Evoked Aggregate Model of Reputation

The evoked aggregate model of reputation asserts that reputation consists of the impressions, beliefs, and evaluations held about the person by reputational network members, whether they have ever been heretofore spontaneously expressed or not. With regard to Figure 3.1, this model high-lights the nodal elements comprised of network members and the substantive content of their relevant person bins. The model has the attraction of yielding a portrait of the person's probabilistic reputational environment and captur-ing its latent aspects.

The evoked aggregate model entails a God's eye perspective on all of the impressions, beliefs, and evaluations concerning the person held by every member of the person's lifelong reputational network. In both cases, various research strategies can be envisioned to yield sensible approximations of these two epistemological ideals.

Reputation as a Probabilistic Social Environment

Persons move among their reputational network members and the implicit person bins concerning them specifically. That is, they live their lives within their probabilistic distributed reputations.

On an ordinary day, a typical person moves through a sequence of behav-ior settings and along the routes connecting them. Some of the other indi-viduals they pass by or encounter may be mutual acquaintances; others may be individuals the person does not know but for various reasons they may identify and know the person. Finally, perhaps most of these other individu-als are strangers and will remain so.

The Comparative Odds of Encountering Acquaintances, Knowing Others, and Strangers

One noteworthy aspect of a person's social environment is the relative break-down of these characters. Obviously, for example, urban life differs from vil-lage life in the relative proportion of mutual acquaintances, other knowing individuals, and strangers that constitute the everyday human milieu. The attributes of a person's environment can be viewed as possessing probabilistic properties (Brunswik, 1956). Thus, for any given person, we can ask what are the odds of the person encountering or passing by acquaintances versus knowing others versus strangers? The tourism slogan "What happens in Vegas stays in Vegas," for example, seems to promise low odds on acquaintances and knowing others that are impossible to guarantee.

A person's social environment is more reputationally imbued to the extent to which acquaintances and knowing others constitute a higher proportion than do strangers. The same notion holds for the type of other individuals who in one way or another make decisions about the person during the course of everyday social life. These decisions about extending credit, inviting to dinner, hiring, engaging in conversation, making a purchase from, striking up some chat in a pub with, and so forth may be more or less consequential for the person. But the relative proportion of acquaintances, knowing others, and strangers within the person's social environment indicates the probability that these decisions by others are reputationally permeated.

The Odds of Favorable or Unfavorable Discourse

Another important aspect of a person's social environment is the extent to which it features some form of ongoing discourse about the person. On any given day, the reputational network of a person may be actively circulating an abundance of discourse concerning the person, who may for some reason or other have become the "talk of the town." But on other days, perhaps most days, the lines are close to being silent.

Perhaps equally important to the probability that something is being said about the person is the probability that what is said is favorable rather than unfavorable in evaluative valence. A high probability that something is being said about the person and that it is favorable generates a distinctive surround through which the person moves, whether accurately attuned to it or not, and similarly for the probability of being awash in the murmurs or noise of unfavorable discourse.

The Odds of Positively or Negatively Disposed Others

The human environment of other individuals can be divided into members of the person's reputational network and strangers. Strangers offer a clean slate for the person to construct a fresh impression upon heretofore unknown other individuals. In contrast, the person and an established acquaintance mobilize their preset impressions of the other as well as taking into account their beliefs about the other's prior impressions of themselves (Kenny, 1994). Finally, the encounter between the person and someone assumed by the person to be a stranger but who is in reality a knowing other may lead to miscalculations and misinterpretations, presumably with the person at a disadvantage of one kind or another.

Thus, from a social ecological perspective, one important question is the probability that when a person encounters a knowing individual, the latter will be positively rather than negatively disposed toward the person, having established predominantly favorable impressions, beliefs, and evaluations. The probabilistic configuration holds also, of course, for instances when the person has not directly encountered the other individual, but this other has third-hand information and is participating in making a decision of some kind about the person. For these instances, the odds for encountering knowing others with negative versus positive expectations must be considered an important factor.

The Distributive Reputation and the Archaeology of a Person's Reputed Development and Change

In Chapter 3, we employed an adaptation of Watts' (2003) network figure to represent the differing amounts of information each reputational network member might have stored about the person. We might now overlay a temporal dimension. Obviously, it is not the case that every reputational network member maintains an updated impression and evaluation of a person. Instead, many network members carry depictions of the person based upon more limited and discrete temporal windows of observation and information flow across the life span of the person and the associated reputational network. At the same time, the person continues to develop and change in various aspects. The windows offer selective views of these developmental phases, such as adolescence versus late adulthood, and upon social changes, such as early versus late career.

The closing of the window by a network member at a certain point is decisive, for then no new information accrues. In contrast, while windows may open at a particular point in the life span, that period of observation allows for receipt of updated hearsay information about prior and missed phases of the person's conduct and life. These temporal tags on the person bins of network members apply not only to direct acquaintance but also to the unseen audience with hearsay acquaintance.

The Reputation Question

The central assertion of our network interpretation of reputation is that individuals who know a person, who have at least minimal recognition identity for the person, function within the person's reputational network. Network members participate in the ongoing discourse about the person through chat and other communications and store their impressions, descriptions, and evaluations of the person. They are engaged members when they suggest to an acquaintance that the person is witty or when they recall their belief that the person is a certified public accountant. This dynamic, ongoing circulation and storage of information about the person is at the heart of a person's reputational network; it is the viable substance of the everyday existence of reputation.

Note that these basic reputational structures, processes, and assertions do not necessarily entail the explicit use of the term "reputation" by the reputational network members themselves.

Nevertheless, on certain occasions, it is sensible to ask the following question explicitly: What is that person's reputation? In these situations, reputational network members are asked to perform very much as we are trying to do, putting on the hat of reputational analysts. In this way, they can and sometimes do step away from inside of the reputational network and view and report upon it from the outside, calling upon a set of their relevant beliefs.

A Third Option: The Belief System Model of Reputation

The belief system model of reputation asserts that to answer the reputation question, one must play at being an omniscient God in yet another way, in this case by stating one's beliefs about the person's reputational network. The task is to convey one's understanding about some or all properties, attributes, and assertions entailed by that person's entire reputational network; about its size; about what is publicly said concerning the person; about what impressions, beliefs, and evaluations its individual members hold regarding the person; about the overall evaluative valence of these elements; and so forth.

If the individual queried happens to be a member of the person's reputational network, then the reputation question does not bear upon that member's ordinary workaday functioning in observing, discussing, and forming impressions, beliefs, and evaluations of the person. Rather, the reputation question entails a meta-task that does not deal with the member's own views about the person but instead with the member's beliefs and understanding about certain aspects of the entire reputational network of the person. That is, this model refers to and encompasses the entire reputational network that Table Intro.1 depicts. Furthermore, if the individual queried is not a member of the person's reputational network, then to answer the reputation question the individual would have to undertake explicit investigation of these various aspects of the person's reputational network.

This model might appear to possess the attraction of relieving us reputation analysts from having to proclaim what any given person's reputation is; the buck can be passed on to others. But, of course, that is not so. As reputational analysts, our professional belief system about a person's reputational network should afford an authoritative and accurate scientific account. We will examine truth in reputation in Chapter 5, with regard to accuracy and validity.

Thus, the belief system model of reputation takes two distinct forms. First, it refers to the formal and objectivity aspiring effort by reputation researchers to achieve a comprehensive and accurate analysis of any person's reputational network. Second, it refers to the beliefs that ordinary members hold regarding these same parameters concerning a given person's reputational network, including their accuracy.

Thus, in the belief system model, to respond to the reputation question, one must be ready to assert one's system of beliefs about some or all facets of the person's entire reputational network.

An abbreviated illustration of this formulation of reputation is found in the procedure sometimes used to introduce the testimony of defense witnesses in criminal court cases. Take, for example, the case of a young man being tried for assault with a deadly weapon, who struck another young man with a hammer during an angry standoff in a nightclub parking lot. The defendant's claim is self-defense. Toward the end of the trial, his attorney presents a high school sports coach as a character witness.

The important point for us is that the coach is initially asked to estimate how many individuals he knows who also know the defendant (e.g., fifteen).

Then, the coach is asked his belief about what the general evaluation of the defendant is among those other individuals. The focus is not upon the coach's testimony about his own impressions, beliefs, and evaluations concerning the young man but, instead, attention is turned to the coach's beliefs about broader aspects of the defendant's reputational network.

From the vantage point of our conceptual analysis of reputational networks, of course, many other questions could be asked concerning the coach's beliefs about other aspects of the defendant's reputational network. And with regard to us as reputational analysts, we can presume that every member of the person's reputational network has parallel belief systems about the many and varied components of any given person's reputational network.

Thus, another analytic challenge is to address this meta-task of gathering and somehow summarizing and integrating these belief systems elicited from all, or a representative sample, of the members of the person's reputational network. Our conceptual analysis of reputational networks affords a systematic framework for directly evoking and probing such beliefs about components and parameters of reputational networks. However, the monitoring of spontaneous expressions in everyday social life of the beliefs about a person's reputational network can also be envisioned, even if they might be rare events. The testimony of a single defense witness represents a naturally occurring belief expression at the individual level. A naturally occurring belief expression can occur at the collective level also, as illustrated when the spontaneous beliefs shaping the discourse at one social gathering—say, a dinner party—concern what is being said about a mutual acquaintance who is elsewhere—say, attending a class reunion.

The final issue raised by the belief model of reputation is the possibility of gauging the extent to which these beliefs are accurate, as determined by the methods appropriate to the specification of network membership, the summary of discourse about the person, and the evoked aggregated views of the person.

Our practice and commitment has been to keep the person as agent out of our conceptual analysis as long as possible. We must constantly bear in mind that reputation is dispersed among a network of other individuals. We must not lose that focus. However, we might acknowledge here that one belief system that will be particularly interesting to explore at a later point is that belief system achieved by the person herself or himself, as one sits alone in a café contemplating the full nature of one's very own reputation. Our analysis suggests that one is faced with a formidable undertaking, to which we will return in Chapters 5 and 6.

Occasions for the Reputation Question

Compared to the pervasive and ongoing functioning of the reputational network itself, the reputation question is a distinctly episodic occurrence. Under what conditions is the reputation question broached, when and where is it raised, who asks it, and for what purposes? And depending upon the context, what counts as an acceptable answer to the question?

The Reputation Question—Rarely Asked?

At the outset, we must acknowledge the possibility that, despite our own intense interest in the concept as reputational analysts, the reputation question may rarely be raised explicitly about persons in their everyday social life. Consider the dignified grandmother still living in her family house in a small town who may have generated a substantial but local lifelong reputational network. Those who are acquainted with her may believe they know a good deal about her life, her personal characteristics, and how she typically spends her days. Her acquaintances individually know her. Nevertheless, occasions to ask the explicit question "What is her reputation?" (or, even more informally, "What do folks believe she is like?") may seldom or ever arise; the reputation question goes unasked. But bear in mind that it could be answered if ever posed, for her reputation network is an ongoing and abiding matter.

Mundane Contexts for the Reputation Question

A variety of occasions can be identified in which the question of a person's reputation does arise. The appropriate form of answer varies among them. For one set of contexts, the person is a stranger in one way or another and the general purpose is to satisfy some form of appraisal or curiosity. For another set of contexts, the person is very well known and the general purpose is to express some form of appreciation or judgment (Craik, 1976). A final set of occasions entail reexamination of a familiar person, leading to a possible revision of reputation (Craik, 1993a).

Occasions of Appraisal

In the first set of occasions, information on what is said and believed about the stranger is gathered from those who already have some form of acquaintance with the person or certain indirect sources of relevant information. In these instances, one's reputation precedes one, but only if it is sought out previously by new acquaintances.

Consider, for example, these illustrative occasions that address the reputation question more or less directly.

1. *The newcomer.* In the case of the newcomer to a workplace, neighborhood, or social circle, the question about the stranger might be readily satisfied by "asking around" and finding some mutual acquaintances who do already know the person to some degree. In earlier days, for example, a traveler might carry a letter of introduction from one mutual acquaintance to be given to another upon arrival in a foreign country.

2. *The applicant for a position.* In modern, mobile societies, applicants for a position are often complete strangers to the potential employer or institution that has a position on offer. Although the legal circumstances surrounding these occasions have been changing rapidly, the practice until fairly recently has included the use references or letters of recommendation. For some sensitive positions, more elaborate inquiries or security clearances are conducted, including direct interviews with many acquaintances of the applicant, the participation of the candidate in a managerial assessment center program (Craik et al., 2002), or a search of files and records of various kinds (U.S. Senate Committee on Governmental Affairs, 1985).

3. *The suitor.* Once again, the nature of modern, mobile societies has had some impact on courtship practices. Within small isolated communities, the suitor—indeed, the full array of potential

suitors—is already known to one and all. Nowadays, in some presumably exceptional instances within urban life, private detectives are employed to conduct discreet background investigations somewhat akin to security clearances, including the gathering of reports from acquaintances.

4. *The candidate.* Questions about the reputation of candidates for public office are typically answered in two ways. First, investigative journalists and other writers contact many members of a candidate's immediate and lifelong circle of acquaintances as a basis for media "profiles." Sometimes competing political camps do likewise, in the form of "opposition research." Increasingly, candidates for high political office seek to introduce themselves to the public through autobiographies or commissioned "campaign biographies." Subsequently, as the general public becomes familiar with these sources and the candidate's background and performance, opinion surveys are conducted that elicit beliefs and evaluations of a candidate's personal qualities as well as policy positions.

Occasions of Appreciation and Judgment

In these situations the person is far from being a stranger and information about the person need not be sought for the purpose. The participants in these occasions are well acquainted, in one way or another, with the person. One purpose of participants in these occasions is to evoke and celebrate their shared common knowledge of the person. Illustrative occasions of this kind include the following:

1. *Testimonials and roasts.* Settings in which the person may be present include testimonial dinners, where several speakers evoke various deeds, stories, characteristics, and life episodes in a fond and celebratory fashion, while the so-called roasts entail a similar format but with a greater degree of more or less good-natured teasing.

2. *Obituaries, eulogies, epitaphs, and biographies.* When the person is no longer alive and present, the reputational network may still function. We will return to these occasions in our analysis of the posthumous reputation in Chapter 9.

Occasions of Reexamination and Revision

The reputational networks of persons may be stable for the most part. Indeed, in the case of reputational inertia, network members may be cut off from contemporary information flows about the person and carry forward outdated impressions, beliefs, and evaluations of the person. Thus, the flow of reputational information forms pools and eddies as well as currents and streams. Perhaps class reunions function as something of an antidote to reputational inertia.

Reputations are also open to revision (Craik, 1993a). For example, a person confronting a time of stress or transition probably gains the renewed focal attention of members of her or his reputational network. How the person deals with the challenge or crisis provides important information and opportunity for the revision of reputation. These occasions include, for example, currently struggling with a severe illness or recently advancing to senior manager.

We have been discussing the reputation question. In Chapter 5, we will consider answers to that question and how to appraise truth in reputation. Specifically, we will delineate the important distinction between reputational accuracy and reputational validity.

5

Truth in Reputation

Accuracy and Validity

How true is the information about a person that flows through a reputational network? This chapter addresses a central feature in most meanings of reputation—the content claims about attributes of the person.

The truth of these claims entails two issues: the accuracy of the claims as representative of what is actually being said and believed about the person and the validity of the claims themselves as checked against other sources of knowledge about the person. In our discussion of legal actions for defamation in Chapter 8, we will deal with the possible harmful consequences of a single false assertion that a person had committed a specific disreputable act. But, of course, the flow of information through a reputational network encompasses a wide variety of kinds of assertions about the person.

Some of the information is factual in nature, such as the person's family name, birth date, occupation, credit rating, and ownership of property and possessions. For various purposes, the accurate compilation of this kind of information is sought out by private detectives, teams conducting security clearances, and citizens sorting out incidences of identity theft.

A second kind of information about a person includes accounts of specific events having to do with the conduct of the person or of others with regard to that person. These event narratives flow through the reputational network in the form of act descriptions, anecdotes, and stories.

A third kind of information is the final topic of this chapter, namely, assertions about what kind of person this individual is. The latter issues might be framed as the big question: What is the relation between reputation and personality? We will address that larger issue in Chapter 7.

By using the term "claims," we highlight the recognition that the content of a person's reputational network constitutes claims to common knowledge. Furthermore, it clarifies the important point that no single answer can be given to the intriguing question of whether a person's reputation is "true" or gives a "true" picture of a person.

A compelling argument can be made that the magnitude of everyday observation and discourse about a person ensures that the reputation affords a "true" portrait of the person. An equally compelling argument can be made that any portrait based upon hearsay, gossip, and fragmented observation establishes that one's reputation is unlikely to provide a "true" portrait of a person.

We will find that specific reputational content claims about a person must face their own distinctive tests of accuracy and validity. No blanket answer to the general question is possible. Before we can discuss the validity of the content claims of a person's reputation, we must deal with a quite different, though parallel, array of issues that also bear upon the truth of reputation. These questions relate to the accuracy of our analysis of a person's reputation. It is necessary to go over these issues carefully so that these accuracy issues do not get mixed up in our minds with the quite separate set of validity questions. It will soon become apparent why these two sets of questions have often been jumbled together in discussions of the nature and truth of reputation.

The Accuracy of Reputational Analyses and the Validity of Reputational Content Claims

In Chapter 8, dealing with legal actions for libel and slander, we will be concerned with the impact of assertions of a disreputable act and how to defend against its harm to reputation. In a central way, truth in reputation is at issue.

In Chapter 6, we will review a wide range of offensive as well as defensive initiatives that a person can undertake in an effort to shape a reputation. In this social arena, the matter may seem to be less about the truth of reputation and more about the process of generating and controlling a constructed and sometimes contested reputation.

In this chapter, we will face head-on the question of how accuracy, validity, and truth become focal matters in the study of reputation.

When we as reputational analysts report on the structural properties of a specific reputational network, the nature of a person's current discursive reputation, or the content of beliefs and evaluations to be found within the person's distributive reputation, how can we appraise the accuracy of our reports? The accurate appraisal of a reputational network structure entails determining and checking its size and membership, the density or interrelatedness among network members, the delineation of clusters or cliques among members, bridging components, and so forth.

In addition, we must examine how we can gauge the accuracy of our reports on the various reputational content domains, based upon study of both the discursive and distributed facets of reputation. Accuracy in this endeavor relates to whether, for example, it is indeed generally said or believed that the person is dominant and bullying, that is, whether that assertion does indeed characterize or represent the content of discourse and beliefs within the person's reputational network. Notice we are using "accuracy" as one term for considering the truth of reputational analyses.

A second question is whether the implicit or explicit claims about the person embedded within the various reputational content domains are valid with regard to the facts of the matter concerning who the person is and what the person is really like.

The structure of issues regarding appraising validity parallels the agenda for appraising the accuracy of reputational analyses, but as we will see, the questions take on an entirely different set of substantive matters. The terms "accuracy" and "validity" are used in varying ways within the field of psychological assessment. For clarity, we will use these terms as consistently as possible in the following ways. The truth of such claims entails two issues: the accuracy of the claims as representative of what is actually being said and believed about the person and the validity of the claims themselves as checked against other sources of knowledge about the person.

The Accuracy of Reputational Analyses

Reputational content encompasses all of the kinds of common knowledge claims about the person that are circulating and stored within the network. For example, reputational content claims can refer to (*1*) social facts and identities, (*2*) anecdotes and act descriptions regarding the person, and (*3*) personality attributes.

Accuracy of What Is Being Said and Believed Regarding Facts About the Person

    A. He was born on March 28, 1970.
    B. She was awarded a medal for bravery during her military service.

Note the issue is whether it is generally thought that he was born in 1970, not whether this date is valid. Also, the issue is whether it is generally held that she received a medal for valor, not whether she in fact did so; that is a matter we will get to later on.

Accuracy of What Is Being Said and Believed About the Person's Conduct: Act Descriptions, Anecdotes, and Stories

    A. A woman dumped a bowl of sugar on his head at the party.
    B. She took charge of the situation after the accident.

Note that the accuracy question deals with whether this story is indeed the one widely circulated throughout this fellow's reputational network. Or is the oft-told story more frequently seen to entail a bucket of ice water rather than a bowl of sugar or that the dumping agent was a man, not a woman. Again, what really happened is moot in this context. The same holds for whether the broadly circulated story of taking charge at the accident concerns the narrative itself. For example, is it said to have been an auto accident or a boating accident?

Accuracy of What Is Being Said and Believed About Depictions of the Kind of Individual the Person Is

    A. She is dominant and bullying.
    B. He is tidy, edgy, and curious.

Finally, these personality descriptions must be checked for whether they capture the beliefs about the traits of these two persons. How we address the issue of whether the individuals are really dominant or curious will be dealt with at a later time. Such questions deal with validity.

The issue now is not whether observer A agrees with observer B but whether, if the study were to be repeated, the degree of agreement—high, moderate, or low—would be the same from one rating occasion to the other. We can conclude this review by asserting that our new field of inquiry does have some sensible means for systematic appraisal of the accuracy of representations of reputational networks.

The Validity of Reputational Content Claims

One may say that the appraisal of the accuracy of reputational analyses deals with our own reputation as reputational analysts. Did we get it right with regard to what we reported about the structural properties of the person's reputational network and about its various content domains? And as a field of inquiry, do we have the means for systematic appraisal of our accuracy?

Now we must relinquish the vantage point of the outside reputational analyst and immerse ourselves into the person's everyday reputational network, taking the vantage point of network members and perhaps that of the person herself or himself.

Here we come face-to-face with reputation's own bad reputation, namely, that it does not convey the truth about a person. Reputation is seen in some quarters as based upon mere rumor and gossip, made up of odds and ends of fleeting observations and tatters of hearsay reports, all twisted by the tendentious aims of reputational network members to bolster or derogate the person.

The team on the opposing side of this debate would hold that as a collective operation in everyday surveillance, the reputational process mobilizes the observations of hundreds of on-the-spot witnesses to the person's conduct and life. A huge investment of attention and communication is devoted to this endeavor, with many potential biases probably canceled out.

We will not settle this argument here or at this time because remarkably little systematic research is available on the question. Indeed, we will use this discussion to outline an agenda for research at a later point. What we must do first is to look at the problem of validity from the standpoint of reputational network members. They realize that the person's prevailing reputation makes certain claims about the person's status and life events and about what kind of person the individual is. They are also aware of the many commonsense ways in which these reputational content claims can be checked and appraised for validity. We will also review the various professional and scientific resources that may address these issues. For each of our three categories of reputational content claims, we will introduce a prototypic inquirer.

*How Valid Is What Is Said and Believed About the Person:
What Are the Real Facts About the Person?*

Prototypic Validity Inquirer: The Detective

A. Was he born on March 28, 1970?
B. Was she indeed awarded a medal for bravery during her military service?

Background Checks

1. Private detective assignments
2. Security clearances
3. Investigative biography

Anybody's reputational network is awash with odds and ends of factual material regarding one's credentials and bureaucratic status, including birth date, credit rating, driver's license, and educational attainments (Nock, 1993). Under certain circumstances, systematic checks of such information might be undertaken. For example, persons applying for various governmental and corporate positions might be subject to security clearances. Journalistic accounts suggest that nowadays both men and women have been known to hire private detectives to conduct background checks on possible mates or persons with whom they are entering a serious relationship. As a guild, biographers have tended to be drawn from history, literature, and the other humanities; but a new cadre of investigative biographers has come from training in journalism and makes much use of intensive scrutiny of public records (Weinstein, 1992).

But even these episodes in fact-checking are not fully aligned with the information flow within the reputational network. A fascinating program of research would examine, first, what array of factual information exists within a typical person's reputational network and, second, what domains of background facts tend to be accurately represented within everyday discourse about persons and within reputational network members' person bins for individuals.

A simple list of fifty background facts could provide the basis for a survey of what knowledge claims about the person might be made by members of differing regions of the person's reputational network. What is the base rate validity of reputational network content claims regarding college education, place of birth, upbringing, and other social/personal facts for which we can readily establish criteria for validity? The kinds of background information that tend to be validly represented would be revealing, as would those that are subject to common misconceptions.

Did Events Occur as Described in Accounts Within Anecdotes, Stories, and Other Narratives?

Prototypic Validity Inquirer: The Historian

A. Did a woman actually dump a bowl of sugar on his head at the party?
B. Did she take charge of the situation following the accident?

Colorful anecdotes about the conduct of historical figures, such as George Washington, often turn out to be more legend than historical narrative.

The problems entailed in establishing the validity of narratives in historical research can also be mobilized for analyzing mundane events of everyday social life. The required steps might include (*1*) gathering witnesses and documented accounts of the incident, (*2*) establishing that a relevant individual event of some kind did occur, (*3*) delineating the context of the event, (*4*) seeking corroboration among witnesses and evidence, (*5*) being alert to biases of various kinds, (*6*) dealing with the ubiquity of multiple descriptions of the same act, and (*7*) taking into account rumor dynamics in the transmission of accounts of an event to third parties (Lowenthal, 1996).

The functioning of the community of historical scholars need not be altogether different from that of a community of reputational analysts. In the case of the validity of storied accounts of the conduct and life of a person, we can examine their prevalence throughout the person's reputational network as well as their validity. However, our efforts to establish some historically sound account of the events themselves will be a challenge to patience and resources. The most interesting results of such research on prevalence and validity may be our general appraisal of how easy or difficult it is to assemble relevant evidence. We might begin validity appraisals with a small set of the most often rendered accounts of specific episodes concerning a particular person.

How Well Do Reputational Depictions of the Kind of Person the Individual Is Match with the Individual's Personality Characteristics?

Prototypic Validity Inquirer: The Personality Assessor

A. Is she dominant and bullying?
B. Is he tidy, edgy, and curious?

In validity matters concerning societal fact, such as whether the person has indeed been divorced, a reputational network member can appeal to various institutional records. And in matters of noteworthy events in the person's life, one can marshal witnesses and other corroborating evidence. In questions about what the individual is like "as a person," the network member, of course, has immediate appeal to her or his own judgments of personality and to those of other reputational network members.

Human observers are sensitive and skillful instruments for monitoring and interpreting information about the personality of others. Furthermore, the ordinary language is rich in descriptive and evaluative terms that are available to observers for portraying and communicating their impressions of other persons.

From the beginning days of personality psychology, observer judgments of personality have been the focus of a long-standing psychological research program.

One objective of this research tradition is to demonstrate that observer-based personality judgments yield substantially valid information about what the person is actually like. That is, personality descriptions gathered from acquaintances of a person tend to agree with each other, and they relate significantly to other sources of information about the person, such as that person's self-descriptions and trends in that person's everyday conduct.

Reviews of this research offer convincing support for these expectations in the contexts within which they have been examined (Funder, 1999; Kenny, 1994; McCrae & Weiss, 2008; Vazire, 2006). Let us review the kinds of evidence that personality psychologists proffer for establishing that a personality characterization of an individual is valid. We will cite exemplary reports for the findings from empirical studies of these topics. And we will pose them as questions for appraising the validity of reputational content claims concerning personality attributes.

Thus, for validity appraisal requirements with regard to a specific personality content claim:

1. Do reputational network members tend to agree about the personality attributes of the person (Funder, 1999)?

2. Do reputational network members having differing relations with the person tend to agree (e.g., parents versus hometown acquaintances) (Funder, Kolar, & Blackman, 1995)?

3. Do reputational network members having longer acquaintance with the person tend to agree more about this personality characteristic (McCrae & Weiss, 2008)?

4. Do personality judgments regarding the person gathered from the same reputational members several years apart tend to agree (McCrae, 1994)?

5. Do personality judgments gathered at year 1 from some reputational network members tend to agree with ratings gathered from different members several years later (McCrae, 1994)?

6. Do personality judgments gathered from reputational network members who have never met each other, such as college and hometown acquaintances, tend to agree with each other as much as those who have met (Funder, Kolar, & Blackman, 1995)?

7. Do the personality descriptions made about the person by reputational network members tend to agree with the person's self-descriptions (Funder, 1999)?

8. Do the personality trait ratings made by reputational network members tend to be associated with trait prototypic act trends in the everyday

conduct of the person (Funder, 1999; Gormly, 1984; Buss & Craik, 1983a, 1983b, 1984)?

This array of validity checks indicates that concurrent consensus among reputational network members is not alone a sure and complete indicator of validity. Both Funder (1999) and Kenny (1994) introduce the important qualification that even complete consensus among judges is not a sufficient condition for the validity of personality judgments. Funder (1999, p. 87) notes "the possibility that everybody might be wrong at once, as difficult as ascertaining such collective error would of course prove to be."

Implications of Reputational Network Tiers

The major implication of our analysis of truth in reputation is that the basic issue cannot be phrased as a single question. It is inappropriate to ponder whether persons "earn" their reputation or to ask whether or not reputation is ill-founded and misleading.

Over the life course, a person generates a steady and diverse flow of information about the kind of person he or she is. In the most general sense, our knowledge of persons derives from this rich variety of sources of information about them. Any and all of these multiple kinds of information about a person can constitute a reputational network content claim. Each content claim can be appraised with regard to how accurately it is embodied within the reputational network and how validly it depicts the person's relevant social fact, narrative, or personality characteristic.

The assertion that a person has a reputation for being courageous can be examined in two ways. First, does this assertion accurately represent a content claim by members of the person's reputational network? That may or may not be the case. Second, if the assertion is an accurately depicted reputational content claim, then is the claim valid? Can independent evidence be assembled in support of the assertion? If so, then perhaps it can be said the person has "earned" a reputation in this particular regard. But no generalization to all the other information domains follows from that demonstration.

In the same way, research may reveal that certain content claim domains are consistently shown to be invalid. For those instances, reputation may be consistently ill-founded and misleading. But once again generalization to other domains is unwarranted.

It is difficult to forecast the lay of the land with regard to these issues. One reason is that most research on interpersonal perception and personality judgments has dealt with close acquaintances or, in the case of laboratory studies, with complete strangers. The large area of peripheral or hearsay network members remains unexamined.

Nevertheless, our network interpretation permits us to sketch out some of these heretofore neglected research issues in a more detailed fashion.

Recall first our differentiation among first-tier, second-tier, and third-tier members of a person's reputational network (see Figure 1.1):

- *First tier*: The first-tier members are directly acquainted with the person. Their personality impressions are formed with a substantial input of direct interactions and observations of the person's everyday conduct. At the same time, these first-tier network members are not sequestered from the ongoing flow of other, indirect information about the person.

- *Second tier*: The second-tier network members are not directly acquainted with the person but share at least one common acquaintance who reports extensively and directly on the person's conduct. Examples include friends and family members of a person's long-term coworker. They have never met the person but have acquired an abundance of secondhand information about the person through the coworker's shop talk and accounts of daily happenings at the workplace. At the same time, they have direct access to information about their hearsay informant and about the relation of this coworker and the person.

- *Third tier*: The third-tier network members have never met the person, nor do they know any first-tier network members who directly know the person. Their sources of information come in the form of second- and thirdhand common knowledge about the person, that is, in the form of social representations of the person's conduct combined with the gist of ongoing discourse regarding the person.

Depending upon how a network member is situated, the processes and skills in generating a personality trait description of a person can be hypothesized to vary in certain ways.

The first-tier network members must draw upon their observational and inferential skills for monitoring and interpreting everyday conduct through use of ordinary language trait descriptors.

The second-tier network members are dependent upon their skills in interpreting the more or less detailed accounts of their informant and their knowledge of this coworker (e.g., is the informant a good judge of others?). Their inferences may be guided by further discussion among other family members who may query the coworker about the workplace context and dynamics.

The third-tier network members must depend upon processes that evoke their savvy in seeking out diverse forms of common knowledge about a person, keeping more or less up-to-date regarding them and possibly weighing the credibility of alternative claims about what the person has done and is like.

Due to these variations, the validity of members' personality judgments may differ according to their tier location and associated processes and skills.

Comparative Analysis

These differentiations segment a person's reputational network into three separate sources of content claims and generate important research questions. The most salient is the question of whether first-, second-, and third-tier members yield similar or different levels of validity in their content claims.

One argument is that we can expect a fall-off in levels of validity as we move from direct observation to more indirect sources. That is, the first-tier members enjoy a privileged access to the reality of the person's trait characteristics, which entails a decrement as one moves from first-tier members to second- and third-tier members.

The counterargument is that the evolutionary perspective establishes the fundamental importance of valid content claims throughout reputational networks. As a consequence, the processes and skills exercised by second- and third-tier members, while different in kind from those employed by first-tier members, nevertheless function adequately to capture, represent, and transmit valid outcomes comparable to those encompassed by the content claims of first-tier members.

Reputation: The Story Thus Far

In this first part of the book, we have established that persons live their lives within a finite but ever-changing and cumulating reputational network. The social network is based primarily on mutual relationships. Among this set of acquaintances, the person recognizes the identities of its members, each of whom recognizes the specific person in turn. However, the reputational network is by definition broader and additionally subsumes those members who know the person even though the person does not know them. For completion, our conceptual framework also encompasses the case of those members the person knows but who do not know the person. In our approach, the reputational network functions primarily on the flow and storage of information about specific persons.

Each member of a person's reputational network accumulates beliefs, evaluations, and impressions of the person based upon a wide array of information gained from direct observation and interaction as well as from hearsay reports from third parties by way of chat, gossip, and more formal accounts and occasions. The structure of reputational networks is founded on a categorization of information concerning everyday acts, anecdotes, and impressions into cognitive person bins. The person bins of each reputational network member are organized around recognition identity for that person over possibly long periods of observation and discourse with others concerning the person. Thus, over the typical life course, a few thousand individuals function as nodes in a somewhat fragmented communication network. We have discussed the various forms of social communication about a specific person that are circulated along this network. These nodes do not simply transmit and direct the flow of information about a person but also entail the cognitive person bins that accumulate and integrate some or all of this information. Finally, by mobilizing this conceptual framework and its components, we are now in a position to examine the concept of reputation and its various meanings in more detail.

Reputation: The Dictionary Meaning

A seemingly direct route to understanding a term or concept is through its dictionary definition and ordinary usage (Bromley, 1993). The *Pocket Oxford Dictionary of Current Usage* (Allen, 1984), for example, defines *reputation* as referring to "what is generally said and believed about a person."

In closing this part of the book, let us unpack some of the notions embedded within this dictionary definition and the issues and implications they raise for a network interpretation of reputation.

What Is Said About a Person

This component of the definition points to the ongoing discourse about persons that takes place informally and spontaneously in chat and gossip and more formally in communications and reports about the person flowing from occasions of privilege.

Issues

This statement might be framed in several ways. First, it can refer to some kind of hypothetical text file of everything that anyone has ever said about the person. This notion raises the problem of how to determine, sample, and then summarize an adequate representation of that text. In any case, it can in this fashion denote a manifest domain of what has at some point or other been spontaneously said about the person. Second, it can refer to what members of a person's reputational network would say about the person if asked certain and various questions about him or her (e.g., How credit-worthy is this person?). This notion refers to a latent domain of what would be said under certain conditions if it were so elicited. Then come ancillary issues about who would be asking these questions, what members of the reputational network would be queried, what questions would be asked, and how the results of the inquiry might be summarized.

What Is Believed About a Person

This distributive component of the definition calls more direct attention to the relevant cognitive person bin maintained by each member of a person's reputational network.

Issues

This statement can be formulated in several ways. First, one implication is that each reputational network member holds a set of beliefs, evaluations, and impressions of the person. Furthermore, these beliefs and so forth tend to guide decisions that each member might make about the person (e.g., Would this person be a good friend? Is this person credit-worthy?). Thus, the beliefs held by reputational network members have consequences for the person which cumulate over the life course. The full set of these individual belief packages constitutes a kind of latent reputational structure or environment, which is activated in ways that must be ascertained by future research and that can have impacts at many and various, more or less critical points during the person's life course. Second, these belief packages distributed among the network members throughout a person's reputational network can be surveyed and summarized in one way or another.

What Is Generally Said or Believed

This component underscores the notion that the impressions, beliefs, and evaluations of a person held by any one particular member of the reputational network do not constitute a reputation. Reputation is something that is pluralistic, collective, pervasive, and multisourced. This facet identifies the problem of how the dispersed processes of information flow and storage, as well as ongoing discourse, concerning a person are to be somehow summed up into a kind of collective reputational portrait or how the multiple beliefs, evaluations, and impressions that prevail regarding the person are to be surveyed and somehow aggregated. Indeed, one prior question is whether there is any point in seeking a summarized reputational portrait, and a second is who does take on this task in everyday social life or who could do so?

Issues

The term "generally" raises a host of questions and alternative meanings. First, the notion of "generally" can point us toward the summarizing task in reputational analysis. That is, does the concept of "reputation" refer to something that characterizes the beliefs, evaluations, and impressions held by each and every reputational network member? Or does it refer to a subset of members, for example, those members who meet certain qualifications (e.g., length of acquaintance, "closeness" of acquaintance) or those members who hold pivotal positions within the network. For example, in *A Dance to the Music of Time* (Powell, 1951–1975), Professor Sillery was often turned to over the years for his take on various figures in Nicholas Jenkins' social circle. Or does "generally" refer simply to all of those network members who happened to have spontaneously made known their views of the person. Second, the term "generally" may refer to a different set of criteria, namely, a threshold level of consensus among reputational network members concerning particular beliefs, evaluations, or impressions concerning the person (e.g., it might be stipulated that at least a majority of network members must find the person to be cowardly before that attribution becomes an element in the person's reputational content).

What About a Person

The "what" component points us to secondary dictionary definitions of reputation that raise the question of what might be thought of as the content domain of reputation.

For example, additional themes found in dictionary definitions of reputation (e.g., *Webster's New Universal Unabridged Dictionary*, 1983) highlight the notion of estimating, judging, or gauging worth, for example, (*1*) "estimation in which a person, thing or action is held by others; character in pubic or popular opinion, whether favorable or unfavorable," and (*2*) "the estimation of having specific qualities," for example, reputation as a thief.

The first formulation focuses squarely upon the evaluative component of reputational network, that is, on the degree of overall favorability (e.g., "a good reputation") or unfavorability. The second emphasizes cognitive and descriptive elements, the substantive content of reputational summaries. This category is potentially boundless, of course, encompassing anything that might be asserted about any person.

Issues

The overall favorability–unfavorability of a person's reputation suggests two quite different ways in which members of a person's reputational network reach such appraisals. In one case, members may maintain a running index of affective valence toward the person that may be only loosely tied to specific information about what the person has said and done. In contrast, members may more or less systematically note the specific social desirability of what the person has said and done, at various levels of description. Specific everyday acts believed to have been performed by the person can each carry a social desirability value. At a second level in the taxonomy, each trait term attributed to the person by a given network member also carries that member's sense of its relative favorability (Buss & Craik, 1983a, 1984; Craik & Gosling, 2001). Thus, the overall evaluative component of a network member's impression of the person may derive in part from some kind of summing across a mix of act information about the person (e.g., Hampson et al., 1987; John & Robins, 1993).

Thus, the "what" of a reputation may refer to various descriptive and evaluative impressions and beliefs concerning the person derived from what members of a reputational network have formed about the specific acts, traits, and life history events associated with the content categorized within the relevant person bin.

In conclusion, we must note that each of the definitional elements found in the dictionary is encompassed by our network interpretation of reputation. However, at the same time, we must note that the key concept of our reputational network is not itself highlighted in the dictionary definitions. That is, our argument that a person's reputation is anchored within an ongoing, dynamic, typically limited, and more or less specifiable network of other persons does not appear. Put another way, to advance the study and understanding of reputation requires going fundamentally and substantially beyond current dictionary definitions.

PART II

Reputation and the Person

6

The Person as Agent and
Resultant of Reputation

The person as an agent of reflexive integrated action is ontologically distinct from the person's reputational network.

We have devoted the first part of this book to formulating a network interpretation of reputation. In this exposition, the person has appeared thus far primarily as the anchoring referent around which the reputational network and its content claims have been spun.

Now that we have articulated a comprehensive formulation of the network interpretation of reputation, we can finally turn to the person as an agent of reputation. Social science theories have emphasized ways in which the person is influenced by reputation and at the same time seeks to influence reputation (Bromley, 1993). In this chapter, we begin to examine a person as an agent of action and, in particular, the agent's dynamic relations with the reputational network.

One argument is that a person more or less explicitly treats the reputational network and its content claims as a major source of self-knowledge. A second argument is that a person recognizes that his or her prevailing reputational network and its content claims shape his or her standing among others and affect decisions regarding how others interact with and what they expect of the person. As a consequence, the person marshals effort and resources to influence the process and its outcomes.

Reputation as a Source of Self-Knowledge

The reputational network and its content claims are the outcome of an extensive effort by those who know the person to formulate their observations and discourse into a social representation that embodies the network members' common knowledge of the person. It is reasonable for the person to treat reputation as a central epistemological resource. In everyday social life, the person is surrounded by others who participate in and manifest their common knowledge of the person. In that way, reputational content claims come to influence a person's own understanding of the kind of individual he or she is. Thus, since those who know us have participated in an ambitious and ongoing process of observation and discussion in generating and maintaining a social representation of us, we can in turn employ this process as an aid as we form our own sense of who we are and what kind of person we have shown ourselves to be. We understand that others offer us a domain of more or less well-founded knowledge claims about us.

We can conclude that one form of our agency is to learn about our reputational network and its content claims.

Learning About One's Reputational Network

Learning about one's reputational network and its content claims is a daunting and, indeed in some specific ways, an impossible task. What is entailed in a person's efforts to learn about her or his reputational network?

First, we must recall that our estimated typical reputational network size of 4,000 means that 4,000 separate cognitive person bins are dedicated to any given person. These cognitive person bins vary in the volume of impressions, beliefs, and evaluations that each contains. For a concrete metaphor, consider the case of a biographer of a famous person. As the biographer builds the archives of material about the person from each of the potentially available network members, an archives room of potentially 4,000 storage boxes might be assembled, each box containing more or less fulsome information from each of these sources or informants. Consequently, in everyday life, the person's task is to form a set of best-guess notions about what will be contained in a biographer's 4,000 archival boxes or in the 4,000 cognitive person bins held by members of that person's reputational network.

At the outset, we must remind ourselves that a major restriction makes this task in a strict sense impossible. The person potentially knows only the 2,000 others who form the members of cell A of Table Intro.1, the social network component. By definition, the person is ignorant of the "shadow side" of the reputational network—the 2,000 others who form cell B, those network members who know the person and form cognitive person bins accordingly but whom the person does not know.

These considerations generate important research questions for reputation analysis. In what ways do cell A members differ from cell B members, for example, in how they are recruited into the reputational network, in their personal characteristics, and so forth. From the person as agent's point of view, the important question is how well one can extrapolate from the 2,000 cell A person bins to the 2,000 cell B person bins.

Another implication from our network formulation is that the challenge of learning about one's reputational network is dramatically open-ended in scope. The topics to estimate include the various parametric properties of the reputational network, such as variations in density and the arrays of cliques among members.

Finally, the domain of content claims encompasses the full range of social facts about the person, the lifelong stream of deeds and narratives, and the broad realm of personality attributes.

Assuming that the person forms best-guess estimates for many of those 2,000 reputational network members, how accurate are these estimates? The kind of research that would address this question is challenging. For an illustrative study, one hundred members of the person's social network might be randomly and representatively sampled. These reputational network members would record their impressions of the person's personality attributes. The person would then record her or his best guess of the others' personality ratings. How accurate are a person's best guesses of the ways reputational network members tend to describe her or his personality traits? Of course, the research program would also want to check the generality of the findings across the large domain of personality trait descriptors. In addition, the domains of beliefs about social facts concerning the person (e.g., age, occupation) must be examined. In addition, network members might be asked to match everyday narratives to the person, while the person might be asked to guess how accurate network members prove to be in this task.

The limited studies available tend to demonstrate that for estimating how others describe one's personality traits the accuracy tends to be substantial (Malloy & Albright, 1990). Does this accuracy derive from the person's direct acuity in attending to feedback from individual reputational network members? Is it enhanced by drawing upon third-person commentary and reports conveyed directly to the person about how others tend to view her or him? Or does the person depend to an important extent upon simply assuming that the way others view him or her is similar to his or her own self-description and then extrapolating on that basis? How this accuracy is achieved is a complex matter (Kenny, 1994).

The primary issue in appraising a person's reputational network knowledge must focus upon accuracy, not validity. That is, we are interested in how accurate are the person's estimates of the reputational network and that encompasses the areas where the network's content claims happen to be invalid as well as those where they tend to be valid (see Chapter 5). Without doubt, a network interpretation of reputation generates a much more extensive and ambitious research program on this issue of "meta-accuracy" in interpersonal perception than has thus far been undertaken.

Reputational Management

Adam Smith (1997) and other social philosophers have argued that humans have an inherent disposition to seek and prize the good regard of others. Furthermore, the general favorability of content claims about the person is a form of social capital and a source of expectations of others about the person's conduct and contributions to social life (Ferris, Blass, Douglas, Kolodinsky, & Treadway, 2003).

Reputational information can precede the person and influence how others will interact with a newcomer. Recently, Logli (2006) has shown empirically that a favorable versus unfavorable reputational portrait is strongly associated with the intentions of others to interact with the newcomer. Logli examined the relation between reputation generated in a naturalistic social setting and subsequent behavioral intentions toward a newcomer. University undergraduates read reputation narratives about ten strangers and then, using only that information, made ratings regarding their behavioral intentions toward the newcomer. The reputational peer reports were gathered in a prior study of reputation among members of a university living group and varied on independently gathered positive–negative ratings.

Logli (2006) reports that the evaluative dimension of the reputational narratives was positively associated with such behavioral intentions as (*1*) to trust the person with a secret, (*2*) to choose the person as a roommate, (*3*) to seek help with a problem, (*4*) to loan money to, and (*5*) to nominate as a leader.

These two features—first, the influence that the person's understanding of her or his own reputation has upon that person's self-conception and, second, the social capital that accrues from a favorable reputation—together generate a deep and vivid sense among persons of the importance of reputation in their lives.

In a moving commencement address at the University of Arkansas School of Law on May 8, 1993, Vincent W. Foster, Jr., told the law students that "[d]ents to the reputation in the legal profession are irreparable" and that "no victory, no advantage, no fee, no favor . . . is worth even a blemish to your reputation for intellect and integrity." He urged them to recognize that the "reputation you develop for intellectual and ethical integrity will be your greatest asset or your worst enemy" (Office of the Independent Counsel, 1997).

Experiencing intense stress and press criticism during his six months in Washington as a counsel to the Clinton White House, Foster later complained to his brother-in-law that he had spent a lifetime building his reputation and now was in the process of having it tarnished. On July 20, 1993, he committed suicide (Office of the Independent Counsel, 1997).

Given their profound significance, what knowledge and capabilities are required to defend and manage one's reputational network and its content claims? What must the person know in order to influence reputation? What must the person be able to effect in order to shape reputation? What parameters of the reputational network do persons try to influence and mold?

Is a self-conscious approach to reputational management more effective than an unself-conscious approach?

Agentic Approaches to Reputation

Two approaches to one's own reputation can be delineated as ideal types. In one case, the person does not take a self-conscious agentic approach to reputation. In the second case, the self-conscious approach to reputation establishes the management of one's reputation as a considered and purposeful undertaking, one of the person's important personal projects (Little, Salmela-Aro, & Phillips, 2006).

The Unself-Conscious Approach to One's Reputation

In the unself-conscious approach, context and conduct are not explicitly attuned to the nature and parameters of one's reputation. Obviously, various factors, in some way or other, must generate the size and membership of this person's reputational network; the flow of communications about this person; the impressions, beliefs, and evaluations formed by members of the reputational network; as well as the favorable versus unfavorable balance. However, a self-conscious intervention or strategic shaping of these processes is not one of those factors. This type of person goes about life meeting and interacting with other individuals, pursuing a host of personal strivings, without regard to, or even attention to, the parameters of reputation that are willy-nilly emerging as a by-product of these endeavors. Many life choices are made along the way that turn out to have reputational impacts and consequences, but these factors are not an explicit consideration for this person in making such decisions, nor are the implications for reputation consciously monitored.

The Self-Conscious Management of One's Reputation

The ideal type of the self-conscious approach to reputation management might be represented by someone already acquainted with our conceptual framework for analyzing reputation. This person would attend vigilantly to the major parameters of reputation. With regard to the flow of information, the person would first strive to monitor what is being said about her- or himself. Second, the person would seek to facilitate selectively the flow of certain kinds of information but not others, either directly or through allies. Third, the person would try to shape the nature of information being circulated by introducing news about the self into the flow or by actually shaping her or his conduct in order to generate certain kinds of reports within the reputational network (Emler, 1984, 1990).

With regard to the size and membership of the reputational network, this person would first make efforts to monitor these parameters. For example, the person would attempt to maintain some awareness of other individuals who know him or her (e.g., friends of friends). Second, this person would initiate proactive steps to expand the size of his or her reputational network, through selective information flows and get-acquainted tactics that recruit new network members (i.e., networking tactics) (Giovagnoli & Carter-Miller, 2000). Third, the person would also attempt to shape network membership by selectively pruning certain individuals through avoidance, dropping them from invitation lists, and so forth. However, as we found in Chapter 1, control over one's reputational network membership may be surprisingly modest and difficult to achieve. Attempting to manage the content claims of the many and various cognitive person bins maintained by members of one's reputational network is also a formidable task. As we have seen, much of these impressions, beliefs, and evaluations held about us by other individuals is latent and may be difficult to elicit, except when prompted by certain social contexts. However, a person may engage in targeted campaigns to augment, supplement, or otherwise shape what he or she infers is already embedded in the relevant person bins of acquaintances.

Finally, the person may attempt self-consciously to influence a reputational "bottom line," that is, the balance of favorable to unfavorable valence that characterizes reputational content claims. The monitoring undertaken here can assume the form of a more or less constant "How am I doing? How am I really doing?" to more subtle forms, including the gathering of confidential soundings made not directly by oneself but indirectly by friends and allies. The focus on the general reputational valence suggests flexibility in its management. For example, social approbation may be sought in forms and venues that reflect the person's particular strengths and resources. On the other hand, dealing with threats of unfavorable tilts in the valence balance may require addressing accusations and offering accounts regarding the commission of quite specific kinds of disreputable acts (Semin & Manstead, 1983).

A notable pervasive challenge in self-conscious programs for reputational management is the need to take pains to conceal these endeavors to some extent. A requirement of subtlety accompanies that of social savvy.

With this general overview from our conceptual framework in mind, we will be able to review some of the specific issues and practices in reputational management. Are the reputations that follow from an unself-conscious approach different in their variety and descriptive parameters compared to outcomes derived from relatively more self-conscious and engaged approaches to reputational management? For example, do self-conscious approaches necessarily lead to more favorable reputations? Not necessarily. The recourse to self-conscious approaches to reputational management may reflect the presence of serious preexisting problems and limitations in reputation that have brought the matter to the focal attention and concern of the person.

Summary: Agency and Reputation

The reputational process is an inescapable and unbidden social fact of life for every person. What degree of awareness does a person have of it, and what kind of attention does the person grant it? To what extent does the reputational process become a focus of the person's purposes and self-reflexive action? These are the kinds of issues to be addressed. The range of possibilities extends from a dim and disinterested recognition of the reputational process and a passive relationship to it, at one extreme, to a vigilant and all-consuming monitoring of the reputational process and an informed, skilled, and perhaps even desperate effort to manipulate it, at the other extreme.

Social Image and Reputation

From a longitudinal perspective, the beginnings of a person's reputational network are established prior to any self-conscious actions of that person as a child. The parents and other caregivers and their own social networks constitute a preexisting context within which the newborn person is encompassed.

The Person as Agent and Resultant of Reputation **105**

Members of this already prevailing reputational network are making observations and forming impressions, beliefs, and evaluations concerning the young person from the get-go. Indeed, the traditional impressions from the expectant mother regarding how active or lively the newcomer seems to be are now being supplemented by high-tech information about other attributes.

The pattern and directions of a person's sense of agency and sense of self are partially determined by more or less constant interaction with others, from which the newcomer gains a sense of personal identity through the feedback of observers—a process captured by G. H. Cooley's (1902) metaphor of the looking-glass self. That is, the newcomer observes the reactions of others to her or his own conduct to see what kind of person she or he seems to be to others.

The person as a young agent of purposive action at some point begins to construe aspirations toward certain kinds of social image—that is, ways in which the person seeks to be viewed by reputational network members. Thus, an ongoing process of self-image communication and feedback takes place, which is constrained by the extent to which the audience is receptive to the intended social image.

The result of this dynamically interactive process is perhaps not a terribly strong influence that the person as agent manages to exert over the individualized social image that is being negotiated with members of the person's reputational network. The extent to which a person's social image is consensual across reputational network members must be determined in each case, as does the degree to which one or several social images are shaped by the intentions and actions of the person.

The processes whereby the person seeks to communicate and negotiate an intended social image have been scientifically studied largely within the framework of impression management. That is, the restricted focus of inquiry has been pointed primarily toward efforts by the person to convey certain impressions of her- or himself to others during immediate, face-to-face exchanges.

Managing One's Reputation

The interplay in the development of self-image and social image, the looking-glass effect, the tactics of impression management, and related topics can all be granted status as background processes impinging upon the issue of current concern to us: reputation management. In his socioanalytic theory of personality, Hogan (1982) posited the maintenance of a favorable reputation as a primary human motive. Emler (1990) articulated the important distinction between the broader goal of reputation management and the immediate, face-to-face processes of impression management within given, situated interactions. Face-to-face impression management impinges upon only a small portion of the components and processes entailed in the generation of a person's prevailing reputation. In the more socially and temporally extended reputational process, a person's conduct in society is constantly monitored, described, and evaluated. This process occurs in a spontaneous, ongoing fashion whether or not the person is self-consciously pursuing explicit reputational goals.

Suppose you have just enjoyed a highly successful business luncheon, during which you believe you have effectively molded the views of your colleagues so that they now see you as operating at the cutting edge of a promising new entrepreneurial venture. That face-to-face accomplishment hardly dents the task of shaping your general reputation along those same lines. What else has to be done? What factors must be addressed?

1. *Reputation network members.* How are the other luncheon partners situated within your reputational network? Are their favorable communications with other individuals likely to be redundant, or do some link or bridge to other more diverse domains of your reputational network?

2. *Communications.* What steps can you take to encourage your luncheon partners to spread the good word about their favorable impressions? What steps can you take to prime other network members to ask your luncheon partners about their impressions of you and your endeavors? What media are available to you for this purpose, such as organizational Internet sites?

3. *Recognition identity.* How effective were you in being sure your promising business proposals were and remain specifically linked with you and your name?

4. *Amplification.* What steps can you take, directly and through intermediaries, to have reports on your luncheon presentation brought to the attention of others at important occasions, such as promotion

meetings or finance meetings? What resources are available to you to ensure the triggering of the good news for the right time, place, and audience?

These considerations represent elementary issues encountered when attention and efforts are expanded from face-to-face impression management to the broader realm of reputation management. Across the life span, social knowledge of the ins and outs of impression management is probably acquired at a developmentally earlier stage than any kind of savvy about the more complex endeavor of reputation management. Nevertheless, persons differ in their knack for managing their reputation and in the strategic social skills and knowledge required to act upon it.

Reputational Awareness

An effective manager of reputation requires some minimal degree of accurate baseline knowledge of the prevailing collective representation within his or her reputational network.

Public figures enjoy professional assistance of various kinds in monitoring their reputations. The Q Index derives from survey research and combines general name recognition and favorability of an individual's public image. Political leaders have access to public opinion results concerning the personal attributes associated with them. Celebrities can track their standing on various lists and rankings of the most admired, the best-dressed, etc. (Rein, Kotler, & Stoller, 1997).

Gross (2001) makes good use of the metaphors of listening and mishearing to capture the efforts of persons to overhear, through the hum of everyday discourse, what is being said specifically about them. The person wonders and surmises and seeks to interpret the partial feedback concerning the communication taking place along the reputational networks. Persons remain curious about and make attempts more or less directly to probe what is contained about them within the cognitive person bins of their reputational network members. Psychological research on self–other agreement (Funder, 1999; Kenny, 1994) has typically dealt with the degree of similarity between self-representations and the aggregate representations held by the person's closest acquaintances. The results reveal at least a modest level of this form of accuracy but with wide individual differences. In contrast, gauging the accuracy of reputational awareness calls for a criterion derived from a much broader, more representative sample of network members than close acquaintances.

Strategic effectiveness in reputation management most likely requires accurate comprehension of the possibly segmented and pluralistic nature of one's prevailing collective representation within the reputational community (Craik, 1985). For example, Tsui (1984) has examined the attention devoted by managers in organizations to the differentiated reactions to them by their multiple constituencies (i.e., supervisors, peers, subordinates, customers).

Reputational Goals and Tactics

For some persons, reputation is a simple by-product of their everyday activities and social life. For these individuals, the very notion that their reputation might be managed would come as a surprise. For others, the extent and substance of their reputation are a preoccupation and a major personal project or striving. For the latter, is their reputational community conceived as extensive, though local, or is a much wider fame, celebrity, or notoriety sought (Frank, 1995)? Is the particular substance of a pursued reputation envisioned in terms of certain exemplary deeds or personality traits (e.g., assertive, imperturbable, clever), as an array of traditionally formulated virtues, or as a social image package selected from the contemporary cultural array (Baumeister, 1986; Emler, 1990; Hogan, 1982; Hampson, 1988)? Or is the goal more simply to maintain a generally favorable reputation?

Appraising the effectiveness of persons in managing their reputations must entail some assessment of their grasp of appropriate tactics. These diagnostic, communicative, and persuasive skills concern, (1) gauging the social visibility and the potential spread of communications regarding daily acts (Bromley, 1993; Petersen, 1965), (2) targeting and timing the flow of reputational information (Emler, 1990), (3) familiarity with the vettings and reviews of relevant prestige systems (Goode, 1978; Whitmeyer, 2000), (4) making use of mechanisms for expanding the size of the reputational community and targeting its membership composition, (5) adapting to the pressures of sudden renown (Berglas, 1986; Schickel, 1985), and (6) marshalling loyal supporters at times of contention or evaluation. We will see that legal actions for defamation deal with attributions of conduct that are likely to do severe damage to one's reputation. Perhaps more frequent in everyday social life are the instances of more ordinary "own goals" in which the person has committed disreputable acts.

Coping with injury to one's reputation due to one's own disreputable conduct can be addressed through a variety of tactics: (*1*) attempting to neutralize the impact of specific acts through the dissemination of apologies or excuses (Semin & Manstead, 1983), (*2*) making public declarations and interpretations ("I am not a crook"), (*3*) performing subsequent socially desirable acts of a highly exemplary and visible kind, and (*4*) engaging in a trend of worthy acts over a prolonged period of observation.

Professional Tips on Managing Reputation

The way in which ordinary persons manage their reputations is an implicit and largely silent—even covert—aspect of everyday social life. It has been the subject of only a scant amount of systematic research (Emler, 1990; Bromley, 1993). The ways in which celebrity reputations are professionally managed have received little in the way of scientific study. However, these practices entail much more overt and explicit endeavors and have gained recent public commentary from sociologists and cultural historians (Braudy, 1986; Cowen, 2000; Gamson, 1994) as well as the growing cadre of professional reputation managers (Fombrun, 1996; Marconi, 2001; Rein et al., 1997; Rojek, 2001).

One approach to explicating what ordinary persons might be doing in everyday social life to manage their reputations is to examine what advice is proffered by professionals who look after the reputations of public figures and others with self-conscious reputational goals. That is, it makes sense to examine first the more overt and exposed enterprise of managing celebrity reputations and then to consider whether we can identify analogous processes and tactics appropriate to the everyday self-management of ordinary reputations.

Managing Celebrity Reputations

Two crucial steps are entailed in moving from ordinary personhood to celebrityhood. First, the individual's visibility and the size of the reputational network are dramatically augmented. Second, the expansion of the reputational network consists overwhelmingly of new and asymmetrical relations, in which other individuals know the person but the person does not know the other individuals. Thus, with regard to Table Intro.1, the reputational structure increases in volume but primarily for the one-way audience depicted by cell B.

In contemporary public life within modern industrial nations, a major financial and technological apparatus is potentially available to those seeking celebrity. Examination of the professional machinery for producing and managing celebrity leads to a number of broad cultural and social policy issues, such as the relation of fame to merit. One view that can be traced to Adam Smith (1997) holds that public approbation is a useful societal invention for promoting good conduct, such as the keeping of promises and the forbearance of cheating in social exchanges. Indeed, in this view public approbation is a cheap and efficient way to bring forth exceptional effort and creativity from individuals (Klein, 1997). One anomaly in this perspective is the option for the individual to gain quick and meritless fame through a notorious act, such as the assassination of a public figure (Cowen, 2000; Rojek, 2001). Finally, more recent developments in technology and increased leisure time seem to be shifting celebrity further and ever more thoroughly into the realm of public entertainment.

We will return to these broad issues, but first let us review the generation and fate of a person's celebrity.

Acquiring and Building Public Visibility

It may not be possible for a person to become known to every human alive on earth, but modern technology through the printing press, radio, television, and now satellite and Internet communication has certainly progressed toward that possibility. These technologies constitute a notable advance over the reproduction and dissemination of coin images, sculptures, and paintings of the fame-seeking person. Acquisition of visibility may come through accident as well as intention. A person can be born into a high-visibility family, such as royalty or the Kennedy family. The person may also unwittingly become associated with someone else's scandalous or criminal act or otherwise become linked to a newsworthy event, such as a coal mine rescue or the performance of a single heroic act. Such persons may merely undergo Andy Warhol's "15 minutes of fame" and then fade from visibility. In contrast, as we shall see, this narrow entry into public visibility might be augmented and sustained through subsequent reputational management.

Access to visibility may also be intentionally sought. One route is through public approbation for merit in a particular field of endeavor. Prestige institutions, including as many as 3,000 halls of fame, abound in modern life, granting well-publicized honors, awards, medals, and other signs of recognition for outstanding performance (Cowen, 2000; Danilov, 1997).

Finally, beginning with Edward R. Murrow's pioneering television show *Person to Person* and continuing through the current success of *People* magazine, a steadily expanding celebrity market has been generated within the entertainment industry that satisfies a seemingly insatiable public interest in the lives of other persons, even those who are simply known for being known (Boorstin, 1961), a category that encompasses society-page figures and the social associates of already established celebrities. As in the case of accidental visibility, initial visibility acquired within one arena of achievement or activity can be built upon by means of a campaign of reputational management.

Shaping and Maintaining a Favorable Public Identity

A wide range of resources is available for maintaining and expanding visibility and for keeping celebrity alive. Celebrityhood requires not only an expanded membership for the person's reputational network but an unceasing flow of chat, commentary, and gossip circulating through it. The hum of social communication about the person can be sustained through a number of channels, including interviews for print, radio, and television media. For their own purposes, gossip columns and celebrity-oriented magazines and television shows readily assist in maintaining the "buzz" about a person. Seemingly intrusive coverage of the daily doings of celebrities provides grist for the media mill.

Celebrityhood itself generates additional occasions for these purposes. Attendance at charity events, publicity opportunities such as film premiers, and various other events such as award nights, celebrity testimonials, roasts, and weddings are not directly related to the core basis of entry into celebrity; but appearances of this kind serve to maintain and expand a person's visibility. Product endorsements not only provide financial gain for celebrities but at the same time assure a specific form of media presence. Joe DiMaggio became almost as well-known for his Mr. Coffee ads as for his baseball achievements and marriage to Marilyn Monroe.

Professional agents and publicists offer services in shaping a public image around the initial basis of access to fame, in which favorable attributes are molded into a public image. Exposure management then guides the selection of communication channels for delivering the image, much in the way other commercial products are advertised and marketed (Rein et al., 1997). Reputation management also entails mobilizing the legal protections of the commercial value of a person's public image (Murumba, 1986).

Reputational Damage Control

Other than those intentionally seeking fame through notorious acts, most celebrities concentrate upon shaping and maintaining a favorable public image. However, persons who earn public approbation through some of their deeds may suddenly suffer condemnation and disdain from others. Reputational damage can arise from two sources. The first source of harm to reputation consists of false attributions of bad acts to the celebrity. The common-law tradition offers some shelter based upon the individual right to protect one's reputation. However, as we will see in our review of defamation law in Chapter 8, the qualified privilege granted to communications concerning public figures has broadened in two ways: first, the category of public figure has been expanded to include many persons who have not sought out public attention and, second, the realm of deeds and aspects of the person's life which now receive qualified privilege has widened.

Nevertheless, legal action for defamation can be successful, gaining vindication and monetary awards and sometimes retraction and apology. Rehabilitation of reputation in these instances may appear straightforward but is very difficult. That is, the good news of vindication and the communication of the falsehood of the assertion must be circulated to the often huge and only intermittently attentive members of the public figure's reputational network. And, of course, the risk of losing the action for defamation carries a heavy cost, including public rejection by a jury that the contentious assertion was defamatory and the self-engendered additional public attention to the assertion surrounding the legal action itself.

The second source comes in the form of "own goals," wherein the person commits disreputable acts that become public. On July 9, 2006, over 300 million astonished viewers of the World Cup soccer final watched on television as Zinedine Zidane (or "Zizou") walked up to an Italian player and flagrantly head-butted him in the chest, sending him to the ground. Zizou was ejected from the game with a red card, and his French team went on to lose to Italy. This single act endangered his reputation for discretion, hard work, and civility (Longman, 2006). In the case of such own goals, the emerging guild of reputation managers is ready to come to the rescue and provide damage control.

As we found in Chapter 3, disreputable deeds encompass a wide range of bad acts, sins, and crimes. In the case of celebrity endorsement contracts, the client is not only making a financial commitment to the celebrity but also associating the firm and brand with the celebrity's presumably good and attractive reputation. An own goal disreputable act committed subsequently by the celebrity is likely to be damaging to all around. Endorsement contracts often spell out the sorts of deeds that will legally terminate the contract.

Response to an Accusation of a Disreputable Act: General Model

Within the everyday hum of social discourse about specific persons, the constant exchange of information entails the repeated shifting of roles in which one person is the possible agent of a described action and another is the reporter or accuser regarding the same act. When acts that can be deemed harmful for reputation are at issue, the information exchange takes on an interesting structure. We will see that this structure parallels the legal form we will later review in detail concerning civil actions for defamation.

In mounting a response or defense for a person accused of a disreputable act, several options are available. First, the person can either admit to the act or deny the truth of the accusation. Note in the latter instance, the accused might also threaten or initiate a civil action for defamation. Second, the accused can challenge the identity of the agent, that is, assert that someone else committed the act or was responsible for it. Third, particularly when the disreputable act is a statement but also when it is an overt deed, the accused can challenge the imputation or description of the act, asserting that the meaning of the statement or deed has been misinterpreted or misconstrued. Fourth, the accused can challenge the legitimacy of the publication of the act report, for example, citing an inappropriate invasion of privacy and claiming that the act was not a public event or matter of public concern—in short, was nobody else's business. Fifth, the accused can claim certain extenuating circumstances or privileges regarding the degree of accountability for the act. These claims typically take the form of excuses, such as acting under stress, impulsively, or otherwise out of character. Sixth, an initial or eventual acknowledgment of being the agent of the statement or deed can be accompanied by an apology for any distress or other impacts of the disreputable act. Seventh, the accused might not only acknowledge the disreputable act but also undertake efforts to remedy the damage caused by the deed, for example, by making amends through specific future acts, the payment of money, and so forth.

Defaming a Person as Itself a Disreputable Act

This general structure of the social problem of responding to accusations of disreputable acts is similar in form to the structure of proceedings in legal actions for defamation. Why have we found this evident parallel? The answer is that civil actions for defamation constitute a meta-instance of the accusation of a disreputable act. For in these cases the core and general disreputable act is the alleged false or inappropriate accusation by the defendant of the commission of another, in this case specific, disreputable act by the plaintiff.

The plaintiff responds to the accusation of a disreputable act by resorting to the first option: denying the truthfulness of the report and suing the accuser for libel. The defendant is now accused of a disreputable act—defaming another person. The accused defamer can then follow the general structure for responding to the accusation of disreputable acts. The defendant in actions for libel can (1) offer evidence that the assertion is true, (2) challenge that the disreputable assertion was made with regard to the plaintiff, (3) demonstrate that the imputation of the assertion was not really defamatory, or (4) show that the publication of the accusation was not inappropriate or did not carry to third parties. The defendant can also claim special circumstances, in this case, the specialized forms of privilege that shelter defamatory statements from successful legal action. Finally the defendant can admit to the defamation and offer (1) an apology and (2) remedies to the plaintiff, in this case, such actions as public retraction of the assertion and payment of monetary damages.

Thus, the legal tradition of defamation law has afforded us a structure that can serve as a useful general model for the response to accusations of disreputable conduct that take place outside the courtroom and within the contexts of everyday social life. At the same time, this connection highlights the nature of civil actions for defamation, in which the defendant is accused of a particular kind of disreputable act, namely, defaming another with regard to a different and more specific kind of disreputable act. Of course, the not infrequent instance of countersuits in libel cases reveals that the meta-level of these relations can be even more complex.

Damage Control Remedies

Professional reputation managers have outlined various pragmatic strategies for dealing with crises regarding negative acts and other self-inflicted damage to reputation (e.g., Fombrun, 1996; Marconi, 2001). The initial crisis is typically accompanied by a frenzy in the media, which, in alignment with the negativity bias, tends to seek out "bad" news. Advisors suggest that the public figure or celebrity must act quickly, avoid attempts at cover-up, take a stand for something worthy, do good deeds, try to mute controversy, and seek goodwill and even sympathy. In contrast to successful defamation actions, the rehabilitation of reputation is more onerous and problematic in the case of self-inflicted damage. Recommended steps include advancing more favorable reinterpretations of the bad conduct; offering excuses and apologies; willingly taking some form of punishment; entering a treatment center or program; announcing subsequently that one has learned from these "mistakes and poor choices" and has emerged as a wiser, stronger, and better person; and producing evidence of public support and testimonials from celebrity colleagues.

The Life Span of Celebrity

However widespread and broad-based celebrity may become for a person, it is a dynamic, rather than a fixed, phenomenon. The size of the reputational network may persist, but the focus of attention and the buzz of communication may wax and wane. Entertainers, for example, may see the venue for their talent disappear, as in the case of silent movie stars, vaudeville performers, and perhaps nowadays stand-up comedians. Efforts at reputation management may try to offer countervailing forces to this expected decline in visibility. For example, competition for attention is natural as one generation of sports stars is followed by another. Nevertheless, some sports stars become television commentators and then product endorsers, thus sustaining and perhaps even broadening their visibility.

Posthumous reputations typically continue to fluctuate. In rare cases, a person who has had little or no expectation of a broad posthumous reputation acquires one, for example, those associated with tragic disasters. In contrast, some persons understandably anticipate a sustained posthumous reputation, although its precise nature may only gradually reveal itself during the person's lifetime. Ted Williams clearly expected his renown as a baseball great to endure for a certain period, but one specific core achievement—being baseball's last .400 hitter—became evident only as the years went by without a successful challenge to that outstanding record. In some instances, forms of posthumous reputational management are not uncommon, as we shall see in Chapter 9. Some persons themselves strategically destroy letters and other materials. Some seek to exercise an influence by selecting at least one biographer. Posthumously, relatives may destroy or selectively hoard documents. Biographers and scholars who specialize in the life and deeds of a particular public figure may contest or promote the enduring nature and high evaluation of the person, as in the case of U.S. presidents.

The Mundane Experience of Celebrityhood

The celebrity and the ordinary person share the experience of their respective social networks, in which they know most of the members, who also know them (Table Intro.1, cell A). They also share the status of being "fans" of certain others they know only indirectly and who do not know them at all (Table Intro.1, cell C). What separates the celebrities from ordinary persons is their experience of having many others know them perhaps quite thoroughly whom they do not know at all (Table Intro.1, cell B). The everyday experience of celebrityhood has its dark side as well as its bright side (Cowen, 2000; Fombrun, 1996; Gamson, 1994; Rojek, 2001).

The rewards of celebrityhood include the ready recognition and attention of other persons. The acknowledgment of others may be accompanied by approbation and deference, even praise and reverence. Financial opportunities can include endorsement contracts, monetary prizes, and career advancement. Social benefits and perks may include queue-jumping, entree into various exclusive venues, entrance into the circle of other celebrities (e.g., sports figures, political leaders, literary figures, entertainers), and the transition from fan to peer, with the frisson of "greenroom" bonding.

The downside of celebrityhood can be substantial. The public attention may become constant and ever-present. Certain fans may become intrusive and commit the category mistake of demanding personal acknowledgment and seeking to become a member of the celebrity's own social network. Some fans may become voyeurs and stalkers, and others may present the threat of violence; indeed, some may strive to gain their own celebrityhood through assassination of a celebrity. The case of John Hinckley, Jr., brings these themes together as he apparently sought the personal attention of one celebrity (a film star) by shooting another (a president).

The asymmetrical relation between celebrities and their audiences is both impoverished and complex. The celebrity may end up greeting fans and doing walkabouts in which the implications of each greeting and hand-shake are heavily imbalanced. At the same time, the fans may adopt varying interpretive approaches to the celebrity. In a traditional stance, the fans may take the public image and identity of the celebrity as a realistic representation of the celebrity as a person. Others may entertain a postmodern stance, in which they view the celebrity's public image as pretence or at least problematic with regard to forming an authentic impression of the celebrity as a person. Finally, other fans may play the game of kibitzing the celebrity's reputation management, providing commentary on the public image, exposure strategies, career moves, and so on (Gamson, 1994). As a consequence, while celebrities have only the barest, minimal notion of the fans as persons, they cannot assume that the fans are treating them as genuine persons either.

Finally, the consequences of public exposure are double-edged. Visibility expands the size of the reputational network. At the same time, transparency leads to losses with regard to individual rights, such as privacy and the legal protection of reputation. Legal status as a public figure removes significant shelter from slander and libel within the framework of defamation law, as we shall see in Chapter 8. The domain of detailed scrutiny of public figures in personality profiles and investigative biographies has steadily expanded to include every aspect of the person's life and deeds. Reverence can quickly give way to disdain, respect to condemnation.

To counter these negative impacts, celebrities take on the services of press agents, publicists, bodyguards, and minders. The celebrity apparatus and entourage has its own impacts upon the everyday life of that person.

A final celebrity hassle, if not crisis, accompanies the almost inevitable decline in the size of the reputational network. Celebrities can readily adapt to, if not become addicted to, constant public notice and the various perks of celebrityhood. Public figures who have lost political office or entertainers whose careers go into decline often experience depressive withdrawal symptoms. The competitive arena of celebrity and its fleeting duration often come as a likely career disappointment to those who have sought or expected enduring celebrity.

A study of American sociologists found that this large field of academic scholars tended to overestimate their own chance of leadership; an implausible 43% expected to be among the top ten in their scientific specialty (Westie, 1973). They also appeared to show unrealistic expectations regarding their "professional immortality" in that an impressive 54% anticipated the survival of their research and writings beyond their own career. At the same time, they granted much more limited recognition themselves with regard to a presumably high-visibility set of other sociologists (namely, former presidents of the American Sociological Association). Over 50% of the respondents failed entirely to recognize either the name or work of nineteen of the sixty-three former leaders, and they found the name only vaguely familiar for quite a few others.

Managing the Reputation of Ordinary Persons

The management of celebrity reputations is a self-consciously strategic and ofttimes professional and team endeavor, supported by a considerable amount of communication and other resources. The management of an ordinary person's reputation is typically ad hoc, implicit, solitary, and unselfconscious. Indeed, outside of our analytic perspective, the term "management" would appear to be overreaching and inappropriate in this context. Nevertheless, by viewing the life span of a person's reputation "as if" it were being managed, we can seek to discern and use potential analogues with the management of celebrity reputations as a means of gaining insight into the development of an ordinary person's reputation. For example, we may find ourselves challenging the assumption that the management of an ordinary person's reputation is really a solitary enterprise or that we are left more or less to our own devices in shaping our reputations. On the contrary, perhaps relatives, close acquaintances, and institutional allies take on various tasks on our behalf that are analogous to those of the celebrity's agents and publicists. Certainly, the notion that reputation management among ordinary persons is always unself-conscious may be hard to support. In addition to persons who self-consciously seek to cross the threshold into the asymmetrical realm of celebrityhood, there are those who simply seek local fame and a broader renown even within the confines of their own social networks.

For the purpose of this analysis, our concept of an "ordinary person" will refer to persons whose reputation resides primarily within their social network, although their complete reputational network may extend somewhat beyond it. With reference to Table Intro.1, their reputation is situated largely, but not necessarily entirely, beyond cell A.

To facilitate our analysis, we will have to distinguish between two prototypic life situations, that of the village dweller and that of the modern urbanite. Prototypic village dwellers of the premodern type may reside, for example, in relatively isolated Mediterranean hilltop villages of 300 to 600 inhabitants and live their lives in highly dense social networks. In these instances, everyone knows everyone else. Little opportunity exists for expanding the size of one's reputational network. Furthermore, few candidates are available to serve as potential members of cell B—those knowing the person but not known by the person. The category of potential members for cell C (celebrity figures) may also have been limited by culture and technology (although decreasingly so). In summary, size and symmetry are given for isolated village dwellers. Most of the parameters of their reputational network are fixed; only specific reputational content claims and general favorable evaluation remain to be managed by the villager.

In contrast, prototypic modern urbanites live within low-density and clustered social networks, surrounded by strangers who might come to know the person while not being known by the person (cell B). Other individuals may become full reciprocal members of the person's expanding social network (cell A). In particular, the low, incomplete, and clustered nature of the structure of an urbanite's social network leaves a host of "fringe" individuals who are acquaintances of cluster members and who become recipients and potential conveyers of news and knowledge of the person, without being known by the person.

In summary, reputational management offers more options and chores for the embedded urbanite, including influencing the size of and structure of one's social network, and remaining aware of the potential asymmetric audience, composed mostly of acquaintances of acquaintances. This latter audience tends, however, to be linked indirectly to an ordinary person's reputational network membership in a way that a celebrity's audience, generated via mass media, is not.

Tasks and Options in Shaping One's Own Reputation

What options and choices do ordinary persons confront in managing their reputations? What resources are available to them, analogous to those afforded by the celebrity industry? Our analytic framework regarding reputation offers several parameters. First, one can aspire to control the size and membership of the reputational network; second, efforts can be made to shape and communicate a particular social image and to inspire parallel reputational content claims; third, tactics can be mobilized to boost the positive evaluative valence of one's reputation and, when necessary, to defend it; fourth, ongoing efforts can be sustained to monitor the state of one's reputation; and fifth, steps can be taken to influence the life course of one's reputation.

Reputation management by ordinary persons depends largely upon individual social skills and knowledge. Nevertheless, persons are typically able to mobilize the efforts of other individuals and the resources of institutions as well.

Generating the Size of One's Reputational Network

If we review the factors influencing the size of one's social network, we will recall that the initial component, the family, is more or less a given. Some persons will enter into a large extended family; others will not. If the extended family is geographically close by, the social networks of the family members will augment a person's own reputational network. With respect to dispersed extended families, persons can differ in the degree to which they seek out and maintain contacts with these relatively remote family members. Marriage represents a more or less indirect choice with regard to the extent of the spouse's family network. Within American culture particularly, the option of joining voluntary organizations offers a wide range of choice for enlarging one's social network. Joiners have varied possibilities in terms of the number of such organizations they can belong to and support. The choice of active participation and subsequent notice in newsletters, reports, and discourse afford opportunities for further networking and attention-getting. Nonjoiners can readily foreclose these opportunities to expand their reputational network.

Vocational choices can either directly or indirectly influence the extent of a person's reputational network. Some vocational arenas generate more reputational network members than others. Fields such as sales and teaching inherently establish relationships with a wide range of other individuals. Even within a vocational domain, the choice of job and firm may have network consequences. A bookkeeper in a small firm is likely to build a narrower vocational network than one employed by a large firm. Even within a large firm, some persons may choose to keep a low profile, limiting relationships to those functionally required and, even in those instances, relatively superficial, while others may cultivate every possible opportunity to establish relationships and keep them current. Tactics for actively and purposefully constructing extensive business networks have been vividly explicated in a host of popular advice books. These guidelines make explicit the amount of everyday social effort that is required to build a large social network. Allies in the cause can often be recruited from those individuals who take an interest in serving as social enhancers and facilitators, seeing to it that newcomers are introduced around and hosting social occasions that help to maintain relationships among other acquaintances.

Village dwellers are fitted within an already established reputational network and the options available mostly entail the depth of acquaintance and frequency of interaction with those they know and who know them. The mobility of modern urbanites and the complexity of urban residential, occupational and recreational arrangements results in reputational networks featuring spatial dispersion and low or clustered density. Prototypic urbanites include military personnel and middle managers of large organizations who are frequently transferred and relocated geographically. Such reassignments requiring the creation of new social networks have sometimes evoked rebellion among other family members and generated the use of special counseling approaches especially tailored to spouses and children.

Increasing the Size of One's Reputational Network

The size of a person's reputational network may fluctuate according to the attention-getting nature of the person's conduct. Various personal projects may generate extensive social initiatives that lead to forming ties with new sets of other persons. These spin-offs may expand reputational network membership size without this outcome being a specific and focal intention of the person.

In other cases, the seeking of fame and renown may become an explicit and self-conscious goal of a person. If a person enjoys a generally favorable level for reputational content claims, then the larger the network membership, the more extensive the associated social capital.

Our network interpretation of reputation suggests several tactics for increasing network size. For example, the person can seek out other individuals who themselves have large networks. This bootstrap approach makes use of the resource of large network building blocks.

Seeking fame for its own sake may derive from narcissistic personality dispositions, as Young and Pinsky (2006) indicated in an empirical assessment of a sample of television celebrities. We will soon turn to institutional contexts for creating and sustaining celebrity, including publicity agents and other professional aides to expanding network size (Rein et al., 1997).

Decreasing the Size of One's Social Network

Carstensen (1992) argued that as persons reach advanced age, they tend to reduce the size of their active social network in order to bring greater focus and depth to their social relations.

Although actions of this kind can shift the density of one's social network, they do not necessarily reduce the overall size of the reputational network. Those network members who receive less attention and a lowered rate of social initiatives from the person may nevertheless maintain an active ongoing cognitive person bin for that person. Indeed, the person's very actions aimed at decreasing the extent of social interactions may prompt increased discourse within the reputational network as members ponder the implications of this shift in the person's conduct.

Another purpose for attempting to reduce the size of one's reputational network derives from the situation in which the person's evaluative level of reputational content claims becomes very unfavorable. One tactic is some form of "leaving town" and "starting anew." The effort here is not to decrease the size of one's reputational network but rather to segregate a major former segment from a newly emerging and isolated network segment. Once again, this social initiative by the person does not reduce network membership and, indeed, may generate lively discourse regarding the implications of the person's "disappearance."

In general, it appears to be difficult to reduce the size of one's overall reputational network. The person's main option is to curtail social initiatives with selective network members. While interactions with certain others may decrease or cease, the associated cognitive person bins maintained by those others persist. And, of course, for cell B members, this option is moot in any case.

Shaping Reputational Network Content Claims

As an agent of one's own reputation, a person can seek to distribute favorable news throughout the reputational network. Structural considerations suggest that one need inform only a few members of relatively dense cliques while at the same time identifying potential weak ties or bridging members in order to achieve more widespread dissemination.

Communicating One's Intended Social Image

As we have seen, identity is a core concept in our understanding of reputation. The bedrock of reputation is the minimal notion of identity of face and name. These recognitions by other individuals are the basis of the cognitive person bins formed by reputational network members. Additional institutional identifiers (e.g., Social Security numbers, passports) are also relevant. Greater detail in the form of associated observations, impressions, beliefs, and evaluations augment the categorized contents of these person bins maintained by reputational network members.

In Chapter 7, when we examine the relation between reputation and personality, we will distinguish among *self-concept* (the way one views oneself), *social image* (the way one seeks to have others view one), *public image* (the way celebrities and their publicists seek to have the public at large view the celebrity), and finally *reputational identity* (the way all those who know the person do view that person). From the point of view of reputational analysis, the identity issues that will concern us have to do with how the ordinary person seeks to shape and convey an image to members of his or her reputational network.

Social scientists have depicted this process in varying ways. Duke (2002) likens the social image shaping efforts to those of an artist in the painting of a picture. That is, in everyday social life, the person, like an artist, seeks to create a set of images by means of dress, posture, utterances, and actions that generates emotional and other reactions in the person as well as in observers of the person's daily "self-painting." For the person, the key affective reaction is one of comfort, acceptance, and familiarity—a feeling of "being oneself" (Duke, 2002; Craik, 2002). Other individuals so encountered are potential patrons or critics of these projected social images; their reactions, in turn, are closely scrutinized by the "self-painter."

The self-consciously projected social image is far from being the only determinant of a person's reputational identity. Many limits constrain the control a person holds over which acts and utterances are potentially observable and which are actually observed by reputational network members and entered into the ongoing discourse about the person. Communication of a projected social imaging is not a one-way process or a matter of passive reception by others. Rather, it entails a process of active negotiation of identity in continual interactions with others (Hampson, 1988). The entire negotiated process raises the question of the relation of reputation to personality, the topic of Chapter 7.

7

The Mutual Relevance of
Reputation and Personality

A person's reputation and the person are distinctly different phenomena. The locus of a reputation is to be found within a person's reputational network, with a focus upon what its members say and believe about the person. In contrast, the locus of a person is situated in and about a specific biological organism displaying intentionality and self-consciousness across a bounded life span of individual development, experience, action, and ultimate death.

Nevertheless, the mutual relevance of reputation and personality remains an open issue within contemporary personality psychology, as it has from the beginnings of this scientific field of inquiry.

Historical Perspective 1: Mark A. May's
Dual Conception of Personality

During a formative period in the emergence of personality psychology as a distinct field of inquiry, a promising community-based and contextual approach was considered but not pursued (Craik, 1986; Craik, Hogan, & Wolfe, 1993). It amounted to a nascent, though partial, formulation of a role for reputation within personality psychology. Specifically, Mark A. May (1929, 1932a, 1932b) and Phillip E. Vernon (1933) advocated the study of a person's reputation as centrally informative regarding an individual's personality. This approach was dismissed by Gordon W. Allport in his highly influential textbook *Personality: A Psychological Interpretation* (1937). Subsequently, reputation has failed to receive the systematic attention it warrants within personality psychology, suffering an interrupted mode of development (Craik, 1986, 2000a, 2007).

Seven decades ago, May (1932b) advanced a dual conception of personality. On the one hand, personality is "the integration of the individual's characteristic and persistent reaction tendencies, modes of conduct or ways of adjustment" (p. 83). At the same time, personality requires a social representation. "An individual's personality is defined not wholly by his responses to others but also by the responses that others make to him as a stimulus" (p. 84).

May considered the personality research of the 1930s to be imbalanced, claiming that 90% of studies were addressing the former conception, while only the remaining 10% could be said to be concerned with the "social stimulus side" of personality. In his own well-known research program, May pursued both conduct-based and reputational studies of personality in his classic investigations of character traits with Hartshorne and Shuttleworth (Hartshorne & May, 1928, 1929; Hartshorne, May, & Shuttleworth, 1930).

May's dual conception of personality has been largely ignored in commentaries on his position. And when noted, he has been almost entirely identified with the notion of personality as only the "social stimulus value" of the individual. This treatment may not be excessively unfair, for despite his efforts to maintain a balanced stance, in his own limited conceptual writings along these lines he tended to convey the social stimulus formulation more vividly and with greater force. At one point he declared, "My view is that the proper object of study is not the individual whose personality is being investigated but rather the responses of others to him as a stimulus" (1932b, p. 85).

In examining the implications of this formulation of personality for the colloquial usage of trait terms by laypersons, Vernon (1933) endorsed and extended May's position by introducing a biosocial conception of personality traits. In his analysis, Vernon viewed trait terms as names for general classes of behavior and concluded that their application in everyday discourse requires laypersons to interpret the agent's conduct accordingly.

Thus, Vernon agreed with May that the agent of conduct does not "possess" the trait; rather, trait descriptions emerge from the interplay of a particular segment of a person's conduct and a set of more or less biased observers. Thus, the agent's behavior trends "are not his traits until they have been apprehended and interpreted by human mentalities . . ." and "traits neither exist in the individual himself, nor merely in the minds of observers" (Vernon, 1933, p. 543).

Historical Perspective 2: Gordon W. Allport's Dismissal of Reputation

In his pioneering textbook, Gordon W. Allport (1937; Craik et al., 1993) scrupulously reviewed forty-nine prior definitions of personality and sought to incorporate forty-five of them within his own influential formulation. Note that May's notion of the person's social stimulus value is explicitly rejected (Allport, 1937, pp. 38–43, Figure 8), and on similar grounds, he put aside the biosocial conception of traits (pp. 287–289).

Ironically, in his critique of this approach to personality, Allport did a better job in contributing a broader delineation of the issues entailed in the reputational analysis of persons than either May or Vernon. He at least hints at network factors that were not explicitly developed at all by May or Vernon. In doing so, for example, he points to important social–ecological facets of reputational analysis.

First, Allport spotlights the issue of social visibility and the extent or size of a person's reputational community. Would a movie queen, he wonders, have "more" personality than a Robinson Crusoe or a poet dwelling "in attic obscurity" (p. 41)?

Second, Allport addresses some of the social dynamics of reputation. He expresses concern that in pursuing this approach an investigator of personality would be "swamped by considerations of reputation, rumor, gossip, erroneous evaluations and social effectiveness" and that in its extreme form "it would not be necessary to study the perceptions, reactions, prejudices and interests of the personality in question at all, but rather, the perceptions, reactions, prejudices and interests of everyone else in his social circle" (pp. 42–43).

Third, Allport poses the problem of social consensus. What is to be done if, due to observer biases or to the agent's varying conduct in response to varying audiences, a multiplicity of impressions of the person prevails throughout the individual's community? On the one hand, Allport cites reassuring levels of consensus among observers (p. 288), but on the other hand, he offers evidence that certain relatively open persons are more consensually rated on personality attributes than are relatively more enigmatic persons (p. 443).

Allport marshals these three areas of concern as ingredients for what he judges to be a solid and convincing case against incorporating the social stimulus value and biosocial trait concepts within a guiding definition of personality for his new field of scientific inquiry.

As a postscript to our historical perspective, we might note that in subsequent treatments of May's formulation of the social stimulus value of persons it has been cited but dismissed (Stagner, 1937) or deemed too narrow to stand alone as a conception of personality (which, of course, May did not propose) (Jones, 1944). These commentators opted instead, along with Allport, for a strictly psychological conception of personality (Mowrer & Kluckhohn, 1944).

In a rare bow to May's dual conception of personality, however, Mowrer and Kluckhohn (1944) implicitly highlight the status of reputation as a collective representation of the person when they acknowledge "that there is a genuine distinction between the individual 'as integrate in action' and his 'reputation' is indicated perhaps most decisively by the fact that when an individual dies, 'personality' in the first sense comes to an end, but in the second sense it may continue or even grow over the centuries (p. 77). As we shall see in Chapter 9, this recognition is a key element in the distinction between personality psychology, on the one hand, and fields that deal primarily with posthumous reputation, such as biographical studies and cultural history, on the other (see, e.g., Longmore, 1988; Schwartz, 1987).

Certainly, we reputational analysts may very well view Allport's same set of contrarian points as simply revealing an important but heretofore neglected research agenda dealing with the collective social representation of persons within their idiographic reputational networks.

But the more fundamental question remains to be resolved: What is the relation of reputation to personality and of reputational analysis to personality psychology?

Historical Perspective 3: William James' Concept of Social Selves

In his influential treatment of the concept of "self," William James is so thoroughly interactive that only a careful reading of his classic exposition of the matter reveals the precise locus of the self to which he is making reference at any particular point (James, 1983, pp. 293–296).

The first locus for a particular kind of self resides in the images within the minds of those other individuals whose recognition and favorable opinion a specific person seeks. In our conceptual framework, these loci are to be found within the cognitive person bins maintained by members of that person's reputational network. (Note, for clarity of exposition, I have reordered some quotations; the italics are James'.)

- *"A man's Social Self* is the recognition he gets from his mates" (p. 281).
- "Properly speaking, *a man has as many social selves as there are individuals who recognize him* and carry an image of him in their mind" (pp. 281–282).
- "The most peculiar social self which one is apt to have is in the mind of the person one is in love with. The good or bad fortunes of this self cause the most intense elation and dejection . . ." (p. 282).
- "To wound any one of these his images is to wound him" (p. 282).
- ". . . we have an innate propensity to get ourselves noticed, and noticed favorably, by our kind" (p. 281).

The second and related locus for the same kind of self resides among the categories or subsets of reputational network members. Here, James highlights the issue of how to monitor or derive some sort of summarizing group image of us held by these others.

- ". . . as the individuals who carry these images fall naturally into classes, we may practically say that he has as many different social selves as there are distinct *groups* of persons about whose opinion he cares" (p. 282).

Thus, James deals here with levels of the reputational network membership, from specific members to groups of members. Subsequently, notions of a generalized or summary image were introduced by Cooley (1902) and Mead (1934).

The third locus of self embodies a dramatic shift from outward to inward, from the images of the person held by reputational network members to a quite different realm: the cognitive, affective, and behavioral components of the person's own inherently multiple social selves. Each of these components is aimed at seeking the favorable attention and shaping of one's social image as it is held in the mind of a particular reputational network member or group.

Depending upon the person's social strategy and the composition of the person's reputational network, the multiple social selves may be organized more or less harmoniously.

- "We do not show ourselves to our children as to our club-companions, to our customers as to the laborers we employ, to our own masters and employers as to our intimate friends" (p. 282).
- "From this there results what practically is a division of the man into several selves; and this may be a discordant splitting . . . or it may be a perfectly harmonious division of labor" (p. 282).

Inward and Outward-bound Social Selves

In James' formulation, the term "social self" is partially an outward-bound concept, referring to the mental images of the person held by members of the person's reputational network. That this aspect of his formulation bears directly upon the notion of reputation is confirmed by a succinct Jamesian footnote on page 282, which is as follows in its entirety: "'Who filches from me my good name' etc." James assumes his readers will recognize that he is referring to one of Shakespeare's classic statements concerning reputation, in Othello, Act III, Scene 3.

But at the same time, James articulates an inward cognitive, behavioral, and emotional component. He clearly implies that the person maintains an inference, whether accurate or inaccurate, regarding the nature of the image of him- or herself that specific others are forming. He describes the behavioral efforts that the person directs to shaping these images, while also taking note of the emotional implications entailed by the person's own perceptions of success or failure in these endeavors. His is a dual outward and inward conception of the social self.

However, although James' formulation features the multiple images of the person held by network members, the overall reputational content claims residing within and throughout the reputational network are not given explicit representation in his analysis.

Prime Social Selves and Best-Guess Social Selves

For each social self in the outward sense, held by a specific reputational network member, the person may have formed a best-guess estimate of that member's image of the person. Thus, presto, James' notion of social selves as social–ecological phenomena is transformed into the cognitive and affective phenomena of multiple social selves in the inward sense.

For the sake of clarity, we will refer to the outward-bound images of the person actually held by reputational network members as the "prime" social selves and the inward versions of them held by the person as the complementary "best-guess" social selves.

Because the best-guess selves derive from the way persons imagine or infer how others are viewing them, Cooley (1902) deemed them reflected or looking-glass selves. In his view, this inferred feedback from others helps to shape the person's self-concept and self-esteem. Miller (1983) has contrasted Cooley's portrait of the person as a relatively pliant object of social pressures with James' depiction of an autonomous self-as-agent, seeking positive self-feeling through effectively influencing or shaping her or his prime social selves, as they are held by others (pp. 324–325).

In James' formulation, the best-guess images constitute only one aspect of the conceptual package he offers. Each best-guess image is linked to the motive to secure a favorable recognition by others, to the subsequent emotional state that follows from good or bad fortune in that regard, and to the kind of distinctive and targeted conduct that the person views as a means to achieving favorable recognition by those network members. Thus, what were initially outwardly oriented referents come to yield a set of dynamic, inwardly located cognitive, affective, and behavioral complexes associated with distinctive network members or subgroups of them. In Chapter 6, we reviewed the many ways that persons as agents of self-reflexive action strive to create, shape, influence, and protect their reputations (or perhaps we should say their best-guess reputations).

Limitations of James' Formulation of Reputation as Social Selves

In his formulation of reputation as social selves, James fails in two ways to articulate a complete network interpretation of reputation.

First, James appears to be of two minds in identifying membership in a person's reputational network. At one point, he refers inclusively to all those "individuals who recognize him and carry an image of him." But at another point, he reduces this scope to those "persons about whose opinion he cares." From the standpoint of our network interpretation, the proper reference is to the entire membership of the person's social network.

Second, as we noted in Chapter 6, our working assumption about typical reputational network size encompasses about 2,000 members from the person's social network and then another 2,000 others from cell B of Table Intro.1, those who know the person although the person does not know them. James gives no acknowledgment of the cell B component of reputational networks.

Reputational Networks Within Models of Personality and Social Systems

From these key historical perspectives on relevant contributions concerning reputation within personality and social psychology we turn to more contemporary conceptual perspectives.

The role of personality research in appraising the validity of reputational content claims (reviewed in Chapter 5) constitutes only one element of a broader issue of the relationship of reputational networks to personality. A major assumption of our theoretical framework views reputational networks as essentially separate from personality, although not unrelated to it.

The concepts of "dynamic systems," "system boundaries," and "system relations" offer a usefully broad perspective for delineating the interactive relations between reputation and personality. The *personality system* refers to the skills, cognitive capacities, values, and psychodynamics of the individual agent of self-reflexive action, while the *social system* comprises the institutional structures, regulatory principles, technological capacities, social networks, and adjustment mechanisms of a society (Smelser & Smelser, 1964; Sanford, 1963; Craik, 1998; Mayer, 1998).

A Generic Reputational Model for Incorporation Within Personality and Social Systems

Reputational network theory yields a generic set of reputation-relevant components for both social system models and personality system models. Figure 7.1 depicts the major reputational components of this conceptual package within a generic model of personality and social systems. Note that Figure 7.1 deals only with reputation-relevant components in a generic sense. We will later embed these generic elements within two contemporary models of personality (Figures 7.2 and 7.3) (Hogan & Roberts, 2000; McCrae & Costa, 1999).

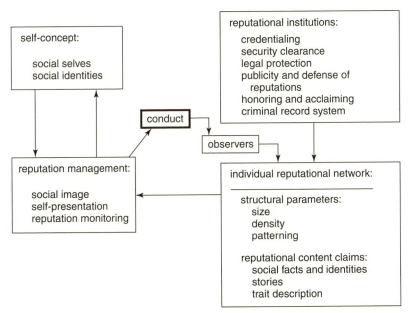

Figure 7.1 Personality and social systems: reputational network theory.

Reputational Components of Social Systems Models

The principal conceptual work is required within a formulation of the social system. First, a social system model must incorporate the multitude of individual reputational networks. Each reputational network consists of all other persons who know a given individual and the membership's structural facets (e.g., size, density). Reputational networks are dynamic, for example, in the changing patterns of communication among members and the addition of new members. The observable conduct of a person, as well as other information about the person, is depicted, evaluated, and communicated by reputational network members, including social facts, stories, and trends in conduct. Trait terminology can be recognized as a natural language for observer descriptions of trends in individual conduct. Reputational information is communicated discursively among network members and stored distributively by specific network members. Thus, reputational content claims are varied and abundant in nature, although sensible approaches are available to attempt summary reputational portraits.

A second focus of conceptualization within the social system deals with reputation-relevant institutions. Among the myriad of institutions of contemporary society, some play a central role in the reputational process.

A. Credentialing institutions that issue reputational information, in the form of credit cards, driver's licenses, educational certificates, and occupational and professional licenses, such as those attained by building contractors and retinal surgeons. These and related institutions grant and objectively maintain evidence supporting reputational claims concerning competence and resources, thereby supplementing or replacing "regular and routine monitoring by our neighbors and friends" (Nock, 1993, p. 73).

B. Security clearance institutions, such as federal screening agencies, detective agencies, psychological assessment firms, and similar units. They deal with evidence bearing upon a person's trustworthiness and dependability, including occupational and financial histories, drug testing, and psychological testing (Nock, 1993).

C. Institutions that deal with the legal protection of reputation (e.g., civil libel court) and the enhancement and defense of reputation (e.g., publicity agencies).

D. Institutions that bestow honor and esteem in the form of special awards and elections (e.g., the hundreds of specialized halls of fame) (Cowen, 2000; Danilov, 1997; English, 2005; Whitmeyer, 2000).

E. Finally, the criminal justice system, whose functions include the identification and recording of those who have committed such disreputable acts as misdemeanors and felonies (e.g., court records, FBI public enemy lists).

A person's reputation is to be found ultimately within her or his specific reputational network. However, reputation-relevant institutions provide social functions that may recognize, endorse, magnify, distort, protect, or evaluate a person's reputation. That is, internal processes within reputation-relevant institutions may generate decisions about record-keeping and certified evaluative judgments that may or may not reflect the individual's reputation, as found within her or his own reputational network.

For example, the selection of individuals for awards, prizes, and honors is typically made by a more or less small panel of judges. Institutionally created fame or notoriety nevertheless gains communitywide attention that is taken note of, in a feedback process, by members of the person's reputational network. Thus, these institutional processes offer a second route to the shaping of reputation, above and beyond the more direct influences derived from the person's own conduct and role enactments.

Reputational Components for Personality Models

Theoretical models of personality typically include elements that represent various interactive and reciprocal relations between personality and reputation. Our generic personality model borrows conceptually differentiated aspects of the self, namely, relational and social selves (Chen, Boucher, & Tapias, 2006; James, 1983; Turner & Onorato, 1999) and social identities (Sarbin & Scheibe, 1983; Tyler, 1999). In addition, self theory incorporates elements of reputation management. The social image constitutes the person's goal or intended outcome in generating and shaping the reputational content domain. Self-presentation deals with some of the means for attaining that aim, including impression management (Bromley, 1993) and reputation monitoring (Emler, 1990; Hogan, 1982).

Reputational Networks Within Contemporary Models of Personality and Social Systems

How can generic reputation-relevant elements be incorporated within specific contemporary personality theories? For our illustrative purposes, any personality theory will do; but two are noteworthy: the socioanalytic theory of personality (Hogan, 1982) and the five-factor theory of personality (McCrae & Costa, 1995).

Within contemporary personality theory, the socioanalytic model grants the most central and explicit role to issues of reputation (Hogan, 1982; Hogan & Roberts, 2000). Our generic formulation of reputation-relevant components of the personality and social systems appears to be compatible with and can be readily incorporated into socioanalytic theory.

Reputational Networks Within the Socioanalytic Theory of Personality

Taking some liberties with the socioanalytic model of person–situation interactions (Hogan & Roberts, 2000, Figures 1.1 and 1.2), our Figure 7.2 sketches this more general model and incorporates the person's reputational network and related elements.

Socioanalytic theory asserts that personality and reputation are best understood within the process of human evolution as it has occurred in the context of small group living (see also Buss, 1991, 1996). Human groups are organized in terms of hierarchies. The two most central adaptive challenges for persons are, first, negotiating hierarchies and attaining status and, second, gaining social acceptance and forming alliances. Persons are motivated to get ahead and to get along with others because status and acceptance generate short-term material advantages and contribute to long-term reproductive success.

Personality from the Observers' Perspective

Hogan (1982) has drawn a basic distinction between personality as viewed from the other or observer's perspective and personality as experienced from the agent or actor's perspective. He focuses upon trait terms as the natural

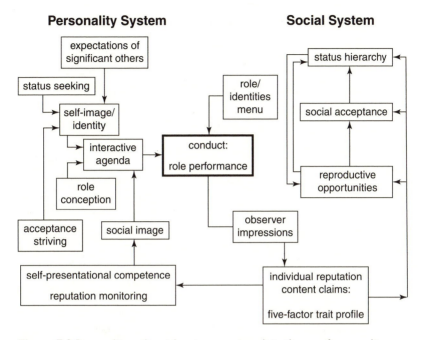

Personality System   **Social System**

Figure 7.2 Personality and social systems: socioanalytic theory of personality.

language for observers to use in depicting what an individual is like as a person; that is, the impressions a person makes upon others are encoded by them in the descriptive and evaluative language of trait terms.

Socioanalytic theory asserts that others who know, observe, and interact with a person will tend to come to a consensus; this agreement can be expressed in the form of a list of trait terms that depict the person's reputation. In its broadest form, these trait descriptors can be categorized to form a profile of the "Big Five" personality dimensions (John & Srivastava, 1999).

Although the social consensus can sometimes be erroneous, individual and group survival depend on our ability to make trait attributions concerning others that are substantially valid. The primary function of trait descriptions and reputational portraits is to appraise persons regarding their potential as resources for the group (e.g., Can this person be trusted? Is this doctor competent?). Through the medium of this informal evaluative process flows the extent to which a person attains status and gains acceptance.

Personality from the Actor's Perspective

In contrast, socioanalytic theory identifies the natural language for actors to use for describing themselves to be that of goals, desires, aspirations, hopes, fears, social skills, values, and social knowledge. Personality dynamics entails a set of interactive elements, including self-images, self-presentational capabilities, role concepts, and interactive agendas.

Our social images constitute the views and identity we want others to credit to us, as well as images that represent the expectations we believe significant others have for us. The self-presentational capabilities are manifested in stylized role performances acquired over the life course and directed at promoting the general adoption by others of our privately held and desired self-image and thereby translating it into our public social image.

Personality from the actor's perspective contributes to explanations of the stable features of a person's social conduct and resulting reputation. Everyday social life consists of structured, more or less predictable interactions guided by rules and roles. These interactions are primarily symbolic, not to be taken at face value; such "texts" have to be interpreted, with more or less skill. Observers assume that a person's actions are intended to tell them how she or he wants to be regarded (e.g., as someone who is competent to treat a medical complaint). Persons differ in their choice of self-images and in the aspirations, efforts, and competence they display regarding this self-presentational endeavor.

Thus, with regard to the personality system, the major components include status-seeking and acceptance-striving, which influence the social image the person seeks to manage and project for adoption by others. Generation of the person's particular social image is partially influenced by the expectations of significant others. The person's broad interactive agenda in social life is derived from the self-image, along with the modes of implementing it via the person's particular role conceptions and self-presentational style and competence. The nexus of the personality and social systems is embodied in role performances, which are influenced by the menu of roles and social images proffered by a particular social system, as well as by the person's own conceptions of those he or she seeks to enact and attain.

Reputation and Personality

The observable role enactments of a person generate the impressions and evaluations of others, which in turn affect the content claims advanced within the person's reputational network. The reputational content claims are commonly deemed to constitute the person's reputation, summarized, for example, by a Big Five personality profile. Reputation, in turn, impacts upon the person's status position and degree of social acceptance. Within an evolutionary framework, these outcomes have a strong general bearing upon the person's ultimate reproductive success.

The feedback from the social system is keenly monitored by the person. Feedback takes the form of the kind of status afforded the person, the amount of social acceptance gained, the extent of reproductive success, and the nature of the prevailing reputation by which the person is represented in social life.

One component of self-presentational skill is general savvy in reputational management, for example, in recognizing how and by whom one is being evaluated and learning the relevant categories of evaluation. The process of self-presentation seeks through strategic interaction to preserve, enhance, and defend one's reputation, especially in key situations, such as job interviews or important social introductions. While impression management deals with episodic face-to-face encounters, reputation management encompasses more distal strategic concerns, for example, to control the flow of information about oneself throughout one's network (Bromley, 1993; Emler, 1990).

Overview: Reputation in Socioanalytic Theory

We are now in a position to consider the formulation of reputation within the current framework of socioanalytic theory.

First, reputation is a crucial component of socioanalytic theory. Reputation is the primary medium through which the person's observable role performances in social life affect how he or she is appraised as a resource by other individuals and the group at large. Reputation in this context is not only personality as viewed by observers but also personality as it affects the major outcomes of an individual's life: status, acceptance, and reproductive opportunities.

Second, in its conception of the personality system, socioanalytic theory delineates how personality from the agent's perspective offers an explanatory account of the individual factors that help to account for how reputations are generated. The person's social image and identity conceptions constitute the goals and project for heeding the perceived expectations of significant others and for acquiring the kind of reputation that may lead to social status and social acceptance, as well as their associated advantages. They combine with the person's role conceptions and self-presentational style and competence to mobilize an interactive agenda that guides the person's role performance and monitors feedback from the social system. In this dramaturgical theory, most social conduct takes the form of role enactments, wherein the critical attention of mutual audiences and associated cast members produces the assorted reputations of their participants.

Third, socioanalytic theory focuses almost entirely upon reputational content claims. It does not provide, although it is compatible with, a network formulation of reputation that includes size, density, visibility, structure, and other network parameters. Nevertheless, given its dedication to understanding individual differences among persons, socioanalytic theory can be readily attuned to incorporate this domain of reputational variations.

Fourth, the theory's treatment of reputational content claims itself is directed primarily to the observers' impressions of the individual as a person, that is, in depictions employing trait terminology. Little or no attention is given to content claims regarding social facts (e.g., credentials) about the person or storied narratives associated with or characterizing the person.

Fifth, socioanalytic theory does not attend to the distinction between discursive and distributive facets of reputation. Indeed, the means of assessing reputation within socioanalytic theory have been directed centrally to the evoked aggregated approach. Reputational network members are sampled in some fashion, and their trait descriptions of the person are recorded and statistically analyzed. Within this theory, adequate consensus is anticipated; and reputation consists of the composite of agreed-upon individual trait terms and the resulting five-factor trait profile (Hogan, 1982). The emphasis is entirely upon more or less settled beliefs about the person and, thus, upon the aggregate person bins of reputational network members and less so upon the buzz of ongoing chat about the person.

Sixth, the distinction between reputational content accuracy and content validity is not explicitly addressed. The issues entailed in appraising and establishing reputational content accuracy are not examined or are implicitly assumed to be obvious and straightforward. Some concern for the validity of reputational content claims regarding trait descriptions is noted, for example, in the assertion that reputations can sometimes be wildly wrong (e.g., Hogan, 1982, p. 59). However, the possibility of important and consequential individual variations among persons in either the accuracy or validity of their network's reputational content claims is not closely explored.

Seventh, socioanalytic theory holds that reputational content claims concerning trait descriptions are stable and predictive but does not examine closely the potential sources of this stability and predictability. In the case of stability, both the personality system and the social system can be seen as eligible sources. In the case of the personality system, stability or change in self-image aspirations, role conceptions, and self-presentational style would lead to accompanying consistencies or shifts in role performance, which observers are expected in this theory to note accurately and encode in corresponding stable or changing trait portraits of the person.

What are not explicitly addressed are sources of inertia and alteration in reputational content claims that can occur independently of the person's role performance. For example, important changes in role performance might be ignored or invalidly assimilated into established representations of the person. Or false reports of the person's social conduct might be invalidly and perhaps maliciously circulated through the reputational network, resulting in reputational content claims not anchored in the person's social conduct. Reputational content claims may also lag behind altered trends in the person's social conduct, in part because not all reputational network members may be "up-to-date" in this regard. In addition, certain life contexts, such as a severe illness or a major shift in occupational status, may provoke in observers a "fresh look" at the person and an occasion for reputational revision (Craik, 1993a).

Within socioanalytic theory, reputational portraits are predictive on two grounds. First, the trait terms employed in reputational accounts of a person are tools for communicating observed trends in a person's conduct which, other things equal, can be expected to continue. Second, socioanalytic theory posits a personality system entailing a stable core of fixed needs and cognitive structures. To the extent that this latter understanding of personality from the actor's perspective possesses predictive power, the reputation of a person can be expected to reflect resulting stability of the individual's social conduct, rather than possible distortions internal to the reputational process.

Reputational Networks Within the
Five-Factor Model of Personality

Our reputation-relevant model may be sufficiently generic to find a place within other personality models as well. For example, the generic reputational network model can be readily embedded within McCrae and Costa's (1995, 1996, 1999) five-factor personality theory, even though its personality system model differs dramatically from that of socioanalytic theory.

Within socioanalytic theory, the five-factor model of personality dimensions appears within the social system as a general summary of a person's reputation. The five factor categories are viewed as the structure of trait descriptors—the terms used by everyday observers in recording their impressions, descriptions, and evaluations of other persons. Individual trait terms are treated within socioanalytic theory as ways of encoding observed trends in the everyday conduct of others (Buss & Craik, 1983a; Wiggins, 1997). Taken together, these trait descriptors, categorized within the five-factor model, constitute a person's reputation and a medium for communicating how a person acts and what we can anticipate about the individual's future conduct.

An alternative theoretical perspective can be found that places the five factor concepts within the core of the personality system (McCrae & Costa, 1995, 1996, 1999). Some liberties have been taken with this model (e.g., McCrae & Costa, 1996, Figure 3.2) to align our Figure 7.3 with our Figure 7.1.

Within this model, the five-factor trait categories serve as basic tendencies, akin to status-seeking and acceptance-striving within the socioanalytic model. Next along the causal pathways, we find aspects of the person's self-concept (e.g., self-schemas, personal myths), which are somewhat akin to the self-image in socioanalytic theory, and the features of the person's characteristic adaptations (e.g., personal strivings, attitudes, habits), which are somewhat akin to self-presentational style and competence in socioanalytic theory. These core components of the personality system result in objective behavior, culminating in the person's objective biography.

The other interactive influences within the model are biological aspects of the five-factor basic tendencies (e.g., genetic factors) and components of the socioenvironmental system (e.g., cultural norms, life events, and situations), which in turn feed back upon the person's characteristic adaptations.

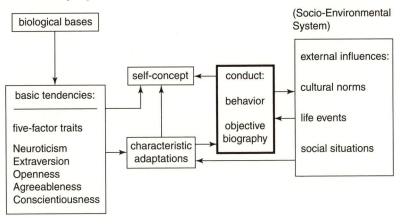

Figure 7.3 Personality and social systems: five-factor theory of personality.

Note that within the five-factor theory of personality, the Big Five dimensions are located as basic tendencies within the personality model. Traits in this model are not encodings of patterns of behavior, nor are they accessible to public observation; instead, "they are deeper psychological entities that can only be inferred from behavior and experience" and "are insulated from the direct effects of the environment" (McCrae & Costa, 1999, pp. 143–144). Thus, traits within this theory are basic causal factors that contribute to an explanation of observed behavior (Allport, 1937; Craik, 1997; Tellegen, 1991). In contrast, within the socioanalytic model, the five-factor model of personality dimensions is situated within the social system, as a reputational summary, representing an encoding of act trends in role conduct that are themselves generated not by personality traits as causes but by the working out of interactions among the pursuit for status and acceptance, the mechanisms of self-image, and the processes of self-presentation.

In most other contemporary models of personality, plenty of conceptual space is available within the largely unarticulated social system to accommodate reputational components, resting upon the basic shared components of observable conduct and attentive and chatting observers.

Conclusions

Within a systems framework, we can conceptually envision an interactive relationship between the personality system and a social system encompassing persons' distinctive reputational networks, along with reputation-relevant social institutions. The personality system can conceptually accommodate within this framework at least two contemporary theories of personality: the socioanalytic theory and the five-factor theory.

In the following chapter, we will examine how persons, enacting the two distinct social roles of plaintiff and defendant, interact with the libel court, a long-standing institution devoted solely to the legal protection of individual reputations.

8

The Risks of Discourse
About Other Persons

Defamation Law from the Plaintiff
and Defendant Points of View

The Libel Court, London

The Royal Courts of Justice are located at the head of Fleet Street in London. They are primarily the civil courts; criminal courts can be found down beyond the bottom of Fleet Street at the Old Bailey.

The entrance to the Royal Courts is a well-known London scene. Winners and losers and their lawyers often hold forth on these steps before a scrum of press and television cameras.

Once inside and past the security checks, you are within a huge and noble hall. Down the middle of this space is a long row of wood and glass display cases giving the times and courtrooms for the cases of the day. Unfortunately, these notices give no hint of the type of legal action at issue. The secret to following actions for libel and slander is to find the handful of courtrooms that contain jury boxes (Courts 13 and 14). Most civil cases are held before judges only, but as we shall discover, the judgments of members of a jury typically form a central part of actions for defamation. These cases are usually open to the public and often receive prominent press coverage. The libel court of London is one the world's liveliest.

We will focus upon the English common-law tradition on defamation which guides it. The English common-law tradition has been a key source for defamation law in the United States and many other countries. Important cross-national variations exist, and change is constant within each country. Defamation law is an important context for considering the nature of reputation. Without legal training, I approach this chapter with trepidation. My intent is to provide only a network-oriented commentary on the structure of civil actions for libel within defamation law and certainly not a technical introduction. For authoritative treatments of libel law in England and comparisons with laws in other countries, see Carter-Ruck and Walker (1985), Milmo and Rogers (1998), and Sack and Baron (1994).

Civil actions for defamation deal with the vulnerable nature of our reputation. Anywhere throughout the members and linkages of one's reputational network, an assertion potentially damaging to reputation can enter and circulate narrowly or broadly and in ways difficult to predict or track.

Defamation Within Reputational Network Analysis

The makings of reputation, we have argued, consist of a person's reputational network, the flow of social communication along it, and the relevant cognitive person bins of its members. In Chapter 6, we reviewed how everyday tactics as well as professional practices and strategies of reputation management can be organized, integrated, and guided by our network analysis of reputation. We now turn to another analytic benefit of a network approach to reputation. In this chapter, we demonstrate how the implicit structure of actions for libel and slander in the common law is brought to light through our network analysis of reputation.

We have seen that in everyday social life information about a particular person flows among members of the person's reputational network. Network members are other individuals, each of whom maintains an identified cognitive information bin for that person and is in more or less steady communication with other members about the person. Each network member's bin for that person may be extensive or sparse, but it is always minimally adequate to sustain a set of beliefs, evaluations, and impressions around a recognized identity for that person.

One way of understanding the function of this hum of communications about specific persons is that it generates an efficient pooling and summarizing of the community's observations and opinions concerning the person. This knowledge resource, however unevenly distributed, serves a generally adaptive function when consequential decisions must be made about the person—whether to loan money, to appoint to an important position, to seek out as a potential friend, and so forth (Hogan, 1996; Buss, 1996; Kenny, 1994).

However, this aspiration to an accurate and useful exchange of information can be sharply constrained by a countervailing tendency for our discourse about other persons to be contradictory and even tendentious, guided not by judicious judgment but by motives to denigrate the person as rival and competitor or to bolster the person as friend and ally (Argyle, 1984; Bailey, 1971; Buss & Dedden, 1990).

Finally, we must once again take note of research findings concerning a prevailing negativity bias in the formation of impressions of other persons. That is, when introduced into discourse about persons, negative assertions, once made, are likely to be more difficult to disconfirm than positive assertions (Rothbart & Park, 1986; Tausch, Kenworthy, & Hewstone, 2007). Negative assertions require more countering instances and evidence to disconfirm. Furthermore, less information is needed at the outset to confirm a negative assertion about a person than a positive assertion. In short, it may be only a bit of an exaggeration to say that, even in the face of a pattern of quotidian decency, a person may be known by her or his most bad deed (Birmbaum, 1973).

A case can be made that, given that the information is accurate, the negativity bias is on balance adaptive. Good deeds from a person are expected, have high base rates, and serve to keep the social system in proper operating order, while bad deeds are less frequent and tend to be problematic and disruptive. Thus, more actionable information is conveyed in using them to identify possible bad actors (Katz, 1997; Moore, 1993).

Nevertheless, the easy confirmability, explosive impact, and difficult disconfirmability carried by negative assertions about persons give rise to the temptation to cheat in the social exchange of information about other persons through false-negative attributions. Furthermore, the ever-present possibility of unintentional but erroneous negative assertions presents all of us with the risk of such unwarranted damage to our reputation.

Legal actions for libel and slander in the English common-law tradition are founded on the presumed individual right of each person to protection or redress from damage to reputation due to negative and defamatory assertions.

Defamation law can be viewed as a countervailing mechanism against the impact of negativity bias in assertions made about specific individuals. In this chapter, we will review the issues in defamation law within our framework of reputational network analysis.

Since the core topic of defamation law is presumably the reputation of a person, viewing that legal tradition within the framework of reputational network analysis should prove to be instructive. In doing so, we will find one notable surprise. Within the traditional legal proceedings in actions for defamation, we learn little about the particular already prevailing reputation of the specific plaintiff in the case. However, our review of the structure and issues of defamation law will reveal the conceptual assumptions underlying this legal tradition. We will also establish a basis for aligning the legal conception of reputation against each of our three formulations of reputation as spontaneous communication, evoked aggregate impresses, and belief system.

Two Forms of Risk in Social Communications About Specific Persons

In social life, we run two forms of risk in our everyday discourse about specific persons. First, we run the risk of having statements made and circulated about us that are harmful to our reputation. In the context of defamation law, this hazard will be termed the "plaintiff's risk." Second, in our almost inescapable participation in the ongoing discourse about other persons, we run the risk, either intentionally or inadvertently, of introducing and broadcasting assertions about other persons that are harmful to their reputation. This hazard will be termed the "defendant's risk."

The Plaintiff's Risk

In defamation law, the plaintiff takes the initiative in bringing a legal action for libel or slander. *Slander* pertains to spoken defamation; *libel* pertains to presumably more permanent written or recorded defamation. When relevant, we will take note of the few legal implications of this distinction.

The plaintiff's risk concerns two hazards: first, letting a defamatory assertion stand unchallenged, with damage to reputation, and, second, the incremental impacts of the civil action itself on the plaintiff's reputation—through publicizing the defamatory assertion anew and in the implication, if the action fails, that the assertion was indeed appropriate. Within the English common-law tradition, access to actions for libel or slander appears to be easy and the legal steps seem to be simple and straightforward. The plaintiff must show simply that the defendant published or circulated to third parties a statement that was defamatory and specifically about the plaintiff. Defamatory imputation, publication, and identification constitute the three elements required for an action for defamation.

Defamatory Imputation

The statement must be one that a right-thinking or reasonable person would interpret as likely to be harmful to the defendant's reputation or, more generally, to any person's reputation. Thus, general harm is presumed to be a likely consequence; specific harm need not be demonstrated as a consequence or outcome of the defamatory assertion.

What rationale is offered for not requiring evidence of demonstrated harm to reputation? In a classic appeals case, defamation was likened by the judge to a poison in the body: It circulates in hidden fashion and may not cause or show damage until much later on.

Within our conceptual framework on reputation, this reasoning is well aligned with the fragmented and possibly tattered fabric of typical reputational networks. The defamatory statement may have been circulated in ways unknown and unknowable to the plaintiff; the information, as a result, may reside latently in the relevant cognitive person bins of a large array of reputational network members. To employ another metaphor, these affected person bins are akin to landmines that may not yet have exploded at the time of the legal action of libel or slander but may detonate years hence, for example, at a hiring committee meeting making an important decision regarding the plaintiff. Thus, the documenting of comprehensive evidence for harm to reputation and its damaging consequences is acknowledged to be often not feasible or even attainable.

The recourse is to a general judgment about the presumed harm or forms of harm to reputation. In Chapter 3, we analyzed a set of illustrative defamatory statements drawn from successful legal actions for libel and slander and, therefore, deemed in each case to have been judged as harmful to reputation (see Table 3.3).

The locus for gauging the defamatory imputation is situated with the jury. A host of minor but interesting psychological puzzles can be generated in interpreting the potential defamatory meaning of specific assertions. For example, satire often—to be effective—must be offered as true, yet within a frame signaling that humor is intended.

From sins to sweets: Historical expansion of the scope of defamatory imputation. The historical evolution of the common-law tradition on defamation has seen a steady expansion of the domain of assertions about specific persons that might be legally deemed harmful to reputation. In fifteenth-century England, actions for defamation were restricted primarily to attributions of actual crimes or actual sins. Formal legal actions regarding accusations of crimes were generally taken to the civil courts, while those concerning sins were considered of comparable importance and taken to the ecclesiastical courts. Often, however, the situation was more complicated than that generalization suggests (Addy, 1989; Helmholz, 1985; Kaplan, 1997).

Gradually, the domain of disreputable attributions broadened to include any acts that threatened a person's reputation in a trade or profession. Subsequently, the domain has widened ever further (Helmholz, 1985; Post, 1986). This trend is illustrated by a case wherein two lawyers were reported in the *Sunday World*, a Dublin newspaper, to have quarreled (i.e., "had words") in a bake shop near closing time over who had first spotted, and therefore held rights to, the last chocolate eclair. The newspaper acknowledged that there was no truth to the report of the alleged core act but denied it amounted to libel. Nevertheless, an award of £50,000 to each plaintiff was made against the newspaper (Lawyer's libel damages, 1988).

Thus, the cultural historical trends can be depicted as moving from the delimited realms of sinful and criminal conduct to a broader domain that appears to encompass the full scope of the personality and any conduct that might be evaluated in a negative manner in society at large (Post, 1986).

Notions of reputation. Of the varieties of conceptual and dictionary meanings we have reviewed, which notions of reputation are found in the legal literature on defamation? The complexity of the concept of reputation is seen in the difficulty in forming a singular definition of defamation (Milmo & Rogers, 1998, pp. 7–8).

First, the term "esteem" is often used in legal writings as a synonym for "reputation" in that defamatory statements tend to lower the plaintiff's standing in the estimation of other members of society generally. Thus, the notion of a general evaluation of the plaintiff appears to be at issue.

Second, the effects of impaired reputation upon the decisions and actions of other individuals toward the plaintiff are noted within references to damaged reputation. That is, the harm to reputation is likely to lead to other individuals shunning, avoiding, or ridiculing the plaintiff or holding the plaintiff in hatred or contempt. The image is that of the plaintiff being ostracized or excluded from friendship, social occasions, business dealings, positions in the community, and so forth. Finally, an important legal assumption makes the kind of evidence highlighted by our more complex and nuanced formulations of reputation moot, namely, the simple presumption of a good reputation on the part of any plaintiff. Thus, an articulated conception of reputation is not required and decisions about defamatory imputation are typically left to the jury.

The default presumption of a good reputation. A good reputation for the plaintiff is assumed. This presumption means, first, that the plaintiff is not required to offer evidence of a prior good reputation or evidence gauging the specific nature or magnitude of harm to reputation that has been inflicted by the circulation of the defamatory statement. By and large, this assumption eliminates any rationale or opportunity for the defense to present evidence of the plaintiff's possible prior bad reputation (except in a later phase concerning mitigation of damages).

In summary, the assumption of a prior good reputation on the part of the plaintiff curtails, while not entirely eliminating, occasions for either the plaintiff or the defendant to give a detailed characterization of the plaintiff's specific reputational network and its content claims. Instead, the alleged derogatory statement is appraised by the jury within a more generalized cultural framework, presumably attending to the kind of assertion that would damage any person's reputation.

In addition, a number of logistical and procedural problems would be raised by any allowance of evidence for a prior bad or good reputation. For example, it has been argued that opening up the issue of prior reputation would give rise to multiple minitrials within the defamation trial as the relevant evidence regarding each and every claim regarding prior reputation would have to be adjudicated in some way.

Publication

The plaintiff must show that the defamatory statement was "published," that is, conveyed to at least one third party beyond the dyad of the defendant and the intended recipient of the communication of the defamatory statement. At first glance, the requirement appears to be an exercise in minimalism. Nevertheless, certain classic defamation cases deal with failed efforts by the defendant to assure that circulation of a statement was indeed restricted to the single intended recipient and to no third party. For example, if the printed statement is mailed with an envelope statement indicating "confidential" or "for the addressee's eyes only," does that shield the defendant from the heedless opening and scanning of the statement by an executive secretary? It does not.

The assumption appears to be that once a third party is part of the communication, the reputational network gates are open for indeterminant and unlimited subsequent circulation of the defamatory assertion. The plaintiff should not be held responsible for the onerous or probably impossible task of tracking down or documenting whatever subsequent communication might have ensued. Clearly, this component of publication resonates well with our network interpretation of reputation.

Identification

Finally, the plaintiff must demonstrate that the subject of the defamatory statement was indeed the plaintiff and not some other person. Thus, just as in eliciting and mapping a person's social and reputational networks, the recognition identity of the specific person at issue must be established (Fischer, 1982; van der Poel, 1993; Milmo & Rogers, 1998, pp. 127–160). Similarly, in gossip sessions, the identity of the specific target person is often explicitly established (Eder & Enke, 1991). And, of course, members of reputational networks must keep their cognitive person bins uncluttered with information about individuals other than the specific person in mind.

Remedy

What is the plaintiff's goal in seeking a remedy from the court regarding the threat to reputation? The plaintiff's "prayer" to the court might consist of any of several options (Milmo & Rogers, 1998, pp. 200–228). The defamatory statement has already been let loose to circulate throughout the plaintiff's reputational network. Nevertheless, an injunction can be sought for the defendant to cease and desist from any further publication of the defamatory assertion. The plaintiff can also seek from the defendant a retraction of the assertion and an apology in open court. This step can be seen as intended to announce to the community the defendant's public confession of libelous conduct, as well as regret for the damaging assertion. Finally, the plaintiff can seek monetary damages of three kinds: (*1*) compensation for the plaintiff's suffering and harm to reputation; (*2*) aggravated damages, for example, if the defendant insists upon repeating the assertion in court during the trial; and (*3*) exemplary damages to signal, for example, to newspapers and other media that there will be financial costs of engaging in such practices.

How effective are these remedies? How should the plaintiff be compensated for defamation? Can reputation be rehabilitated? Does any remedy balance the risk of increased publication of the defamatory assertion that is generated by the public attention to the legal action itself and the ensuing trial? We will return to these issues after reviewing the nature of the defendant's risk.

The Defendant's Risk

It is impossible to participate in social life without running the risk of becoming a defamer of others. Our information about other persons is frequently secondhand and not necessarily accurate or trustworthy. Even our direct observations of others' conduct are subject to our own mistaken construal or at least to differing construals (Rommetveit, 1980). In addition, almost all of our comments about the conduct of other persons have an evaluative tilt, in a positive or negative direction. Thus, what we might judge to be mildly negative in valence may strike others as truly shocking conduct.

As a consequence of these interpretative nuances, the information about a specific person that we convey to other individuals may be false, misleading, or in other ways harmful to reputation. Finally, even when we communicate strongly negative information about a person that is completely true and accurate, we may be implicitly or explicitly defaming the person, attacking reputation and speaking ill of him or her. But at the same time, the information may be interesting or amusing and thereby capable of enlivening an idle conversation. Furthermore, as we have argued, chat about other persons is not always idle and merely diverting. We may feel impelled or obligated to pass on disturbing information about another person. Once we have entered the murmur and noise of everyday social life, we may not consider it proper to remain silent ourselves. Finally, we may give way to the temptation to attack, punish, or disadvantage another person through placing a negative "spin" on a report of that person's conduct or even by circulating a completely fabricated report of a negative act by that person.

The defendant's risk concerns two hazards: first, the danger of doing harm to another person's reputation, either intentionally or inadvertently, and, second, the damage to one's own reputation in becoming known as a slanderer or libeler or as someone seriously negligent in social communication about other persons (Gross, 2001; Kaplan, 1997).

The Defendant's Defenses

If we find ourselves as defendants in a civil action for libel or slander, we might succeed by challenging the evidence for the basic elements and premise of the plaintiff's case. That is, we might argue that the assertion was not in reference to the plaintiff, who is mistaken on that count. Or we might successfully hold that the evidence offered by the plaintiff is insufficient regarding the publication or circulation of the assertion to third parties and beyond. Finally, we might present a convincing case that the imputation of the assertion was different from that offered by the plaintiff and that a proper interpretation of the meaning of the assertion was not defamatory.

If these premises cannot be challenged, then the defendant has recourse to several possible lines of defense. First, we might argue for justification, that is, that the assertion about the plaintiff is substantially true even though damaging to reputation. Second, we might argue that the nature of the assertion is one of fair comment on a matter of public interest. Third, we might argue that the assertion was made in an occasion of qualified privilege or was a communication enjoying absolute privilege.

The "rumor repetition rule" should be noted to highlight a little understood consideration regarding one seemingly plausible line of argument that does not constitute a defense (Milmo & Rogers, 1998, p. 236). Proving that a prior rumor exists or even some other source exists for your defamatory assertion is not generally a defense; rather, you carry the full burden of the defamatory assertion. The argument that you were simply saying what others had already said will not suffice as a defense. In the United States, however, newspapers can seek shelter through an argument of "neutral reportage" (Sack & Baron, 1994, 7.3.2.4.3).

Justification

The aim of this defense is to establish that the imputation or assertion is substantially true. In the English common-law tradition, the truth of an assertion about a person constitutes an absolute defense and a bar to successful civil action by a plaintiff (Milmo & Rogers, 1998, p. 233). One ordinary implication of the meaning of this defense is that one must bear up to public communications that accurately report upon our past expressions and actions, even those "own goal" incidents that entail damage to our reputation. Apparently, even defamatory assertions with evident malicious intent are absolutely defensible in the common-law tradition, if they are substantially true (Milmo & Rogers, 1998, p. 233).

The burden of proof that the defamatory assertion is substantially true about the plaintiff is carried by the defendant. This requirement is sometimes seen as unfair. After all, in most legal actions the defendant is considered innocent until proven guilty. But in civil actions for defamation, the other side of the argument is that the defendant has taken the initiative by accusing the plaintiff in some sense of a disreputable expression or action and, thus, it is the plaintiff who should be deemed innocent unless the defendant can present evidence to the contrary.

The evidence for the truth of a defamatory assertion must be substantial; nevertheless, inaccuracies in details might be tolerated in the view and judgment of the jury. The success of the defendant using a defense of justification carries a heavy risk for the unsuccessful plaintiff, of course, who has attracted public attention to the defamatory assertion and then may suffer to have seen it, at least by implication, validated in a public jury trial.

Justification as a defense deals with one aspect of the larger issue of truth–falsity in actions for libel (Post, 1990). Although the matter is now somewhat unsettled, a general presumption of falsity has been made in the common law in favor of the plaintiff: "it is presumed in all actions for libel that the matter complained of is untrue" (Carter-Ruck & Walker, 1985, p 31). That is, "the concept of actual falsity—the underlying truth or falsity of the published statement—has been infused into the tort. At common law actual falsity, if relevant at all, was presumed from a well-pleaded defamation complaint" (Bezanson, Cranberg, & Soloski, 1987, p. 183).

Thus, in civil actions for libel, England follows the common law in that "a defamatory imputation is presumed to be false and that the burden is upon the defendant to show that it is substantially true" (Milmo & Rogers, 1998, p. 235). Nevertheless, falsity remains a presumption, rather than one of the elements of the tort, which consists only of identification, publication, and defamatory imputation.

Empirical research on media libel actions in the United States in the 1970s and 1980s found that what upset plaintiffs about the alleged libel was their belief that the published assertions were false (63%) compared with their violating privacy (4%), damaging personal reputation (7%), damaging business or professional reputation (20%), or other (3%). From the plaintiffs' viewpoint, "Their chief concern is with falsity, and their chief interest is in setting the record straight" (Bezanson et al., 1987, pp. 175, 285, Table 4).

Alas, the plaintiff's aspirations are usually thwarted. In part because actions are often defended and resolved on defenses of fair comment or privilege, well over half of the examined cases were not directly adjudicated on the falsity issue.

The issue of falsity, even if it turns out not to play the role anticipated for it by ordinary plaintiffs, can be seen as reflecting a folk concept that emphasizes validity in the flow of reputational information. In the same spirit and within our network interpretation, the importance of validity in reputation is also highlighted by the justification of truth as a defense.

The remaining defenses include fair comment, occasions of qualified privilege, and statements enjoying absolute privilege. The defenses derive from a willingness of society to tolerate the risk of circulation of defamatory assertions about a specific person because such communications serve general social purposes and bring benefit to the community as a whole.

Fair Comment

In one case, individuals are shielded from successful actions for defamation when they are participating in a discussion of issues attracting broad public interest, including statements of belief and inferences about the expressions and actions of public figures. In this instance, the risk of harm to the reputation of specific persons through defamatory assertions is balanced against the fundamental right of free speech concerning matters of public interest.

This defense may cover assertions of opinion reasonably linked to relevant facts; however, the core facts on which comments are made must be substantially accurate. In considering the use of this defense, the jury or judge must weigh questions concerning what are matters of public interest, who is a public figure, what is opinion and what is fact, and how accurate are the relevant facts at the core of the assertions.

In addition, the jury must make a major inference of its own regarding the degree to which malice was involved in the defendant's defamatory assertion about the plaintiff. Heretofore, the jury's inferences have dealt with a relatively external and public matter, the question of whether harm is likely to have been done to the plaintiff's reputation. Now, in considering malice, the jury must make inferences of a quite different kind, regarding the state of mind of the defendant (Milmo & Rogers, 1998, p. 248).

We have noted that the range of assertions that may be deemed defamatory has broadened historically from issues of sin to those of sweets. Similarly, on the defense side of the courtroom, the domain of persons who might be considered public figures has expanded. Indeed, it is beginning to appear that any one of us drawn by happenstance and unwillingly into a feature news story can become a public figure, with attendant loss of certain protections to our reputation. At the same time, the realm of assertions about public figures that might be deemed of public interest has also expanded (Post, 1994).

Earlier in the historical evolution of this defense, defamation actions were a favorite and intimidating device of those in power and authority to stifle political criticism and opposition (Addy, 1989; Helmholz, 1985; Kaplan, 1997). In this sense, the defense of fair comment represents progress in free expression and political liberty.

In contrast to that of civil libel, the traditional law on criminal libel deals with a hybrid of seditious and defamatory libel, entailing the publication of severe vilification of persons in public positions and authority (Milmo & Rogers, 1998). Here, an overriding interest in maintaining public order or control is clearly evident in those circumstances in which even the truth of the assertion is not deemed a defense (Milmo & Rogers, 1998, p. 544).

Qualified Privilege

The defense of fair comment entails communications in the public forum, the marketplace of ideas and opinions, and other open venues. These are occasions where the societal aim is the full and wide-ranging discussion of matters of interest and concern to the public. In contrast, the defense of qualified privilege deals with more restricted occasions, featuring circumspect communications and very circumscribed publication or circulation of assertions about specific persons.

As we found in Chapter 2, these occasions of qualified privilege deal with situations in which one participant is deemed to have a social, moral, or legal duty to respond to the inquiry of another person with regard to a specific third person. In turn, the recipient is considered to have a right or interest in this information. Examples include a former employer or teacher providing references to a possible employer or a relative or advisor providing information about someone's potential suitor or future spouse. In other cases, the occasion of qualified privilege arises out of the reciprocal benefits for two individuals to share information about another specific person in reaching a decision of mutual interest, for example, in considering a future business or professional associate.

Typically, occasions of qualified privilege appear to entail as one purpose the making of more or less consequential decisions about the person in question. We have already cited several social scientists who view this kind of exchange of information as one of the primary adaptive functions of the ongoing discourse about specific persons. This defense within the common-law tradition seems to acknowledge the general benefits that accrue to the social welfare from relatively unfettered communication about specific persons for certain purposes.

The defense of qualified privilege shelters these occasions of communication from action for defamation even if the derogatory assertion proves to be wrongheaded or false or cannot be shown to be true about the person. This tolerance of the risk of mistakes harmful to the reputation of particular individuals carries the qualification that the communication was made with "honesty of purpose" and without malice (Milmo & Rogers, 1998). An aura of conscientiousness and expectations of good intention surrounds this defense. As in the case of fair comment, recourse to this defense can be countered by the plaintiff's demonstration of malice on the part of the defendant. Malice in this legal context seems to carry two meanings, one having to do with negligence and irresponsibility and another dealing with cruelty and selfishness; it need not refer to the emotional state of the defendant.

Note that it is the occasion, and not the nature or content, of the communication that enjoys qualified privilege. Access to this defense requires restraint in that the content of the communication bears closely on the purpose for which it is to be used and discretion that the report circulates only to those with a right or interest in receiving it. Negligence with regard to these limitations can deprive the defendant of successful recourse to this defense. The communication cannot carry purposes other than those that make the occasion privileged. For example, if a relative communicates something defamatory to a wealthy nephew regarding the latter's potential spouse to be that turns out to be both derogatory and false, the occasion can nonetheless be privileged. But if that relative is shown to have known that the assertion is false or if the relative is shown to have a self-interested purpose of promoting the competing prospects of a friend, then recourse to this defense may fail.

As in the case of fair comment, the issue of malice requires considerable inference on the part of a jury concerning the knowledge and intentions of the defendant. But, as we have seen previously, defamation can be viewed as a destructive recourse to social cheating in the exchange of information, particularly in those instances in which malice is found to be present.

Absolute privilege. The availability of the defense of absolute privilege offers a remarkable but limited set of contexts in which the contested statements about specific persons are public, defamatory, false, and even guided by malice yet nevertheless become sheltered from successful civil action for libel and slander. Statements of this kind pertain to those made in (*1*) judicial proceedings, including communications by witnesses, lawyers, and judges, and (*2*) legislative bodies such as parliamentary proceedings.

Individuals who are the subject of these public, false, and defamatory statements are left without legal remedy because these essential public activities might not function at all if participants in them were constantly subjected to defamation lawsuits.

Prior to 1600 and the historical development of these notions of privileged contexts of communication, the realm of criminal accusations was quite muddled and risky. A citizen might properly accuse another community member of a crime, such as theft. If the accused was found not guilty, then the accused could turn around and bring a defamation action against the accuser. The risk thereby entailed in reporting possible crimes could constitute a severe constraint upon the identification and prosecution of criminal conduct (Helmholz, 1985; Kaplan, 1997).

Summary: What Discourse About Other Persons Is Sheltered and What Is Not?

What Is Sheltered?

The truth about specific other persons, by and large, is sheltered. A member of the community can with confidence and security communicate information about another person that is substantially valid. However, if that report is valid and unfavorable in content, then in conveying news of disreputable utterance or conduct, the individual runs the risk of being seen by others in the role of the accuser, a social role that carries its own social risks (Gross, 2001; Kaplan, 1997).

Defamatory reports about specific persons are sheltered under certain circumstances. If the target person is a public figure or has become associated with an issue of public interest, then a defamatory assertion may be sheltered from successful legal action (via fair comment). If the target person has become the subject of interest of one kind or another to certain other individuals, then a community member may be considered (via qualified privilege) to have the moral, social, and legal duty to convey derogatory information to the interested parties, even if it turns out to be mistaken. However, if these defenses are misused, the individual can be considered a social cheater in the exchange of information. For example, the informant cannot communicate the defamatory assertion with knowledge that it is false or with malice.

Defamatory reports constitute fair comment only if they are guided by honest intention to contribute to the discussion of public issues. And no occasion of qualified privilege obtains if its circumspect and discreet prerequisites are not met; for example, if the information exceeds the focus and domain of mutual duty and interest or if it is circulated beyond the specific individuals who are properly entailed in those duties and rights.

Only a handful of public activities shelter statements with absolute privilege. They include proceedings where defamatory assertions whose truthfulness is uncertain must be publicly entertained, such as judicial settings, and where full and unfettered expression of beliefs and opinions is considered essential, as in legislative deliberations.

What Should Be Sheltered, from the Perspective of Reputational Network Analysis?

Occasions of qualified privilege are particularly interesting in relation to the broader notion that one social function of everyday chat and gossip is to circulate and pool information about persons that may at some later time become useful in making decisions about them. Under the traditional scope of qualified privilege, the sheltered occasions arise only when certain information and certain purposes form a specific and narrow nexus of duty and right to know. From our conceptual framework, one might argue that all informal, nonmalicious communication about specific other persons should be sheltered from actions for defamation, under an expanded articulation of qualified privilege.

First, in the interests of full disclosure, it might be argued that all occasions should be privileged occasions and all reports, including those dealing with possible disreputable conduct, should be open to full and wide-ranging discourse. After all, how are we to establish and know when we have or will come to have a moral, social, or legal duty to share information with another individual about a third party? How are we to determine when and whether we can seek out such information from other individuals? How do we decide when our mutual interests with another person allow us to exchange such derogatory information about a third party?

Given the difficulties in delineating occasions of qualified privilege and anticipating a jury's judgment, why not simply declare all exchanges of information to be sheltered from defamation action? Our slogan might be "A duty by all to convey and a right by all to receive any and all information about other persons." What may not be relevant today may become relevant in the future. What may be important for a particular individual to know about a specific other person may be more likely to reach that individual if information is broadly circulated. The nexus of information and need to know is unforeseeable. When it occurs, the wider the prior circulation of available information, the more likely that it can be usefully mobilized for the relevant occasion.

But is it not unfair and harmful to circulate possibly false and defamatory reports? Perhaps, but bear in mind that what is false may be more readily disconfirmed if it is also circulated broadly rather than narrowly and selectively. What is false may more readily come to the attention and knowledge of the target person if it is widely circulated, allowing the person to take informal corrective steps prior to, or rather than, resorting to risky civil actions for libel or slander.

To counter the social cheating entailed in false defamatory assertions about others, we might augment and mobilize greater use of the legal remedy for malicious falsehood.

Certain trends appear to be moving us in the direction of this reformulation. The occasion of qualified privilege that traditionally sheltered letters of recommendation has proven steadily less effective. Lawsuits centered on defamatory inaccuracies have focused on negligence and have led former employers and teachers to limit their reports to the barest facts (e.g., confirmation of dates of employment and position).

At the same time, the category of public figure within the defense of fair comment has steadily grown to encompass persons who have not sought out public attention, while the range of information deemed to be in the public interest about public figures now has almost no limits. Indeed, like it or not, we are becoming a transparent society (Brin, 1998).

This radical proposal would make everyone a public figure and would shelter all nonmalicious exchanges of information about other specific persons from civil actions for defamation, with no boundaries on content and without restriction to occasions of mutual duties and rights. Despite its alarming implications, this radical approach recognizes our network theory's emphasis upon the free circulation of information.

In contrast, network theory also places a strong emphasis upon the individual right to the protection of reputation and the adaptive value of accurate and valid information flow. Thus, a less radical, even traditional, proposal would call for continued support of the English common-law approach to defamation and, indeed, for the strengthening of its protection of individual reputation.

In this regard, contentious issues have arisen from the 1964 *New York Times v. Sullivan* case, and related cases, in which the U.S. Supreme Court dramatically shifted the focus from reputational harm to the plaintiff to whether the action of the defendant showed, for example, active malice, negligence, or knowledge of inaccuracy of the assertion at the time of publication (i.e., subjective falsity). These issues and the focus on constitutional privileges have resulted in "the receding emphasis on reputation" (Bezanson et al., 1987, pp. 195–196).

Aligned with this shift is the enormous legal infrastructure sustained by newspapers and other mass media to protect their interests as defendants. In contrast, plaintiffs are typically one-time players in the libel arena and, consequently, little organized plaintiff pressures counter the self-protective lobbying efforts of the media. The spirit of our network interpretation of reputation supports reform efforts to restore the English common law's primary attention to the plaintiff's reputational harm (Dill, 1993; London, 1993).

Rehabilitating Reputation

In actions for defamation, the plaintiff's presentation typically ends with a prayer for relief, that is, the set of legal remedies sought. The goal is to restore the plaintiff's reputation as well as to recognize the plaintiff's distress during the publication of the defamatory assertion, as well as during the trial itself.

How can a reputation be rehabilitated? At a minimum, one goal would be that the news of the plaintiff's legal vindication should be communicated to everyone in her or his reputational network who might have been exposed to the original defamatory assertion.

In village life in sixteenth-century England, the remedy was straightforward. At Sunday morning church service, for example, the defendant would stand before the congregation, announce that he or she had sinned against the plaintiff, perhaps acknowledge the falsity of the assertions, publicly apologize, and seek forgiveness (Helmholz, 1985). Thus, this news was fully and efficiently communicated to most of the plaintiff's reputational network. But as we have seen, in modern segmented and mobile social life, reputational networks are much more fragmented and geographically extended.

Juries have been allowed to make large monetary damage awards in part because the full extent of injury to reputation from a public and defamatory assertion cannot be completely ascertained (Milmo & Rogers, 1998; Dill, 1993; London, 1993). Due to the distributive facets of reputation, years later the false report might arise at a committee meeting to determine the plaintiff's well-being or future career prospects.

Large monetary awards can also be seen as intended to bring media attention to a plaintiff's vindication. One successful libel plaintiff, the entertainer Carol Burnett, won an award of $1.6 million 1981 in a libel suit against the *National Enquirer*, which she claimed had reported that she was drunk in a restaurant, had a boisterous argument with Henry Kissinger, and spilled wine over another diner (Carter-Ruck & Walker, 1985, Appendix III, p. 501).

Defamatory assertions cannot be traced in the way infectious diseases are tracked in public health investigations. The communication link within a reputational network can skip any identifiable routing, for example, through overheard gossip. Nor can such defamatory reports be "recalled" as in the case of defective products because no record of all of the "buyers" exists.

In the abstract, the procedures entailed in the case of pretrial settlements in the plaintiff's favor may seem attractive. Typically, a public retraction and apology are made in "open court" before the judge; arrangements for monetary awards and the plaintiff's legal costs are often made, which may or may not be made public. However, anyone who has attended one of these sessions in a libel courtroom at the Civil Court in London will realize the striking contrast between this venue and the setting of a sixteenth-century village church.

In 2001, David Soul, former star of the TV series *Starsky and Hutch*, won a pretrial settlement for a libel suit he brought against a newspaper,

The Mirror, claiming a theater review of his show in a West End venue inaccurately reported that attendance was small, ushers were instructed to try to prevent audience members from leaving early, and his personal financial investment was at risk (Kelso, 2001). Late one afternoon, in a large but nearly empty libel courtroom at the Royal Courts of Justice in London, the judge announced a pretrial settlement in open court, which entailed an apology from *The Mirror*, a "considerable sum" in damages, plus his legal costs. These announcements by the defendant's lawyers were made before the judge, the plaintiff, a few of his associates, various legal staff, perhaps a journalist or two, and seemingly not more than two members of the general public (who happened to be my wife and myself). The occasion was a far cry from sixteenth-century England, when the convicted defamer was expected to stand up in the village church on Sunday and denounce her or his own false accusations directly to the entire relevant community.

In the instance of a celebrity case, the scrum of journalists and photographers at the entrance to the Civil Court on Fleet Street might provide a narrow window of opportunity for a plaintiff eager for broadcast of the vindication on the daily news shows. However, if the case entails a small-time businessperson, for example, falsely reported to have made dishonest use of a client's funds or property, the open court announcement would likely also be made in a nearly empty courtroom but likely with no media scrum available on the sidewalks to provide any modest amplification of the vindicating news.

Public retractions and apologies in newspapers and other media may be partially effective. The award of large monetary damages may also be somewhat attention-getting and thus facilitate the dissemination of the news of the plaintiff's vindication. However, even in the case of the actor cited above, the overlap between readers who scanned the original false and defamatory account of his stage production and those who might have noticed the outcome of the legal case months or years later might be surprisingly small.

Monetary damages may be viewed as a compensation for this inevitably ineffectual means to rehabilitate reputation. Often, another aim of plaintiffs is to affect the decisions of publishers in ways that effectively put a stop to further publication or circulation of the defamatory assertions. In small towns, for example, a plaintiff can gain some relief if the local newspaper desists from repeated publications of the same defamatory assertions (Bezanson, 1986, p. 794).

Defamation Law and Concepts of Reputation

One of our purposes has been to increase our understanding of how the structure of civil actions for libel mutually illuminates our conception of reputation. One of the properties of the English common-law tradition has been its long, piecemeal, and pragmatic evolution. In attempting to clarify the theoretical nature of the common-law tradition, Post (1986) offered three concepts of reputation that address differing facets of defamation law. The distinct concepts of reputation as property, as honor, and as dignity speak not only to the individual right to protect reputation but also to images of how persons are interrelated in society.

Different concepts of reputation resonate to varying facets of defamation law. In order to place concepts of reputation within this comparative approach, an array of the facets of defamation law is presented in Table 8.1.

Reputation as Property

The concept of reputation as property presupposes that persons are linked to each other through the institution of the market, which determines the value of property. The merchant known for her credit-worthiness and the carpenter known for the high quality of his workmanship represent forms of property

Table 8.1 Issues in Defamation Law

Elements required of the plaintiff
    Identification
    Publication
    Defamatory imputation

Additional features
    Presumption of good reputation
    Presumption of general damages
    Presumption of falsity
    Justification: Truth as a defense
    Remedy: Publication of verdict
    Remedy: Retraction
    Remedy: Monetary awards
    Corporate entities can sue

resulting from individual effort and labor. Unjustified aspersions on these valued characteristics deprive persons of the market value of their efforts. Such injuries can be assessed in monetary terms and remedied through monetary awards.

Post argues that certain facets of defamation law can be understood by the concept of reputation as property. One is the use of monetary rewards as a remedy. Another is that corporations and other nonpersonal entities can sue for defamation.

Other facets of defamation law do not resonate well with the concept of reputation as property. One example is the fact that defamatory imputation is a required element in actions for defamation. As a consequence, untrue communications that cause damage to a person's credit or business opportunities but lack defamatory imputation do not entail redress, even though demonstrated monetary loss is involved.

A second instance follows from the irrebuttable presumption of general damages. In the spirit of reputation as property, it may appear to be inexplicable from a potential defendant's point of view that monetary awards can be made in compensation without any proof of actual and specific harm.

Reputation as Honor

The concept of reputation as honor presupposes that individuals are linked within a hierarchical structure of well-defined social roles and positions. An individual identifies with and personifies a given social role and expects to receive from others the regard and status that society accords to the associated social position.

According to this concept, the element of defamatory imputation is central and involves distinguishing between communications that are relevant to honor and those that are not. Dishonor entails a loss of face in the community as well as a loss of status and identity.

Since honor is generated from shared social understandings that transcend the conduct of specific persons, it is a public good as well as a private possession. The common-law presumption of damages can be viewed as a process of reinforcing the hierarchical status structure of ascribed roles and positions as well as vindicating the plaintiff's honor.

Reputation as Dignity

A person's dignity resides in the nexus of the public and private components of the self. Its locus is the reciprocal ceremonial process of deference and demeanor, as delineated by social theorists such as Cooley (1902), Mead (1934), and Goffman (1967).

For Goffman (1967), the rule of deference identifies conduct by which a person conveys respect and appreciation of another person. Rules of demeanor identify the conduct of an individual in conveying to others that he or she is a person of certain desirable or undesirable characteristics. This demeanor image is similar to what we have called the person's "social image" (see Figure 7.1).

The law of defamation "can be conceived as a method by which society polices breaches of its rules of deference and demeanor, thereby protecting the dignity of its members" (Post, 1986, p. 710).

One element of defamation law that appears not to resonate with the concept of reputation as dignity is the requirement of publication of the contended communication to third parties. Goffman's (1967) theoretical focus is primarily upon dyadic face-to-face interactions, which tend to escape libel liability. Thus, it must be acknowledged that in the all-important dyadic context, the issue of libel remains at best ambiguous and of equivocal significance, with both participants threatened. With third parties, an audience enters the scene.

As Post (1986, p. 712) argues, a defamation trial is "an arena in which the parties are free to present 'competing interpretations of behavior': the plaintiff contending that the defamation should be explained by the social incompetence and inappropriate behavior of the defendant; the defendant urging that the lack of respect implied by the defamation should be understood as justified by the plaintiff's conduct."

Thus, to rescue this concept of reputation as it relates to defamation law, two functions are assigned to it. First, the plaintiff's dignity is rehabilitated when the court authoritatively determines that the defendant's defamatory communication constitutes an unjustified departure from the rules of civility. Thereby, the verdict signals the plaintiff's worthiness of respect and continuing membership within the community. At the same time, a verdict serves a second function of maintaining and enforcing the community's general rules of civility. Monetary awards can aid in, but cannot alone serve, this dual function.

In summary, Post's (1986) comparative analysis delineates the differential relevance of three concepts of reputation to facets of defamation law. The concept of reputation as property encounters difficulties in accommodating the required element of defamatory imputation as well as the presumption of general damages. On the other hand, this concept assimilates the feature that permits corporate entities to sue for libel as well as the remedy of monetary awards for damages. The concepts of reputation as honor and reputation as dignity readily assimilate the defamatory imputation requirement and the presumption of general damages. However, they must seek out ancillary functions for the award of monetary damages. Finally, the concept of reputation as dignity encounters an initial objection that this theoretical framework does not immediately assimilate the required element of third-party publication.

The Network Concept of Reputation in Comparative Context

Each concept of reputation within this analytic framework presupposes broad societal functions. The concept of reputation as property encourages personal exertion, labor, and self-creation. The concept of reputation as honor encourages adherence of personal conduct to social roles and positions and supports a hierarchical system of position and status. The concept of reputation as dignity encourages and protects a reciprocal system of demeanor and deference.

As we have found, the concept of reputation as network seeks to promote and protect the validity of the adaptive flow and storage of information about specific persons. The network interpretation of reputation resonates with a considerable number of the features of defamation law listed in Table 8.1.

The element of identification fits well with the focus upon information regarding specific persons. It not only is an individual right to the protection of reputation but deals with particular individual characteristics of specific persons.

The element of publication accords with the network characteristics of the flow and dispersed storage of information. Three features of defamation law are also accommodated by the network interpretation of reputation. The presumption of general damages can be justified specifically by the difficulties of tracking the flow and spread of the defamatory assertion throughout the person's reputational network. The remedy of publication of the verdict through announcement in open court promotes the flow of information concerning a settlement or verdict, whatever it might be. Finally, the remedy of large monetary awards can be viewed as having the ancillary purpose of gaining the attention of reputational network members to the plaintiff's vindication.

Facets of defamation law deal with the potency of negative assertions about specific persons. The required element of defamatory imputation assures that the contested assertion falls within the domain of the negativity bias and acknowledges its power, which we reviewed in Chapter 3. The presumption of a good reputation also protects against the discounting of negative attributions on irrelevant grounds, such as possible prior bad reputation. The latter only becomes relevant in the issue of mitigation of damage.

Finally, two facets of defamation law address the issue of validity in reputation. The presumption of falsity of contested communication challenges the validity of information flow and storage. Similarly, justification—that is, truth as a complete defense—recognizes the adaptive value of the validity of information flow and storage.

A New Venue for Defamation: The Internet

The worldwide development of Internet communication has generated a new venue for defamation and novel complexities for defamation law (Collins, 2001; Solove, 2007).

A fascinating matter is the relevance of Internet communication to the distinction between slander and libel within the legal tradition of defamation law. Spoken defamation has been partially sheltered through a higher threshold for bringing civil action (Carter-Ruck & Walker, 1985; Milmo & Rogers, 1998). Actions for slander have required evidence of specific and special damages to reputation, while libel has been actionable per se and injury to reputation is inferred or presumed, in the manner we have discussed.

Why this differentiation? Why has slander been treated as a somewhat lesser action than libel?

First, a difference can be seen in the form of publication: Slander is transient, but libel entails a more permanent record and a broader array of possible subsequent consequences. Second, slander is considered to be more spontaneous and less considered than libel. Assertions made in the heat of the moment enjoy a certain degree of shelter from actions for defamation, in the form of a higher evidentiary hurdle. Thus far, most civil actions for defamation that entailed Internet communications have tended to be treated as libel rather than slander (Collins, 2001).

The determining factor seems to have been the permanent and potentially widely disseminated scope of Internet communications. However, various characteristics of Internet communication appear to take on the spontaneous attributes associated with direct oral communication. Indeed, the misleading imagery of the term "chat room" is used to refer not to permanency but to a nexus of immediate interactive communication in informal and minimally edited style.

The parallel may come closer with the advent of visual and auditory components to Internet communication. Thus, defendants may have new openings for arguing that such defamation actions be considered slander rather than libel. However, at the same time, the addition of visual and auditory components may reduce the anonymity of the sender and make easier the establishing of identity recognition.

Serious difficulties are faced by potential plaintiffs in bringing Internet actions for defamation. One problem is establishing that the plaintiff is the person about whom the defamatory assertion was made, especially if one carries a common name (e.g., John Smith). Related elements of the Internet are the search engines, which may turn up voluminous accumulations of items for a given personal name (Brin, 1998). An even more serious matter is the identification of the defendant, given the seeming anonymity of Internet communication. Apparently, specific computers and their messages can be linked via ID numbers (Collins, 2001). But even then, having the ID number for the computer source does not ensure ID evidence for a particular user/sender, especially with the rapid development of Internet cafés and computer sections of public libraries. Given the worldwide nature of the Internet, fixing legal jurisdiction also presents problems.

The issue of publication takes on a new potential with the Internet, whereby communication is worldwide and messages can be downloaded and then sent along on further, disconnected routings. Observers of the Internet scene are reporting an increase of false and defamatory attacks that are stored and then disseminated by networking sites and search engines. The legal tension between libel rights and free expression remains fluid in this new context. A market appears to exist for services such as ReputationDefender. com, which offers for set fees to search out and attempt to remove Internet items that are harmful to a client's reputation (Badkhen, 2007).

Conclusion: Relation of Defamation Proceedings to Models of Reputation

We have learned about how facets of defamation law map onto our three models of reputation. The spontaneous communication model has the widest set of ties to defamation law. On the plaintiff's side, the evidence for publication and identification bears directly upon the circulation of defamation information within the plaintiff's reputational network, while the remedies of injunction and damages relate to gaining the cessation of such information flow and the circulation of the news of the plaintiff's vindication. On the defendant's side, the defenses of qualified and absolute privilege and fair comment speak to the countervailing interests of the community to ensure and shelter the circulation of information about specific persons within particular occasions and circumstances.

Our two other models of reputation appear to have less relevance for defamation law. If evidence for prior reputation were a more salient feature of defamation proceedings, then the evoked aggregate model and belief systems model would gain greater relevance. As it stands, the belief system model makes a cameo appearance in a generalized form, with regard to the issues of defamatory imputation and the assumption of a good reputation for the plaintiff.

Finally, we should note that, in any case, defamation law in an important sense deals with only one-half of the domain of reputation, namely, its defensive dark side. In undertaking efforts to protect reputation through civil action for defamation, the person has emerged as an agent of action, specifically as an agent of reputation. In Chapter 6, we saw how the person can also serve as a pragmatic promoter of the bright and positive side of reputation. In both cases, we have insisted that the neglected components of reputation require us to look beyond the person, to the members of the person's reputational community. Reputation resides within the impressions, beliefs, and evaluations that they have formed and communicated regarding the person.

9

Posthumous Reputational Networks

The phenomenon of posthumous reputation establishes an intrinsic distinction between personality and reputation. The concept of personality treats the individual as an agent of self-reflexive and integrated action; its locus centers in the mind and body of the person. Reputation is comprised of what is generally said and believed about the person; its locus resides in the person's reputational network of other individuals. With death, the former ceases but the latter need not do so. Some of the most interesting implications of a network interpretation of reputation point us toward a better understanding of posthumous reputation. For without posthumous reputational networks, there can be no posthumous reputations.

A network interpretation affords a new and systematic understanding of posthumous reputation. This framework identifies not just one but three general stages in the evolution of a person's posthumous reputation: the surviving lifelong network, the posthumous network, and, between them for several decades, their overlapping coexistence as a transitional posthumous network. Scholarship in the humanities dealing with the lives of noteworthy persons establishes the significance of this general sequence in the evolution of posthumous reputational networks.

The Prerequisites for an Enduring Posthumous Reputation

A posthumous reputation must entail the same set of elements as a lifetime reputation, along with other elements. They include a reputational network of other individuals who hold at least minimal recognition identity for the person, a flow of information throughout the network via person chat and other informal and formal occasions, and the storage of information about that person within the specific and relevant person bins of reputational network members.

The Three Stages of Posthumous Reputational Networks

A person dies within the midst of her or his lifelong reputational network. Its surviving members afford immediate continuity to the person's posthumous reputational network.

A. The lifetime reputational network encompasses the surviving network membership generated during the person's own life. The eyewitness time span of surviving lifetime network members can be roughly specified. Following a person's death, direct eye witnesses may continue to live and contribute accounts about the person through ongoing social communication for perhaps seventy years or so (i.e., from 10-year-old acquaintances and onward), while secondhand or second-tier accounts may extend another seventy years. However, as they are also mortal, this cadre of surviving lifetime reputational network members will steadily diminish and disappear. As Deborah Solomon (2007, p. 17) notes, "Many people believe that our lives end not when we die but when the very last person who knew us dies." Nevertheless, through the printed word, biographies and similar media can extend a person's posthumous reputation even longer and augment the lifetime reputational network in several distinctive ways.

B. The transitional posthumous reputational network comprises the surviving lifetime reputational network members plus overlapping but new members including, for example, ongoing familial generations or those recruited through an evolving biographical network. Studies in biography and cultural history will allow us to illustrate the dynamics of this sequence in the evolution of enduring posthumous reputations. Any enduring long-term posthumous reputation is ultimately dependent upon the steady recruitment of new members who have had no direct experience or encounters with the now deceased person. As those new recruits arrive, they will initially overlap during this transitional stage with surviving lifetime members. These posthumously recruited new network members are in some sense in a similar position to second- and third-tier members of the surviving lifetime reputational network, both lacking direct encounters with the deceased person. The difference is that at some point all of the members of the enduring posthumous reputational network will have that status and will be mutually aware of sharing that status.

C. Ultimately, the thoroughly posthumous network will spin off and prevail as the sole site of the person's enduring posthumous reputation, along perhaps with some continuing representation within an oral tradition, for example, within families. Thus, the purely posthumous reputational network ultimately comes to encompasses those who know the person only indirectly yet continue to hold and discuss their beliefs, evaluations, and impressions of the person.

Posthumous Reputational Information Flow

How does the death of a person affect the content claims of the surviving lifetime reputational network? The recognition that actions initiated by the person have ceased may "carry over to the inference that death also should end the impression-building process," and thus, the posthumous reputation becomes "frozen in time" (Eylon & Allison, 2005, p. 1716). From this point of view, the reputational content claims regarding a dead person are finished and relatively static. Recent research suggests, for example, that as a consequence new inconsistent information, whether favorable or unfavorable, has more impact upon the reputations of living persons than upon those of dead persons (Eylon & Allison, 2005).

In contrast, from the point of view of our network interpretation of reputation, far from coming to a halt at death, the flow of information about a person is likely to be accelerated through a series of posthumous events and occasions, including death notices, obituaries, eulogies, and memorial services.

Brief death notices are posted in newspapers and other outlets. Newspaper obituaries nowadays appear in an array of differing formats. Some appear in local publications largely in the form in which they are supplied by family or acquaintances. Some are compiled by newspaper reporters on assignment. In larger newspapers, the obituary beat has become a journalistic genre, and these more ambitious obituaries are based on a variety of sources, including telephone interviews with informants. Persons earning these broader notices range from interesting ordinary persons to those with an offbeat life history experience or achievement to others who are famous celebrities and public figures (Johnson, 2006; Siegel, 1997). By and large, these journalist obituary writers tend to be strangers to their subjects.

A second set of occasions, including eulogies and memorial services, entails family and acquaintances. In these instances, the contributors and participants are individuals who knew the person well and seek to evoke a distinctive appreciation of the deceased. As we learned in Chapter 2, the death of any person activates communication throughout the reputational network. Formal and informal exercises of remembrance take place. Furthermore, information and anecdotes that were once intentionally or unintentionally held closely and confidentially now receive broader circulation. At memorial services, heretofore unacquainted subsets of the individual's reputational network are brought together socially in ways that can encourage broader exchange of beliefs, evaluations, and impressions of the person (Craik, 1985).

As one result, the distribution of information about the person throughout the reputational network is likely to shift dramatically. In life, the person may have more or less self-consciously sought to allocate certain of this information to particular subsets of network members, through conversation and correspondence. Now, it flows more broadly.

A second and related result is that the surviving members of the person's reputational network may consider the restraints of privacy and discretion to be relaxed now to varying degrees, unblocking new sources of information flow. And, as we noted in Chapter 8, the individual's right to the protection of reputation, available through legal actions for libel and slander, by and large disappears at death. Thus, the posthumous buzz is due in part to this domain of new and perhaps once confidential information about the person.

Information Flow: Unblocked or Frozen in Time?

One point of view is that death brings a freezing of the reputational process, sealing the impressions that the surviving reputational network members have formed of the person. This research has contrasted impression formation regarding dead persons with that of living persons. Whatever impact this frozen-in-time effect might have must be placed in the context of quite different processes of impression formation regarding persons prior to death and following death. In this comparative case, countervailing posthumous processes, on the contrary, point to an unblocking of important domains of reputational information. The outcome is likely to be new and differently configured information about the person (e.g., the result is a burst of sometimes strongly contested impression-building and revision).

Posthumous Reputational Information Storage

We have argued that reputational networks are a prerequisite to enduring posthumous reputations. Their members necessarily shift over time, beginning with surviving members of the person's lifetime reputational network, then becoming intermixed with posthumous newcomers, and then consisting entirely of these posthumous recruits.

We know almost nothing scientifically about how or whether the general nature of information that flows through and is stored within the posthumous reputational network differs from that within the lifetime reputational network.

Major personality research programs, discussed in Chapter 5, have focused upon the issue of stability and change across the life span, based upon repeated longitudinal observer ratings by family and acquaintances (McCrae & Weiss, 2008). One attractive research strategy would be to continue these longitudinal projects for a decade or two after death.

Consider the following hypothetical but not implausible project, which I call the "Professors Study." At major universities, a steady stream of senior professors moves from (*1*) a preretirement status to (*2*) retirement, then to (*3*) a postretirement stage as professor emeritus, and then, with death, to (*4*) posthumous status. A longitudinal study of content claims by their reputational network members would be undertaken. A sample of senior professors would volunteer to have personality descriptions of them collected at the these points in time (with two or three posthumous assessments) from departmental staff members, graduate students, faculty colleagues, family, and friends.

Does the volume or richness of reputational content claims tend to decline during the posthumous period? Are certain domains of personality descriptors more enduring than others during the posthumous period? Are there trends in the evaluative valence of descriptions across the living and posthumous periods, for example, a favorable tilt in the immediate posthumous period, followed by a more critical corrective, and then a final or stable level?

Very preliminary empirical research on these topics has suggested a death positivity bias in evaluations of the dead compared to evaluations of the living, with dead subjects rated as significantly more likeable, competent, and inspiring than equivalent living targets (Allison & Eylon, 2005). These trends held for dispositional inferences of hypothetical laboratory targets as well as in judgments of a wide range of real-world targets.

Posthumous Reputations of Biographical and Cultural Figures

We now turn to two fields of inquiry whose primary, though not necessarily sole, focus is the posthumous reputations of persons. They are biographical studies and cultural history.

The genre of biography and the field of biographical studies examine the detailed conduct, impact, and lives of persons and typically gather, collate, and circulate more generally a great deal of information about a person, much of which has otherwise been held by and perhaps carefully distributed among relatively few members of the person's lifetime reputational network. Thus, biographies compile and make public information that was not previously encompassed among what was generally said about the person.

As we have noted in reference to the eyewitness time span, following an individual's death, direct eyewitnesses may continue to contribute accounts about the person through ongoing social communication for seventy years or so, while secondhand accounts may extend another seventy years. Through the medium of the printed word, biographical accounts extend a person's posthumous reputation even longer and augment the posthumous reputational network in several distinctive ways, which we now explore.

Thus, for many persons, their posthumous reputation is sustained in the form of biographical reputation. For another, overlapping class of persons, their posthumous reputations are extended even further, though possibly more thinly, as broadly held social representations that become established as basic elements of cultural knowledge and legacy, taught to successive generations from the earliest years of schooling. We can refer to them as persons enjoying "posthumous cultural reputations."

In this context, our focus extends to reputational network members among segments of the general public who show at least a minimal commitment to knowing about and discussing the person primarily as a part of their shared cultural history and heritage (Lowenthal, 1996).

Of course, certain historical figures sustain both biographical and cultural posthumous reputations. Biographies of George Washington continue to appear; at recent count, 672 are catalogued in the Library of Congress ("Founding Favorites," 2004), while schoolbooks and the mass media steadily focus upon general features of his life, character, and accomplishments.

We now turn to a broader discussion of posthumous reputation as analyzed within the realms of biographical studies and cultural history.

Posthumous Reputation in Biographical Studies

In this section, we will bring our network framework to bear upon understanding the relation between reputation and biography. After reviewing relevant historical trends in the development of the biographical enterprise, we will examine the nature of biographical networks. Our analysis will then be directed to the continuing flow of information and impressions about biographical subjects throughout the network and the resulting generation of an evolving discursive biographical reputation. We will then sketch the possibilities for systematic study of the individual cognitive person bins held by contemporary biographers possessing expertise regarding a given subject and the methods available for recording and depicting distributive biographical reputations.

A central topic will be the role played by a person and the person's associates—both keepers of the flame and perhaps enemies—in seeking to shape and manage the person's posthumous reputation.

The Enterprise of Biography

Historical Trends in Biography

Modern biography emerged from a highly evaluative atmosphere, excited by and sustained within a culture of scandal and slander (Holmes, 1993; Kaplan, 1997; Mascuch, 1996). Nicolson (1928) has traced a similar but broader trend, also moving from a highly evaluative approach found in the early lives of the caesars and the saints to a more balanced aspiration in the twentieth century.

Contemporary biographies continue to show traces of commemorative goals as well as debunking purposes. The move toward Nicolson's ideal of the objective biography can be seen in several developments. One is the rise out of journalism of investigative biography (Weinberg, 1992), which devotes notable resources to assembling biographical information from all sorts of private collections and public archives and records, as well as from a very wide range of informants. Another is seen in the contributions of psychological perspectives to biographical analysis (Elms, 1994; Roberts, 2002; Runyan, 1982, 1988).

The latter can be tied to the emergence of life history analysis as a multidisciplinary area of study. This field seeks to bring the processes and standards of historical inquiry to the study of individual lives (Craik, 1996b; Runyan, 1982). Such an endeavor requires a community of scholars sustaining a shared inquiry (Lowenthal, 1985; Pompa, 1990).

Our network analysis of posthumous reputation will reveal that the biographical enterprise is less individualistic than commonly assumed. The dynamic functioning of a communal and self-critical guild is organized around understanding the lives of specific persons.

The Realm of Biography-Worthy Persons

Only a small portion of the general public becomes the subject of a biography. Nevertheless, within the world of publishing, the biography as a product has maintained a strong position of interest and sales.

Mascuch (1996) reminds us that the popular subjects of the emerging genre of biography, as well as autobiography, were often shaded by scandal. During the first half of the eighteenth century they were "dominated by criminals, courtesans, castaways, comedians and other peculiar characters, accounts of whose personal activities momentarily satisfied the seemingly insatiable popular appetite for novel (that is deviant) experience" (p. 163). These written biographical narratives provided abundant material for the nascent market in the printed book.

Eventually, a greater diversity of biographical subjects received attention. Jean Strouse (1978) discerns three categories: famous persons, semiprivate persons, and ordinary persons. The first group "become famous, usually, because they do interesting things: write novels, formulate theories about gene codes, rob banks, rule empires, scale peaks, get burned at the stake" (p. 113). The second group, falling between the famous and the obscure, is located "in a twilight zone, a semiprivate realm occupied by minor poets, lesser dignitaries, hands that rocked important cradles, single flashes of success or fame, and the friends, relatives, and disciples of great men and women" (p. 114). The third group is comprised of ordinary persons whose lives are obscure and thinly documented, sometimes limited to census reports and institutional records. Yet, they have been found by social historians to be "exemplary precisely because they were commonplace" (p. 114) and, thus, informative about how "life was lived day to day, about work, about life's conditions in distant times and places" (p. 113).

In all three cases, network relations are relevant, especially so in the case of the second group, whose prominence is frequently dependent upon their membership in the reputational network of a more famous person.

Nowadays, biographies steadily appear dealing with newsmakers and celebrities. Presidential campaigns generate an array of supporting and critical accounts of the lives and conduct of candidates. Major and intriguing literary figures often enjoy a steady stream of biographical treatments (Aaron, 1978). Some notable subjects of biographies, such as Samuel Johnson, have been biographers themselves, as in his volume on the poet and murderer Richard Savage (Holmes, 1993).

Many biographies deal with persons of more local or circumscribed note, yet their lives and conduct remain of provincial interest within particular locales, organizations, or professions. One learns, for example, that a former Berkeley police chief and pioneering criminologist is to be the subject of a biography now in progress.

Biographical Reputational Networks

Our argument is not simply that the posthumous reputations of persons can be found in printed biographical treatments of them, reiterated in a more or less enduring but quite static fashion, but that biographical practitioners, experts, and readers constitute a living, dynamic reputational network whose members demonstrate a substantial commitment to speaking, writing, and reading about a specific person and to discussing formally and informally their beliefs, evaluations, and impressions of the person's conduct and life.

Biographical Networks as Eventual Successors to Lifetime Networks

To capture the dynamics of biographical reputations, we must recognize our distinction among three reputational stages. First, the lifetime reputation obtains during the person's own life; it typically does not overlap with biographical endeavors, although occasionally a subject will begin to work directly with a designated or authorized biographer. Second, during the transitional stage, a complex interplay comes about between an emerging cadre of biographers and a chorus of surviving members of the person's lifetime reputational network. Strictly speaking, this stage extends at least to the end of the eyewitness span but features most prominently the members of the person's surviving generational cohort. Third and finally, the posthumous biographical reputational network spins free of eyewitnesses to the person or even beyond any secondhand witnesses. The person's posthumous reputation now comes to reside primarily within the biographical reputational network and perhaps secondarily within the person's family oral tradition.

In summary, we identify three general stages in the evolution of a person's reputation. First, the living reputational network encompasses the network generated during the person's own lifetime. Second, the transitional posthumous reputational network comprises the posthumous surviving lifetime reputational network members plus new members, including those recruited through the evolving biographical and scholarly network. Third, the purely posthumous reputational network encompasses those who know the person only indirectly yet continue to hold, exchange, and discuss their beliefs, evaluations, and impressions of the person.

The Biographical Guild

It is easy to form the impression that biographers work as independent and isolated scholars and writers. No strong and distinctive academic field of biographical studies yet exists, although efforts in that direction have been increasingly apparent in recent years, with the advent of several relevant academic journals. Even so, professional biographers tend to move from subject to subject, guided by personal interests or advice from literary agents. Thus, often, no systematic connections can be discerned from one given biographical subject to others across a biographer's career.

While vigorous social networks may not be found among them, biographers do function to revive and revise their subjects' reputations and to sustain and augment their subjects' reputational networks. We can depict this process as it is revealed by application of our conceptual framework for analyzing reputational networks.

In doing so, we must distinguish between two kinds of biographer networks. The first is biographer-oriented and would encompass each biographer's own social and reputational network. The second and more pertinent for us is the subject-oriented network of biographers, reviewers, and readers who form around a specific biographical subject. In some cases, such as Washington and Napoleon, a sequence of biographers may not overlap within their own lifetimes but they would count toward and function as members of, say, Washington's biographical network. In other cases, such as John F. Kennedy or Philip Larkin, multiple biographers of the subject may be acquainted with each other and may thus form a subset of their own networks. Our emphasis will be upon the role of biographers, reviewers, and readers in constituting an evolving posthumous reputational network for a particular biographical subject.

At a minimum, the publication of one biography of a deceased person will directly and immediately extend the subject's reputational network, through the reviewers and readers of the biography. Indeed, in seeking out, assembling, and interpreting as much information as possible, the biographer becomes one of the most active members of the person's reputational network, probably as enterprising as any member encountered during the person's own lifetime.

For the biographer, this typical acquaintance at a distance can become intensely intimate and emotionally engaging. During her work on a biography of Alice James, Jean Strouse (1988b) experienced times when she would become so frustrated and distressed by Alice James' actions and life choices that she would have to take a walk around the block to regain her receptive attentiveness and muster and sustain a professional openness to her subject.

Unless the subject of the biography has been deceased beyond the eyewitness span of seventy years, the biography's readership is likely to include a chorus of surviving members of the person's lifetime reputational network. Thus, a renewed buzz may be prompted throughout the remaining reputational network. The biographer may be caught up in this enlivened discourse and, of course, may already have consulted directly with some of the surviving network members. We will return to this dynamic process in addressing the nature of a person's posthumous discursive reputation.

In the case of individuals such as George Washington, who are subject to multiple biographies, an entire biographical guild becomes organized around the subject, comprising a large number of biographers, scholars, reviewers, and informed readers. Thus, this process generates a posthumous reputational network that complements that of the surviving members and then subsequently persists and evolves beyond the original lifetime network's necessarily and ultimately limited duration.

The Sequence of Biographical Reputational Networks: Living, Transitional, and Posthumous Reputational Networks

Occasionally, biographies are undertaken during the subject's own lifetime. In some cases, these are authorized biographies whose development occurs with the active cooperation and endorsement of the subject. In other cases, biographers work independently. These biographies appear amid the ongoing life of the subject and among the subject's lifetime reputational network, into whose membership the biographer willy-nilly enters.

More typically, biographies are posthumous endeavors, with many being written and published relatively soon after the death of the subject. For this transitional category, the biographer appears among the surviving members of the subject's lifetime reputational network. The one or many biographers who publish in the immediate posthumous scene constitute the germination of a parallel biographical reputational network. This nascent biographical reputational network initially coexists with the surviving lifetime reputational network for perhaps several decades. Ultimately, the biographical network will separate and prevail as the major locus of the person's posthumous reputational network, along perhaps with a continuing remembrance within the oral tradition of the families of the subject and of the subject's associates.

Posthumous Reputational Network Size

The size of a person's immediate posthumous reputational network is initially an inertial effect of the size of that individual's lifetime network. The exceptions include Emily Dickinson, who lived a secluded life in Amherst, Massachusetts, within a notably constricted social network. However, through leaving a large corpus of unpublished work, she soon emerged as a world-renowned poet after her death. For ordinary persons, the duration of posthumous network size is partly a function of age at death. For a death at age 50, for example, the active generational cohort will persist for several decades. For a death at age 80, a depleted generational cohort means that the size of the posthumous network depends upon steadily recruited younger members and a larger overall lifetime network structure.

The generation and size of a person's biographical network are somewhat separate and distinct from the lifetime network. Of course, biographers, literary agents, and publishers are likely to focus upon subjects with immediately posthumous networks of substantial size. They seldom pluck subjects out of obscurity. Even so, within the realm of biographer-worthy persons, the typical case is likely that of the one-biography subject. But even just one biography entails a biographer, reviewers, and readers who may accumulate over several decades.

With two or more biographies, scholarly interaction between the biographers becomes a possibility. One-way interaction can take place when the second biographer comments on the interpretations of a much earlier biographer. When the biographers are contemporaries, formal and informal communication is likely. Furthermore, reviewers and readers of the second biography may be inspired to seek out the first. For example, John Paul Jones, the founder of the U.S. Navy, has been the subject of a handful of biographies, two of them major efforts by Samuel Eliot Morison (1939) and Evan Thomas (2003).

One biographical issue concerns John Paul Jones' paternity. His assumed father, John Paul (the naval hero himself added "Jones" to his last name), was the gardener for a landowner and pioneering landscaper, William Craik (no relation to your author). William Craik's estate, Arbigland, is located in Kirkbean on the Solway coast in southwestern Scotland. Craik's son, James, a contemporary of John Paul Jones, later became a friend of George Washington, as well as Washington's personal physician and the chief hospital physician and surgeon in the Continental Army. James Craik was actually an illegitimate son of William Craik, who had acknowledged and educated him. Morison treats in detail, but gives no credence to, local stories that John Paul Jones was in fact an unacknowledged illegitimate son of William Craik, or perhaps the son of some other high-status local landowner (p. 7, Appendix 1). Four years later, Lorenz (1943) appears neutral on the issue but adds other paternity possibilities and a report that Jones himself tended to believe certain of these rumors (p. 7). Sixty years later, in his recent extended discussion, Thomas (2003) draws upon Morison's account and adds new information based upon his own research but leaves the matter unresolved (pp. 16–17). Issues of this kind illustrate the network flow of new information and evolving interpretations among biographical treatments of the same person.

Of course, a smaller number of the biographical elite warrant a steady stream of biographies, generating a partially concurrent and partially serial cadre of biographers, biographical experts, reviewers, and readers. This new community is organized around the conduct and life of the subject and the intermittent flow of sometimes surprising and reorienting information about a given subject. Such posthumous biographical networks may communicate at scholarly conferences, in academic journals (e.g., *The James Joyce Quarterly*), and nowadays on Internet sites (e.g., Jane Austen websites).

Furthermore, overlapping circles among biographical subjects them-selves can serve to generate scholarly networks. An excellent example is the Bloomsbury Group, a network of friends in England during the first half of the twentieth century who had an impact upon a wide array of endeavors, including fiction, biography, literary criticism, economics, painting, journal-ism, publishing, and public policy (Rosenbaum, 1995). The group included Clive Bell, Vanessa Bell, Roger Fry, Duncan Grant, John Maynard Keynes, Desmond MacCarthy, Lytton Strachey, Leonard Woolf, and Virginia Woolf (Edel, 1979). This core group has been the subject of a host of individual biographies; indeed, one member, Virginia Woolf (1940), quickly wrote a biography of Roger Fry, the first of the group to die. In addition, a cot-tage industry of writings and commentaries on the group per se has emerged (Markert, 1990), and it has been the subject of at least one group biography (Edel, 1979).

The boundaries of the network extend beyond the original core. As Edel (1979) notes, "Bloomsbury had other members, who led quiet lives and played marginal roles in its annals. There are some who have been labeled 'Blooms-bury,' but were simply 'friends of the friends'" (p. 12). Edel treated his group biography as a longitudinal portrait of a committed group of friends: "My Bloomsbury personages met in youth; they became friends; they struggled to maturity; they courageously faced the world's turmoil; their lives became intertwined. There are many novels that tell such a story . . ." (p. 13). Indeed, we have already encountered one in the form of Anthony Powell's *A Dance to the Music of Time* (1951–1975).

Similar biographical circles can be found. Individual biographies are available of Alice James (Strouse, 1988a), Henry James (Edel, 1953–1972), William James (Allen, 1967), and their father Henry James, Sr. (Habegger, 1994). R. W. B. Lewis (1991) has offered a biographical history of the Jameses as a family. Individual biographies are amply available of this country's vari-ous founding fathers, but Ellis (2000) has shifted the metaphor in treat-ing the "founding brothers" as a network within a generational cohort (see also Wood, 2006). Freud's circle and Darwin's circle present additional examples.

One point underscored by group biographies is that authors of individual biographies often work implicitly, if not explicitly, within such overlapping networks of biographical subjects. Indeed, scholars of a specific person typically have mastered these associated networks and consider the common and joint source materials as important academic topics.

Discursive Posthumous Reputation

As we learned in Chapter 2, the death of any person activates communication throughout the reputational network. Formal and informal exercises of remembrance take place. Furthermore, information and anecdotes that were once intentionally or unintentionally held closely now receive broader circulation. At memorial services, subsets of the individual's reputational network are brought together socially in ways that can encourage broader exchange of beliefs, evaluations, and impressions of the person. The impact of biographical agents and activities serves to amplify these processes.

First, the distribution of information about the person throughout the reputational network is likely to shift dramatically. In life, the person has more or less self-consciously sought to allocate certain information to particular network members, through conversation and correspondence, often recorded in others' diaries and in correspondence received from third parties. Now, the biographer comes along to assemble what has been strategically and perhaps delicately dispersed and to make public what was to a greater or lesser degree kept private. Thus, it is not simply the content of these materials that becomes public but also their configuration. Biographical treatments will reveal the organization of information through the person's lifetime reputational network and what this now public overview reveals about the person.

Second, the surviving members of the person's reputational network may also consider the restraints of privacy and discretion to various degrees now relaxed, providing more grist for the biographer's mill. In addition, the individual right of protection of reputation embodied in actions for defamation largely ceases for the deceased (Milmo & Rogers, 1998; De Baets, 2002).

Thus, the buzz due to new and in part once confidential information about the person is enhanced by the anticipation of biographical publications, and then their appearance sparks new spikes and alterations in what is being said and what is believed about the person.

The Chorus of Survivors

We have emphasized that during the transition period the emerging biographical network of writers, scholars, reviewers, and readers overlaps with the surviving lifetime reputational network. The latter members can become a chorus that comments vigorously about whatever biographical activities and products are under way. This discursive process may entail a buzz of speculation about what personal papers, diaries, correspondence, unpublished works, and so forth exist; who has control of these materials; and when and how they may be made public, if ever. Commentary may ensue about how access to sources and publication is being handled as a result of the person's prior planning and by the actions of executors and heirs.

The chorus of survivors may also hold firm convictions about what form biographical narratives of a person's life should take. In the case of Robert Louis Stevenson, for example, two distinctively different storylines were championed. Among his literary friends in Great Britain, tales of Stevenson's exuberant young adulthood were viewed as a featured and essential component and one of their colleagues was identified as the suitable biographer. In contrast, his widow, who had taken Stevenson off to America and the Pacific islands, wished to see a biography that ignored those tales and instead dealt largely with his second life in exotic places. While writer's block settled in on the first potential biographer, his wife managed to select another who did the job as she envisioned it (Hamilton, 1992).

Another impetus for continued discourse about a person is the irregular and unpredictable posthumous flow of information, despite the cessation of the person as an agent of intentional action. Letters and diaries must be found before they can be published or made use of by biographers. One of the most dramatic cases is that of James Boswell, whose dignified family was not eager to see further letters, diaries, or other writings by him published and remained uncooperative in locating such material. As a result, two major caches of his documents—upon which much of his current literary reputation is founded—were not made public until over one hundred years after his death (Hamilton, 1992).

At the same time, other new information about the person can enter posthumous circulation as a result of the availability of materials from the estates of colleagues and relatives. This prospect of an evolving and dynamic flow of information and interpretation serves to sustain and augment the posthumous biographical network over time and generations.

Managing Posthumous Reputation: Keepers of the Flame and the Bonny Bonfire

The cultural invention of the literary and artistic estate has given institutional organization to the many decisions entailed in allowing access to unpublished materials, arranging publications, and supervising copyright matters (Hamilton, 1992; Salvesen & Cousineau, 2005).

A number of what might be called "pre-posthumous" tasks can be undertaken by a foresighted person. These decisions include making a will; selecting a literary or artistic executor; leaving instructions for the executor; authorizing a biographer; writing, selecting, and destroying correspondence with an eye for posterity; and perhaps preparing for one's deathbed utterances. Also, Lowenthal (1996) takes note of the autobiography masquerading as biography. A striking case is Thomas Hardy, who spent years ghostwriting his official biography and then having it passed off as his wife Florence's memoir (Lowenthal, 1996, p. 145).

The social and legal roles of the literary or artistic executor remain complex and require many difficult judgments. The mission, as keeper of the flame, is to ensure that some sort of representation of the person endures into posterity, but what kind? What is to be made public and what is to be suppressed? What is to be embargoed and what actually destroyed? And if embargoed, then for what period of time? Implicit in these decisions is often the matter of what is disreputable and what is not. What are the real and settled wishes of the deceased—for a full representation in posterity or for one that reflects the boundaries of a "good" reputation? And within the spirit of the common-law notion of qualified privilege, what right to know is to be granted to posterity?

Hamilton (1992) effectively marshals the actions of the poet Philip Larkin to illustrate these issues. Larkin shaped a social image of himself as that of a retiring, even reclusive poet. At the same time, from his early teens onward, he had maintained a long-standing and frank diary and carefully assembled and catalogued every personal paper and document—foreshadowing and in keeping with his subsequent career as a university librarian. What was to become of this biographical treasure following his death? Larkin thoughtfully selected his literary executors and struggled to provide them with full authority and clear guidance concerning his wishes, especially with regard to disclosure versus reticence.

But the upshot was not as foreseen. Close reading of his unsettled instructions yielded a deep-seated ambiguity regarding disclosure to posterity versus everyday discretion. And in any event, at the very end, Larkin had short-circuited his careful assignments of posthumous responsibilities to posterity by asking the main beneficiary of his will to destroy all of the diaries, which she did.

In another case, Hamilton recounts how Henry James had thought and written extensively about the biographical enterprise and had been consulted by other writers and their heirs concerning sensitive matters regarding literary estates and executors. For himself, James resolved to be the keeper of his own bonfire by carefully reviewing, editing, and selectively destroying material from his personal papers, correspondence, and other documents. Yet, despite his program of bonfires out in the back of Lamb House, his residence in Rye, more than sufficient grist for the mill remained in the possession of contemporaries and others to support Leon Edel's (1953–1972) classic five-volume biography.

Posthumous Social Images: Reputation and Posterity

In Chapter 7, we examined a generic framework for the reputational elements of both social system and personality system models. Within this context, the social image constitutes the person's goals or intended outcome in generating and shaping a reputational content domain (see Figure 7.1).

By and large, the person's typical target audience for the social image project is comprised of members of her or his lifelong reputational network, that is, members of her or his contemporary generation. However, another potential social image target is posterity, that is, members of future generations.

Our founding fathers are generally portrayed as being deeply concerned about fame as it entailed securing their intended social image among future generations (Adair, 1967; Wood, 2006). Leaders such as George Washington explicitly sought to guide their own conduct in ways that would embody and be seen to embody the Enlightenment ideals of a gentleman: civility, politeness, learning, and a disinterested manner in their approach to important issues of the day. Their remarkable generation succeeded in displaying these modes of exemplary conduct and seemed to have earned the expectation that subsequent generations of Americans would appraise them by these lofty standards and acknowledge their achievements in this regard.

However, Wood (2006) has argued that those founding fathers, such as Adams and Jefferson, who had lived long lives and thereby gained a glimpse of the coming generations were disheartened by what they perceived. The substance of their accomplishments in promoting popular democracy, an egalitarian spirit, and broader political participation turned out to be at odds with any continuation of their preferred Enlightenment style of political conduct. The status of the standards they had adhered to and had expected to be appraised by had now shifted dramatically—posterity had altered the predominant political style to one that was considerably ruder, rougher, and more robust (Wood, 2006).

These experiences of the founding fathers highlight the difficulties in managing reputation for posterity. Effectiveness in this project requires not only a shaping of conduct in accord with one's intended social image for posterity and a sustained visibility across generations but also an ability to forecast and accommodate the changing standards and ideals of future generations.

Distributive Biographical Reputation

Recognizing the viability of a dynamic and evolving discursive posthumous reputation makes the monitoring and examination of a person's distributive reputation plausible. The continuing posthumous network and its flow of informal and formal communications about the person creates a community of more or less expert informants, each of whom possesses cognitive person bins encompassing their beliefs, evaluations, and impressions about the target person.

The procedures for the analysis of distributive reputations remain the same as those delineated in Chapter 3. In the case of posthumous reputation, two more or less distinctive populations of network members are available for this purpose: first, the surviving members of the person's lifetime network and, second, the newer members of the biographical network. Eventually, the latter will prevail, and acquaintance with the person will come to be only at a distance.

Few studies have systematically explored biography-oriented reputation. Certainly, large numbers of biographical experts are available on figures such as George Washington and Virginia Woolf. Biographical experts occasionally engage in public exchanges concerning particular issues about a person, for example, the impact of Woodrow Wilson's neurological condition while serving as president (George & George, 1981–1982; Weinstein, Anderson, & Link, 1978–1979) and the many alternative interpretations of van Gogh's act of cutting off his ear (Lubin, 1972; Runyan, 1981).

The task of assessing posthumous distributive reputations requires the cooperation of a panel of experts who independently record a comprehensive portrait of the person, using such techniques as character sketches, personality descriptions, or adjective checklist impressions (Craik, 1988; Simonton, 1991; Song & Simonton, 2007).

Differences among biographers in their approach to a subject have often been noted and have inspired speculation that such "countertransference," whether negative or positive, may color or bias a biography (Loewenberg, 1983; Tucker, 1988).

Sigmund Freud and William C. Bullitt, an American diplomat, had both formed a strong antipathy toward Woodrow Wilson during the Paris Peace Conference following World War I. They later wrote a biography of Wilson, which was not published until after their deaths and that of Wilson's widow (Erikson, 1967). To examine the possible influence of this predisposition, I asked members of a panel of university students to record independently a personality Q-sort description based upon their own reading of the Freud and Bullitt (1967) biography. A second panel did the same based upon a well-regarded and more balanced biographical treatment by George and George (1956). Although considerable convergence was displayed in the overall personality characterization of Wilson, the portrait derived from the Freud and Bullitt volume shows him as notably less resilient and competent compared to that emerging from the George and George interpretation (Craik, 1988; Historical Figures Assessment Collaborative, 1977).

Using expert judgments by biographers, Rubenzer and Ones (2000) have reported personality comparisons among U.S. presidents, including Washington and Lincoln, based upon personality Q-sort descriptions and ratings on the five-factor personality dimensions. This research team was successful in recruiting the participation of 115 experts who had published a biography of at least one of the presidents serving through 1960. Thus, for example, their personality profiles are based upon the independent judgments of ten biographers of Washington and seven biographers of Lincoln.

Posthumous Reputation: From Biographical Studies to Cultural History

The Case of George Washington as Cultural Symbol and Legacy

Certain historical figures attain a posthumous reputation that stretches far beyond the biographical guild. Take the case of George Washington, who generated an enormous lifetime reputational network within Europe and throughout the colonies that were to become a new nation. Over 650 biographies have taken him as their subject. But beyond biography, Washington has continued to be represented more broadly for generation after generation of Americans as an enduring symbolic figure whose life story and conduct form a central part of the nation's cultural legacy.

History and Heritage

Cultural and historical figures such as George Washington emerge as the focus of two approaches to treating the past: as history and as heritage (Lowenthal, 1996). Historical knowledge, according to Pompa (1990), constitutes a consensually received but evolving system of beliefs about the past, open to continuing scrutiny and shared by mutually critical scholars alert to the risks of a variety of methodological biases. This collective process is sensitive to the selective survival of records and is marked by a commitment to attaining valid chronological and causal accounts of events, to textual skepticism, and to the use of distinctive modes of analyzing evidence, such as close attention to corroboration, sourcing, and context (Lowenthal, 1985; Novick, 1988; Wineburg, 1991).

Within this communal process of inquiry—not in its narrative products—resides the aspiration to historical objectivity that, according to Novick (1988), embodies the "noble dream" of most practicing historians.

Lowenthal (1996) has drawn an instructive distinction between history and heritage. In his formulation, the purpose of heritage is the construction of a past that advances the ideals of group allegiance and pride in an imagined past, whereas history is dedicated to the ideals of truth and impartiality. Heritage embellishes upon the good and valued of the group's past. Heritage tends to be exclusive and geared to the current social uses of the constructed past for strengthening present group identity and enhancing group morale. In contrast, history, in the Pomparian view, seeks an open and testable truth concerning the past. Heritage tolerates anachronisms and upgrades, invents, forgets, and excludes accounts of events. The preferred medium for heritage is vivid depiction, whereas that for history is consensually established evidence.

We have noted already that biography and life history analysis may reasonably aspire to the noble dream of historical objectivity (Craik, 1996b). Washington's deeds have certainly been the focus of historical inquiry (e.g., Middlekauf, 1982; Fischer, 2004). And he has been the subject of many biographies, including the well-regarded seven-volume biography by Freeman and associates (1948–1957) and the four-volume treatment by Flexner (1965–1972).

But beyond biography and within the realm of heritage, Washington has been a subject for cultural historians as well. Just as family roots form part of our personal legacy, so also the abiding recollections of such admirable and exemplary personages as Washington come to be a part of our collective legacy (Lowenthal, 1996).

The basis of Washington's enduring resonance for citizens of the United States is now being traced by cultural historians. Schwartz (1987, p. 3) has made the case for why inquiry must move in this direction, beyond biography: "Although Washington's life is now documented in excruciating detail and treated more dispassionately than ever, we know little about why that life was the object of such intense veneration. Such are the limits of biography."

In examining this issue, Schwartz (1987, p. 3) establishes a clear distinction between biographical and cultural approaches to understanding Washington: "Biographical statements are intended to show what Washington did and why he did it; they are not intended to illuminate in any systematic or detailed way how Washington's achievements and motivations were perceived by his contemporaries, and how these perceptions were shaped by the cultural or social circumstances . . . in which he and his admirers lived."

To document and analyze the venerational practices of Washington's contemporaries and their successors, Schwartz (1987, p. 8) examined a wide array of private and public sources, including private correspondence; newspaper articles and commentaries; poems, orations, and eulogies; the display of his portraits and naming of towns in his honor; and the widespread public occasions commemorating his birth and death.

As Lowenthal (1996, p. 174) notes, being a father figure—being the new nation's first commander in chief and then first president—was a key element in Washington's image as a cultural figure: "Metaphors of priority pervade patriotic maxims. 'First in war, first in peace, first in the hearts of his countrymen' was Washington's archetypal accolade."

Furthermore, Washington has served as a symbol of certain enduring values including the private virtue of self-mastery and the public virtues of strength of will, sacrifice for the public good, and, most of all, the restrained use of power (Schwartz, 1987). In his posthumous reputation, Washington has moved through and beyond biography into the realm of cultural legacy. "Recovering the memory of Washington, we recover a part of ourselves and feel more complete. Recovering the memory of Washington, we regain fuller possession of that heritage of liberty that has tamed the growing power of America" (Schwartz, 1987, p. 207).

Washington as Agent and Object of His Cultural Image

In advocating a cultural analysis of reputation, Schwartz (1987) identified certain limitations and boundaries of biographical studies. In doing so, he examined the social and institutional structures that served to shape and sustain Washington's reputation and image as a cultural symbol.

In turn, a Washington biography by Paul K. Longmore (1988) reasserts the function of biographical analysis by offering an extended account of how Washington's own more or less self-conscious choices and actions contributed powerfully to the ultimate cultural image that Schwartz has documented and provided the bedrock for its content and substance.

In his cultural analysis, Schwartz (1987) stressed the yearning among Washington's contemporaries for a leader displaying restrained use of power.

Indeed, he suggests that, except for this attribute's almost happenstance fit with his seeming reluctance and modesty, Washington did not appear to have the makings for his later ascendance and high regard. "It is the range and significance of Washington's shortcomings that makes it difficult to understand his veneration on the basis of his personal qualities alone" (p. 5). Rather, "the worship of Washington entailed not the recognition of greatness inherent in the man, but the transformation by society of ordinary talents and unremarkable characteristics into an image of heroic proportions" (p. 6).

In turn, Longmore (1988) does agree that something must be explained, namely, "the historical process by which the revolutionary generation of Americans made an individual leader into an heroic personage who incarnated their republican and nationalistic beliefs. That is, the story of how a man became a myth" (p. ix). However, Longmore holds that Washington himself must be recognized as a key agent throughout that very process.

Longmore (1988) argues that Washington was widely acquainted with the political values and aspirations of his contemporaries and did much that was deliberate and skillful in responding to them throughout his long career in public life. Longmore salutes "Washington's conscious and purposeful role in that process, his intentional shaping of his public and historic self, a talent . . . amounting to genius." Furthermore and ironically, "precisely because of his skillful embodiment of contemporary ideals, this is perhaps his least recognized and least appreciated gift" (p. ix).

Two endeavors must be undertaken, Longmore (1988) maintains, to explain "how an ambitious frontier soldier and provincial politician became the 'Father of his Country.'" First, in accord with Schwartz, the linkage must be established between Washington's public self-fashioning and the predominant cultural values and political ideology of the time. But, second, one must describe Washington's "own deliberate part in these historical events, recounting his increasing skill and sophistication as a political leader" (pp. ix–x). He delineates in detail a series of occasions when Washington actively shaped and communicated the symbolic meaning of his actions.

In summary, Longmore's revised biographical and cultural interpretation of Washington and his career amounts to an assertion regarding Washington's own subtle and successful knack for reputation management. In supplementing the standard biographies of Freeman (1948–1957) and Flexner (1965–1972), Longmore (1988) has established a Washington who is "politically shrewd, closely in touch with the beliefs, aspirations, and fears of his contemporaries, a consummate political leader and public actor who sought to embody and to be perceived to be embodying their highest ideals" (p. x).

Posthumous Cultural Reputational Networks

Cultural reputations of the kind that George Washington continues to enjoy entail a huge expansion of the person's reputational network onto a national or international scale and cumulatively from generation to generation. Thus, the math alone demonstrates that the size of the posthumous reputational network in these cases transcends that of the lifetime network.

As Schwartz (1987) has shown in the case of Washington, sustaining cultural reputations is the result of organized institutional activities and processes. Thus, the posthumous reputational network of someone like Washington is structured to encompass the biographical and historical guilds, the heritage establishments, the school systems, the mass media, and the continuing discourse and beliefs of the general public.

Relevant institutions monitor these trends in cultural reputations closely. For example, the administrative unit of Mount Vernon, Washington's estate in Virginia, has been reported to be distressed recently by research finding that school textbooks used today allocate only 10% of the space to Washington that was assigned to him in textbooks of the 1960s. The institutional response at Mount Vernon has been the planned development of a new theater and education complex that will use holograms, computer imagery, and a live-action film to communicate an updated representation of Washington. Stephen Kinzer (2002) reported Washington's new incarnation in the *International Herald Tribune* as "the action hero of the 18th century, the swashbuckling warrior who survived wild adventures, led brilliant military campaigns, detected spy rings and fell in love with his best friend's wife" (p. 16). A related computer-aided learning program is planned, intended for use by every 5th-grader in the country. Social and intellectual trends are leading cultural decision-makers such as teachers, curriculum planners, and textbook authors and publishers to grant greater attention to coverage of women, minorities, and social trends. "There's a tendency to downplay the importance of the individual, and it has hurt Washington," said Peter Henriques, a history professor at George Mason University (quoted in Kinzer, 2002, p. 16).

Kinzer (2002) finds that Washington scholars, however reluctantly, are ready to go along with this "celebrity package." He quotes historian Joseph Ellis, who was preparing a biography of Washington: "I recognize that there's an audience out there that needs to know about him and can only be reached by devices that are a little off-putting" (p. 16).

The assumptions that Washington needs to be known by new generations and is "hurt" by diminished attention, as well as the counteractions under way at Mount Vernon, suggest that his posthumous network remains viable, even if threatened. And whatever the shifting prominence among the founding fathers, Washington ranks first in visitation to his historic home (for 2003, Mount Vernon, 791,596) in comparison to Thomas Jefferson (Monticello, 464,733), John Adams (Adams Historical Park, 217,000), and Alexander Hamilton (Hamilton Grange, 13,413). And he remains first in biographies catalogued in the Library of Congress (672) compared with Jefferson (606), Adams (186), and Hamilton (184) ("Founding Favorites," 2004). But these matters are temporally dynamic; Washington's unrivaled symbolic importance and veneration were quickly challenged by Lincoln, in the postassassination period (Schwartz, 1987, pp. 196–198).

Cultural Reputation and Social Representation

In this discussion of cultural reputations, we have come full circle. In Chapter 4, we adopted the macro-level concept of social representations and argued that it offered useful guidance in thinking about and analyzing the reputations of specific ordinary persons as micro-level social representations. Now, we find that the broadest conceptual levels of the reputations of specific persons—their cultural reputations—qualify as full-fledged social representations within Moscovici's (1984b) original formulation. Our terminology for differentiating the discursive and distributive versions of reputation grew out of the literature on social representations.

Conclusion

Prospects for Reputational Analysis

A network interpretation of reputation locates it within a finite and idiosyn-cratic set of other individuals who have recognized and known that specific person. Reputational network members are more or less connected with each other. Information about the person flows through portions of the network. And information is stored within the beliefs, evaluations, and impressions of the person maintained by each reputational network member.

A major contribution of our network interpretation of reputation is a rich package of conceptual distinctions that promise a more articulated and coherent program of future research on reputation.

The Concepts of Social Networks and Reputational Networks

The network interpretation situates reputation within person-centered, idio-syncratic, lifelong reputational networks. The concept of reputational net-work encompasses the person's social network of mutual acquaintances, both core and peripheral, who recognize and know the person and are known by the person. However, reputational networks also encompass those other individuals who recognize and know the person, however minimally, but are not known to the person.

The Concepts of the Small Village and the Small World of a Person's Reputational Network

On the one hand, compared to the global population, any person's reputational network is relatively small and interrelated. In this sense, a reputational network is akin to a person-centered village or community, with focus upon the density parameter of network structure. On the other hand, reputational information courses through network bridges that tie together and expand a person's own network to others. This feature of network structure generates the capacity for rapid, widespread, and probably untraceable reputational information flow. In this sense, a global scale for the scope of a person's reputational network appears to be plausible.

Two Aspects of Reputational Information: Information Flow and Information Storage

Person-centered information has two properties within reputational networks. First, information about a person flows through relational networks as chat, gossip, and talk. Second, information about a person is stored in specific cognitive bins to a greater or lesser extent by each member of the person's reputational network.

Two Facets of Reputation: Discursive Versus Distributive Reputation

The distinction between reputational information flow and storage generates two modes of reputational network analysis. The discursive facet of reputation requires the analysis of spontaneous occasions of chat, gossip, and talk, drawing upon methods from the fields of social linguistics and communication studies. The distributive facet of reputations calls for elicitation methods and the systematic sampling of reputational network members, drawing upon techniques from the fields of survey research and personality assessment.

Two Structural Features of Reputational Networks: Network Parameters and Network Content Claims

Moving to a network interpretation of reputation draws attention to structural properties of reputational networks, including size, density, and various forms of patterning. These concerns contrast with the popularly held focus upon reputational content claims, for example, whether the person is consensually believed to be a credentialed accountant.

Two Issues Regarding Truth in Reputational Content Claims: Accuracy Versus Validity

Our analysis identifies two forms of truth in reputation. In the way these terms are used for our purposes, the accuracy issue concerns how well the content claims prevailing within the reputational network are characterized. Is the person generally held to be shrewd and broad-minded? The second question concerns the validity of the content claim with regard to that person. Even if generally claimed to be a shrewd and broad-minded person, how can these claims be appraised for their validity with regard to this person?

Reputational Networks in the Context of the Personality System and Social System

A primary tenet of the network interpretation of reputation is that the reputation of a person resides within the social system. At the same time, constructs such as the self-concept and tactics of reputational management can be formulated as reputation-relevant elements of the personality system. A generic model of reputational concepts as they are situated within the personality and social context can be accommodated within a variety of contemporary personality theories.

Three Sequential Stages of Reputational Networks

The network interpretation anchors reputation within three temporal networks: the lifetime reputational network, the transitional reputational network, and the posthumous reputational network. Heretofore, the nature of reputation has been addressed primarily with regard to an implicit notion of the reputational network that prevails during the person's lifetime.

Scholarship in biographical studies and cultural history dealing with noteworthy persons has revealed two additional networks. The transitional network constitutes a mixture of the steadily decreasing surviving lifetime network as it overlaps with the emerging and more or less enduring posthumous network with its new and perhaps renewing membership. These patterns warrant analysis in their own right as well as for their guidance in the study of the reputational networks of ordinary persons.

Research Agenda

Future Inquiries

Along the way throughout this exposition of a network interpretation of reputation, we have taken note of specific research ideas and opportunities. A few lively brainstorming sessions among any set of readers would quickly augment these specific possibilities, demonstrating the potential for a productive program of interdisciplinary research.

For example, we have stressed the central need for research comparing the kind of reputational content claims about a person advanced by direct or first-tier reputational network members with those asserted by indirect or second- and third-tier members. The relative degree of validity must also be systematically delineated.

Historians and biographers dealing with posthumous reputations should be especially interested in the outcomes of this line of investigation. As we have recognized, posthumous reputations eventually become anchored entirely within the realm of second- and third-tier reputational network members. Thus, these research findings will help to characterize the extent to which posthumous reputations differ, if at all, from lifetime reputations. Thus, we have here an important linkage between the fields of person perception and person memory, on the one hand, and history and biographical studies, on the other.

Unfinished Business

Our treatment of reputation has been wide-ranging. Even so, certain topics have fallen by the wayside, such as rumor, corporate reputation, and character.

Rumor

From the vantage point of our concept of discursive reputation, one would expect to find research on rumor to be relevant. After all, rumor and gossip have certain overlapping affinities. Both deal with the flow of information. The information often takes the form of hearsay and other unverified or unofficial communications. They share also a general sense-making function. However, the definitional endeavor of the gossip research guild tends to be preoccupied with the favorability of communication content, while the rumor research guild is concerned with the validity of communication content. And, of course, the object of gossip is more readily and narrowly specified (i.e., other persons), while the object of rumor encompasses the entire realm of common knowledge and curiosity.

Recent overviews of research on rumor could provide the occasion to explore the potential value of a close and systematic examination of the mutual relevance of rumor and reputation (DiFonzo & Bordia 2007; Solove, 2007). One useful approach might be the micro-analysis of a particular case of the transmission and spread of rumors throughout a person's reputational network.

Corporate Reputation

Corporate reputation has been mentioned only in passing. We noted in Chapter 8 that from the earliest period of the English common law on defamation, corporate entities enjoyed legal standing in the libel courts and could sue, along with individual plaintiffs. In our review of reputation management in Chapter 6, we readily borrowed professional tips from organizational analysts who look after the reputations of corporate entities, as well their brands and products.

Similarities between the analysis of reputations among persons and among corporate entities are most evident in the systematic comparisons of impressions recorded by observers employing trait-like descriptive and evaluative attributes and dimensions (Bromley, 1993, 2001, 2002; Ferris et al., 2003). This domain of attributes would fall within what we have termed "reputational content claims."

At the same time, we can recognize from the vantage point of our network framework that the reputations of persons are embedded in a much more complex and thicker set of relations and processes than are those of corporate entities. A major distinction is that the members of a person's reputational network are of the same category, namely, other persons. In the case of corporate reputation, network members must ultimately also be persons. Or can a case be made for them to be conceptualized as other corporate entities?

Along another line, we might explore the implications of our network interpretation for organizational analysis. For example, consider the nature of posthumous reputations of defunct corporate entities (e.g., automobile companies) or discontinued brands and products (e.g., newspaper comic strips). In these instances, what are the differing functions of the lifetime, transitional, and posthumous reputational networks? What is the role of keepers of the flame, and how does it differ in the case of corporate entities compared to persons?

A systematic attempt to apply the full framework of reputational networks to corporate entities seems promising.

Character

I have removed character from a central place in my network interpretation of reputation. In doing so, I have followed the lead of Gordon W. Allport, just as he set character aside in his psychological interpretation of personality.

Allport declared, "Character is personality evaluated" (1937, p. 52). But personality evaluated by whom? This obvious follow-up question suggests that character as a concept might also be situated within the person's reputational network. In this sense, we would consider character to do a minor conceptual job in signifying the overall evaluative facet of all reputational content claims regarding that person. That is, character can be reputation evaluated.

In contrast, another approach is to consider character to constitute a particular subset of personality traits or reputational content claims, such as steadfast, honest, and principled. Similarly, if character is considered to bear upon the entire realm of morality, then it becomes situated primarily within the personality domain. Facets of moral thought and conduct may be more or less opaque to members of a person's reputational network. For example, rather than covert and concealed, a delinquent's acts of bad conduct are often quasi-public and locally self-reported by the delinquent as a means of reputational management and promotion. However, other aspects of moral reasoning and disposition may be more or less opaque to reputational network members (Emler, 1984; Emler, Tarry, & James, 2007).

Thus, while character is not a conceptual component of our network interpretation, a thorough analysis of its relation to reputation remains an important bit of unfinished business.

Reputational Analysis as a Distinct Field of Inquiry

In developing our network perspective on reputational analysis, we have drawn upon ideas and findings from a host of scholarly and scientific fields of inquiry, including anthropology, biographical studies, cultural history, evolutionary theory, law, media studies, medieval history, organizational studies, personality psychology, social network analysis, social psychology, and sociology.

We have discovered that none of these fields of study, not even those most relevant, grants sufficient attention to reputation to sustain a productive program for reputational analysis. Social network analysis provides a basic framework and one of the three key components for reputational analysis. However, research in this field has concentrated upon such phenomena as forms of acquaintance, modes of influence, and social and emotional support afforded to close network members. While it has addressed the nature of person-centered networks, it has not treated them in detail as the focal point of the person's lifelong and posthumous social circle.

The flow of communication about persons and other entities remains an amorphous field of inquiry. The theory of social representations offers the broadest formulation of this topic, but its application to the reputation of individual persons has just barely gotten under way. The interdisciplinary study of gossip in anthropology, psychology, and sociology is still trying to sort out a workable definition of "gossip." Its most conceptually structured formulation primarily encompasses negative communications about persons, while the effort to broaden its domain has generated a still vague notion of "good" gossip. The modest amount of empirical research has focused on the gossipers rather than the individual targets of gossip. The promising advocacy of talk studies from a historical cultural perspective, initially in the field of medieval history, enriches our explorations but may remain more general than what reputational analysis requires.

The scientific investigation of cognitive person bins has attracted an active program of laboratory-oriented empirical research on the topics of person memory and judgments of personality. The approach of researchers has thus far been excessively individualistic, examining how one individual independently forms impressions of another. These impressions are analyzed as if none of the ubiquitous everyday social communication among community members plays a significant role in the mundane process of person perception. The closely related but distinct study of personality judgments treats person perceptions as in part affording valid input within the impressions, judgments, and evaluations that others form about a person. Because researchers in this venue seek to extract valid and predictive data or measures relevant to testing theoretical hypotheses about personality, they tend to privilege and attend to a narrow subset of the members of a person's reputational network. One focus, for example, is upon direct and close acquaintance with the person. Yet, evidence that acquaintance is generally linked to valid information is not well established, and network analysis suggests that information among these close members may be limited and redundant. To make contributions to reputational analysis, the scientific study of cognitive person bins must be extended throughout the person's reputational network and focus upon network issues and processes—a challenging but necessary endeavor.

The fields of the law, reputation management, biographical studies, and cultural history present the opportunity to apply a network perspective upon reputational analysis to fields where reputation is a central concern but not a focus of broad and systematic analysis. We have attempted at least to illustrate the benefits of these lines of inquiry and application.

The common-law tradition concerning libel and slander is organized within an implicit network framework. The assertion of a defaming claim about a person is treated as a threatening and consequential event, in part because of the particularly damaging impact of negative assertions and in part because of the potentially widespread, uncontrollable, and unknowable circulation of a defaming assertion of disreputable conduct. Reputation management attacks the dilemma posed by assertions of disreputable conduct that, regrettably, happen to be true, as well as those that may be false. Reputation management can be viewed currently as an amalgam of crafts and trades emerging from such realms as publicity and organizational behavior, media analysis, and public affairs. These professional guilds would benefit from a systematic framework of reputational network analysis to illuminate and guide reputation-building programs and defensive interventions. At the same time, reputational analysts will benefit from pragmatic experience and rules of thumb emerging from this arena, which can be envisioned as applied reputational analysis.

Biographical studies and cultural history devote a notable amount of effort to depictions and commentaries of matters that bear upon essential aspects of posthumous reputation. These fields aspire to the achievement of highly contextualized accounts, embedded within the individual and social specifics of historical periods and cultural conditions. As a consequence, they draw upon many other areas of scholarship but are not organized toward the development of a new and general field, such as reputational analysis. Instead, systematic analysis of the surviving posthumous networks of a person provides a useful framework and workshop for gaining deeper understanding of the often contentious and strongly motivated efforts of others to sustain and shape a specific person's posthumous reputation. At the same time, these fields provide the resources of detailed descriptions and the basis for cross-cultural and transhistorical comparison.

Finally, the fields of personality psychology and social psychology have perhaps the most intimate relations to reputational analysis. After all, we have been dealing with the reputation of specific persons. Although we have taken pains to reiterate that the reputation of a person resides in the flow of communications among and within the person bins of reputational network members, these conversations and these cognitions are typically sparked by some aspect or at least some report of that person's conduct. Personality psychology seeks to understand the person as a self-reflexive agent of action but has not yet succeeded in adequately situating that agency and conduct within a community or network context.

The mission of the personality psychologist is to gain an understanding of the person as a whole. Examining more generally how personality interacts with a person's reputational network is a formidable and heretofore neglected undertaking. Certainly, this task will entail the nature of the social self and the ways in which social psychologists have conceptualized the social image as both a goal and an outcome of the interplay between person and reputational network.

The history of personality psychology and social psychology suggests that these fields have continually dropped the ball in providing a broadly delineated formulation or central place for reputation within their research programs. The most promising strategy for gaining greater knowledge of the interaction between reputational network and personality is through first creating reputational analysis as a distinct and fully formed field of inquiry.

Over the past four decades, I have had the privilege to serve as a close observer and participant in the emergence and evolution of the interdisciplinary field of environmental psychology (Canter & Craik, 1981; Craik, 1970, 1973, 1990, 1996a). I have learned that the successful launching of a new and distinct field of intellectual and scientific inquiry requires the efforts of many researchers and diverse forms of institutional support. But the fundamental prerequisite is a core concept that is complex and intriguing, such as environment and reputation, and is situated at the nexus of manifold varieties of human concerns.

One exciting promise of a theoretical framework centered in the concept of reputational networks lies in its integrative capacity to sustain new forms of interdisciplinary analysis.

I hope that this book has made a strong case by showing how sociologists, cultural historians, personality psychologists, legal scholars, social psychologists, and students of biography all share a stake in understanding the phenomenon of reputation and how each has something important to contribute to its analysis. So many factors must be considered in addressing the concept of reputation that it is easy to be daunted by the task and to call desperately for interdisciplinary approaches simply on the basis of its complexity alone.

However, the network interpretation of reputation goes beyond that generic argument. It offers a comprehensive model for addressing the subject. It links the most disparate phenomena, extending from evolutionary psychology, on the one hand, to historical biographies, on the other. It appreciates reputation as immensely intriguing and always contestable.

References

Aaron, D. (Ed.). (1978). *Studies in biography.* Cambridge, MA: Harvard University Press.

Adair, D. (1967). Fame and the founding fathers. In E. P. Willis (Ed.), *Fame and the founding fathers: Essays by Douglass Adair* (pp. 24–52). Bethlehem, PA: Moravian College.

Abrams, D., & Hogg, M. A. (Eds.). (1990). *Social identity theory: Constructive and critical advances.* New York: Springer-Verlag.

Addy, J. (1989). *Sin and society in the seventeenth century.* London: Routledge.

Allen, F. (1954). *Treadmill to oblivion.* Boston: Little, Brown.

Allen, G. W. (1967). *William James, a biography.* New York: Viking Press.

Allen, R. E. (Ed.). (1984). *The pocket Oxford dictionary of current usage* (7th ed.). Oxford, UK: Clarendon Press.

Allison, S., & Eylon, D. (2005). The demise of leadership: Death positivity biases in posthumous impressions of leaders. In S. Messick & R. Kramer (Eds.), *The psychology of leadership: New perspectives and research* (pp. 295–317). Mahwah, NJ: Erlbaum.

Allport, G. W. (1937). *Personality: A psychological interpretation.* New York: Holt.

Allport, G. W., & Odbert, H. (1936). Trait names: A psycho-lexical study. *Psychological Monographs, 47* (No. 211).

Altman, I., Brown, B. B., Staples, B., & Werner, C. M. (1992). A transactional approach to close relationships: Courtship, weddings, and placemaking. In W. B. Walsh, K. H. Craik, & R. H. Price (Eds.), *Person–environment psychology: Models and perspectives* (pp. 193–242). Hillsdale, NJ: Erlbaum.

American Law Institute. (1985). *Model penal code.* Philadelphia: American Law Institute.

Anouilh, J. (1967). *Traveler without luggage* (J. Whiting, Trans.). London: Methuen. (Original work published 1936)

Aquinas, T. (1952). *The summa theologica of Saint Thomas Aquinas.* Chicago: Encyclopedia Britannica.

Argyle, M. (1984). The components of long-term relationships. In K. M. J. Lagerspetz & P. Niemi (Eds.), *Psychology in the 1990s* (pp. 474–481). New York: Elsevier Science.

Badkhen, A. (2007, May 6). WEB can ruin reputation with a stroke of the key. *San Francisco Chronicle,* p. A-1.

Bailey, F. G. (Ed.). (1971). *Gifts and poison: The politics of reputation.* Oxford, UK: Basil Blackwell.

Bamm, P. (1968). *Alexander the Great: Power as destiny.* London: Thames and Hudson.

Barker, R. G. (1968). *Ecological psychology: Concepts and methods for studying the environment of human behavior.* Stanford, CA: Stanford University Press.

Barker, R. G., & Wright, H. F. (1951). *One boy's day: A specimen record of behavior.* New York: Harper & Row.

Barkow, J. H. (1992). Beneath new culture is old psychology: Gossip and social stratification. In J. H. Barkow, L. Cosmides, & J. Tooby (Eds.), *The adapted mind: Evolutionary psychology and the generation of culture* (pp. 627–638). Oxford, UK: Oxford University Press.

Bauer, M. W. & Gaskell, G. (1999). Towards a paradigm for research on social representations. *Journal for the Theory of Social Behaviour, 29,* 163–186.

Baumeister, R. F. (1986). *Identity: Cultural change and the struggle for self.* New York: Oxford University Press.

Baumeister, R. F., Zhang, L., & Vohs, K. D. (2004). Gossip as cultural learning. *Review of General Psychology, 8,* 111–121.

Berglas, S. (1986). *The success syndrome: Hitting bottom when you reach the top.* New York: Plenum Press.

Bergmann, J. R. (1993). *Discreet indiscretions: The social organization of gossip.* New York: Aldine de Gruyter.

Bernard, H. R., Johnsen, E. C., Killworth, P. D., McCarty, C., Shelley, G. A., & Robinson, S. (1990). Comparing four different methods for measuring personal social networks. *Social Networks, 12,* 179–215.

Bezanson, R. P. (1986). The libel suit in retrospect: What plaintiffs want and what plaintiffs get. *California Law Review, 74,* 789–808.

Bezanson, R. P., Cranberg, G., & Soloski, J. (1987). *Libel law and the press: Myth and reality.* New York: Free Press.

Billig, M. (1993). Studying the thinking society: Social representations, rhetoric, and attitudes. In G. M. Breakwell, & D. V. Canter (Eds.), *Empirical approaches to social representations* (pp. 39–62). Oxford, UK: Clarendon Press.

Birmbaum, H. M. (1973). Morality judgments: Test of an averaging model with differential weights. *Journal of Experimental Psychology, 99,* 395–399.

Blamires, H. (1988). *The new Bloomsday book: A guide through Ulysses* (2nd ed.). London: Routledge.

Blomberg, H. H. (1972). Communication of interpersonal evaluations. *Journal of Personality and Social Psychology, 23,* 157–162.

Bloom, P. (2004). Postscript to the special issue on gossip. *Review of General Psychology, 8,* 138–140.

Bloomfield, M. W. (1952). *The seven deadly sins: An introduction to a theological concept, with special reference to medieval English literature.* East Lansing: Michigan State College.

Boissevain, J. (1974). *Friends of friends: Networks, manipulators and coalitions.* New York: St. Martin's Press.

Boorstin, D. J. (1986). *The image: A guide to pseudo-events in America.* New York: Atheneum.

Borkenau, P. (1990). Traits as ideal-based and goal-directed social categories. *Journal of Personality and Social Psychology, 58,* 381–396.

Bowman, L. (1959). *The American funeral: A study in guilt, extravagance, and sublimity.* Washington, DC: Public Affairs Press.

Braudy, L. (1986). *The frenzy of renown: Fame and its history.* New York: Oxford University Press.

Breakwell, G. M. & Canter, D. V. (Eds.). (1993). *Empirical approaches to social representations.* Oxford, UK: Clarendon Press.

Brennan, N. (1974). *Anthony Powell.* New York: Twayne Publishers.

Brin, D. (1998). *The transparent society: Will technology force us to choose between privacy and freedom?* Reading, MA: Addison-Wesley.

Bromley, D. B. (1993). *Reputation, image and impression management.* New York: Wiley.

Bromley, D. B. (2001). Relationships between personal and corporate reputation. *European Journal of Marketing, 35,* 316–334.

Bromley, D. B. (2002). Comparing corporate reputations: League tables, quotients, benchmarks or case studies? *Corporate Reputation Review, 5,* 35–50.

Brown, B. A. (1948). *The numerical distinction of sins.* Washington, DC: Catholic University of America Press.

Brunswik, E. (1956). *Perception and the representative design of psychological experiments.* (2nd ed.). Berkeley: University of California Press.

Burt, R. S. (2000). Decay functions. *Social Networks, 22,* 1–28.

Burt, R. S. (2002). Bridge decay. *Social Networks, 24,* 333–363.

Buss, D. M. (1991). Evolutionary personality psychology. *Annual Review of Psychology, 42,* 459–492.

Buss, D. M. (1996). Social adaptation and five major factors of personality. In J. S. Wiggins (Ed.), *The five-factor model of personality: Theoretical perspectives* (pp. 180–207). New York: Guilford Press.

Buss, D. M., & Craik, K. H. (1983a). The act frequency approach to personality. *Psychological Review, 90*, 105–125.

Buss, D. M., & Craik, K. H. (1983b). The dispositional analysis of everyday conduct. *Journal of Personality, 51*, 393–412.

Buss, D. M., & Craik, K. H. (1984). Acts, dispositions and personality. In B. A. Maher, & W. A. Maher (Eds.), *Progress in experimental personality research: Normal processes* (Vol. XIII, pp. 241–301). New York: Academic Press.

Buss, D. M., & Craik, K. H. (1985). Why not measure that trait? Alternative criteria for identifying important dispositions. *Journal of Personality and Social Psychology, 48*, 934–946.

Buss, D. M., & Dedden, L. (1990). Derogation of competitors. *Journal of Social and Personal Relations, 7*, 395–422.

Campbell, K. E., & Lee, B. A. (1991). Name generators in surveys of personal networks. *Social Networks, 13*, 203–221.

Canter, D. V., & Craik, K. H. (1981). Environmental psychology. *Journal of Environmental Psychology, 1*, 1–12.

Carstensen, L. L. (1992). Social and emotional patterns in adulthood: Support for socioemotional selectivity theory. *Psychology and Aging, 7*, 331–338.

Carter-Ruck, P. F. (1990). *Memoirs of a libel lawyer.* London: Weidenfeld and Nicolson.

Carter-Ruck, P. F., & Walker, R. (1985). *Carter-Ruck on libel and slander.* London: Butterworths.

Cassidy, J. (2006, May 15). Me media. *The New Yorker, 82*, 50–59.

Cheek, J. M. (1988). Identity orientations and self-interpretations. In D. M. Buss, & N. Cantor (Eds.), *Personality psychology: Recent trends and emerging directions* (pp. 275–285). New York: Springer-Verlag.

Chen, S., Boucher, H. C., & Tapias, M. P. (2006). The relational self revealed: Integration, conceptualizations and implications for interpersonal life. *Psychological Bulletin, 132*, 151–179.

Collins, M. (2001). *The law of defamation and the internet.* Oxford, UK: Oxford University Press.

Connerton, P. (1989). *How societies remember.* New York: Cambridge University Press.

Cooley, C. H. (1902). *Human nature and the social order.* New York: Charles Scribner's Sons.

Coriden, J. A., Green, T. J., & Heintschel, D. E. (Eds.). (1985). *The code of canon law: A text and commentary.* New York: Paulist Press.

Cosmides, L., & Tooby, J. (1992). Cognitive adaptations for social exchange. In J. H. Barkow, L. Cosmides, & J. Tooby (Eds.), *The adapted mind: Evolutionary psychology and the generation of culture* (pp. 163–228). Oxford, UK: Oxford University Press.

Cowen, T. (2000). *What price fame?* Cambridge, MA: Harvard University Press.

Craik, K. H. (1970). Environmental psychology. In K. H. Craik, B. Kleinmunst, R. L. Rosnow, R. Rosenthal, J. A. Cheyne, & R. H. Walters, *New directions in psychology 4* (pp. 1–122). New York: Holt, Rinehart and Winston.

Craik, K. H. (1973). Environmental psychology. *Annual Review of Psychology, 24,* 402–422.

Craik, K. H. (1976). The personality research paradigm in environmental psychology. In S. Wapner, S. Cohen, & B. Kaplan (Eds.), *Experiencing the environment* (pp. 44–69). New York: Plenum Press.

Craik, K. H. (1985). Multiple perceived personalities: A neglected consistency issue. In E. E. Roskam (Ed.), *Measurement and personality assessment* (pp. 333–338). New York: Elsevier Science.

Craik, K. H. (1986). Personality research methods: An historical perspective. *Journal of Personality, 54,* 18–51.

Craik, K. H. (1988). Assessing the personalities of historical figures. In W. M. Runyan (Ed.), *Psychology and historical interpretation* (pp. 196–218). New York: Oxford University Press.

Craik, K. H. (1990). Environmental and personality psychology: Two collective narratives and four individual story lines. In I. Altman & K. Christensen (Eds.), *Environment and behavior studies: Emergence of intellectual traditions* (pp. 141–186). New York: Plenum Press.

Craik, K. H. (1993a). Accentuated, revealed and quotidian personalities. *Psychological Inquiry, 4,* 278–281.

Craik, K. H. (1993b). The 1937 Allport and Stagner texts in personality psychology. In K. H. Craik, R. Hogan, & R. N. Wolfe (Eds.), *Fifty years of personality psychology* (pp. 2–20). New York: Plenum Press.

Craik, K. H. (1996a). Environmental psychology: A core field of psychological science. *American Psychologist, 51,* 186–187.

Craik, K. H. (1996b). The objectivity of persons and their lives: A noble dream for personality psychology? *Psychological Inquiry, 7,* 326–330.

Craik, K. H. (1997). Circumnavigating the personality as a whole: The challenge of integrative methodological pluralism. *Journal of Personality, 65,* 1087–1111.

Craik, K. H. (1998). Personality system concepts and their implications. *Psychological Inquiry, 9,* 145–148.

Craik, K. H. (2000a). Personality psychology: Methods of study. *Encyclopedia of psychology* (Vol. 6, pp. 133–140). New York: American Psychological Association and Oxford University Press.

Craik, K. H. (2000b). The lived day of an individual: A person–environment perspective. In W. B. Walsh, K. H. Craik, & R. H. Price (Eds.), *Person–environment psychology: New directions and perspectives* (pp. 233–266). Mahwah, NJ: Erlbaum.

Craik, K. H. (2002). On the mutual relevance of art theory and personality theory. *Journal of Research in Personality, 36,* 58–71.

Craik, K. H. (2007). Taxonomies, trends and integrations. In R. W. Robins, R. C. Fraley, & R. Krueger (Eds.), *Handbook of research methods in personality psychology* (pp. 209–223). New York: Guilford Press.

Craik, K. H., & Gosling, S. D. (2001). Disreputable acts. Berkeley: Institute of Personality and Social Research, University of California at Berkeley.

Craik, K. H., Hogan, R., & Wolfe, R. N. (Eds.). (1993). *Fifty years of personality psychology.* New York: Plenum Press.

Craik, K. H., Ware, A. P., Kamp, J., O'Reilly, C. III, Staw, B., & Zedeck, S. (2002). Explorations in construct validity in a combined managerial and personality assessment. *Journal of Occupational and Organizational Psychology, 75,* 171–193.

Danilov, V. J. (1997). *Hall of Fame museums: A reference guide.* Westport, CT: Greenwood Press.

Deaux, K., & Philogene, G. (Eds.). (2001). *Representations of the social: Bridging theoretical traditions.* Oxford, UK: Blackwell.

De Baets, A. (2002). Defamation cases against historians. *History and Theory, 41,* 346–367.

DiFonzo, D. J., & Bordia, P. (2007). *Rumor psychology: Social and organizational approaches.* Washington, DC: American Psychological Association.

Dill, B. (1993). Libel law doesn't work, but can it be fixed? In M. London & B. Dill, *At what price? Libel law and freedom of the press* (pp. 33–73). New York: Twentieth Century Fund Press.

Dodd, P. S., Muhamad, R., & Watts, D. J. (2003). An experimental study of search in global social networks. *Science, 301,* 827–829.

Doise, W. (1993). Debating social representations. In M. Breakwell & D. V. Canter (Eds.), *Empirical approaches to social representations* (pp. 157–170). Oxford, UK: Clarendon Press.

Doise, W., Clemence, A., Lorenzi-Cioldi, F. (1993). *The quantitative analysis of social representations.* New York: Harvester Wheatsheaf.

Duke, M. P. (2002). Theories of personality and theories of art: A budding consilience. *Journal of Research in Personality, 36,* 32–58.

Dunbar, R. I. M. (2004). Gossip in evolutionary perspective. *Review of General Psychology, 8,* 100–110.

Edel, L. (1953–1972). *Henry James* (5 volumes). Philadelphia: Lippincott.

Edel, L. (1979). *Bloomsbury: A house of lions.* Philadelphia: Lippincott.

Eder, D., & Enke, J. L. (1991). The structure of gossip: Opportunities and constraints on collective expression among adolescents. *American Sociological Review, 56,* 494–508.

Ellis, J. J. (2000). *Founding brothers: The revolutionary generation.* New York: Knopf.

Ellison, N., & Lampe, C. (2006). Social networking notes. Social Software Symposium, Chapel Hill, NC. Retrieved February, 28, 2007 from www.ibiblio.org/sss/index.php/Social Networks Session Notes.

Elms, A. C. (1994). *Uncovering lives: The uneasy alliance of biography and psychology.* New York: Oxford University Press.

Emler, N. (1984). Differential involvement in delinquency: Towards an interpretation in terms of reputation management. In B. A. Maher & W. B. Maher (Ed.), *Progress in experimental personality research. Normal personality processe*s (Vol. 13, pp. 174–241). New York: Academic Press.

Emler, N. (1987). Socio-moral development from the perspective of social representations. *Journal for the Theory of Social Behaviour, 17,* 371–387.

Emler, N. (1990). The social psychology of reputation. *European Review of Social Psychology, 1,* 171–193.

Emler, N. (2001). Gossiping. In W. P. Robinson & H. Giles (Eds.), *The new handbook of language and social psychology* (pp. 318–338). Chichester, UK: Wiley.

Emler, N., & Ohana, J. (1993). Studying social representations in children: Just old wine in new bottles? In G. M. Breakwell, & D. V. Canter (Eds.), *Empirical approaches to social representations* (pp. 63–89). Oxford, UK: Clarendon Press.

Emler, N., Tarry, H., & James, A. (2007). Post-conventional reasoning and reputation. *Journal of Research in Personality, 41,* 76–89.

English, J. F. (2005). *The economy of prestige: Prizes, awards, and the calculation of cultural value.* Cambridge, MA: Harvard University Press.

Erikson, E. H. (1967). Review of Freud, S., & Bullitt, W. C., Thomas Woodrow Wilson: A psychological study. *International Journal of Psychoanalysis, 48,* 462–468.

Eylon, D., & Allison, S. F. (2005). The "frozen in time" effect in evaluations of the dead. *Personality and Social Psychology Bulletin, 31,* 1708–1717.

Farr, R., & Moscovici, S. (Eds.). (1984). *Social representations.* Cambridge, UK: Cambridge University Press.

Fenster, T., & Small, D. L. (2003a). Introduction. In T. Fenster & D. L. Small (Eds.), *Fama: The politics of talk and reputation in medieval Europe* (pp. 1–14). Ithaca, NY: Cornell University Press.

Fenster, T., & Small, D. L. (Eds.). (2003b). *Fama: The politics of talk and reputation in medieval Europe.* Ithaca, NY: Cornell University Press.

Ferris, G. R., Blass, R., Douglas, C., Kolodinsky, R. W., & Treadway, D. C. (2003). Personal reputation in organizations. In J. Greenberg (Ed.), *Organizational behavior: The state of the science* (2nd ed., pp. 211–246). Mahwah, NJ: Erlbaum.

Fife-Schaw, C. R. (1993). Finding social representations in attribute checklists: How will we know when we have found one? In G. M. Breakwell, & D. V. Canter (Eds.), *Empirical approaches to social representations* (pp. 248–271). Oxford, UK: Clarendon Press.

Fischer, C. (1982). *To dwell among friends: Personal networks in town and city.* Chicago: University of Chicago Press.

Fischer, C. S., Jackson, R. M., Stueve, C. A., Gerson, K., & Jones, L. M. (1977). *Networks and places: Social relations in the urban setting.* New York: Free Press.

Fischer, D. H. (2004). *Washington's crossing*. New York: Oxford University Press.

Flexner, J. T. (1965–1972). *George Washington* (4 vol.). Boston: Little, Brown.

Fombrun, C. J. (1996). *Reputation: Realizing value from the corporate image*. Boston: Harvard Business School Press.

Foster, E. K. (2004). Research on gossip: Taxonomy, methods, and future directions. *Review of General Psychology, 8,* 78–99.

Founding favorites. (2004, July 11, p. 17). *New York Times Magazine*.

Frank, R. H. (1995). *Choosing the right pond: Human behavior and the quest for status*. Oxford, UK: Oxford University Press.

Fredricksmeyer, E. (2000). Alexander the Great and the kingdom of Asia. In A. B. Bosworth & E. J. Baynham (Eds.), *Alexander the Great in fact and fiction*. Oxford, UK: Oxford University Press.

Freeman, D. S. (1948–1957). *George Washington* (Vol. 7) by J. A. Carroll & M. W. Ashworth . New York: Scribner.

Freeman, L. C., & Thompson, C. R. (1989). Estimating acquaintanceship volume. In M. Kochen (Ed.), *The small world* (pp. 147–158). Norwood, NJ: Ablex Publishing.

Freud, S., & Bullitt, W. C. (1967). *Thomas Woodrow Wilson: A psychological study*. Boston: Houghton Mifflin.

Funder, D. C. (1999). *Personality judgment: A realistic approach to person perception*. New York: Academic Press.

Funder, D. C., Kolar, D. C., & Blackman, M. C. (1995). Agreement among judges of personality: Interpersonal relations, similarity and acquaintanceship. *Journal of Personality and Social Psychology, 69,* 656–672.

Gamson, J. (1994). *Claims to fame: Celebrity in contemporary America*. Berkeley: University of California Press.

Gaskell, G. (2001). Attitudes, social representations and beyond. In K. Deaux & G. Philogene (Eds.), *Representations of the social: Bridging theoretical traditions* (pp. 228–241). Oxford, UK: Blackwell.

George, A. I., & George, J. L. (1956). *Woodrow Wilson and Colonel House: A personality study*. New York: John Day.

George, J. L., & George, A. I. (1981–1982). Woodrow Wilson and Colonel House: A reply to Weinstein, Anderson, & Link. *Political Science Quarterly, 96,* 641–664.

Giovagnoli, M., & Carter-Miller, J. (2000). *Networlding: Building relationships and opportunities for success*. San Francisco: Jossey-Bass.

Goffman, E. (1967). *Interaction ritual*. Garden City, NY: Doubleday.

Goode, W. J. (1978). *The celebration of heroes: Prestige as a social control system*. Berkeley: University of California Press.

Goodman, R. F., & Ben-Ze'ev, A. (1994). *Good gossip*. Lawrence: University Press of Kansas.

Gormly, J. (1984). Correspondence between personality trait ratings and behavioral events. *Journal of Personality, 52,* 220–232.

Gould, S. J. (1995). Cordelia's dilemma. In S. J. Gould, *Dinosaur in a haystack. Reflections in natural history* (pp. 123–132). New York: Harmony Books.

Granovetter, M. (1973). The strength of weak ties. *American Journal of Sociology, 78,* 1360–1380.

Granovetter, M. (1974). *Getting a job: A study of contacts and careers.* Cambridge, MA: Harvard University Press.

Gross, K. (2001). *Shakespeare's noise.* Chicago: University of Chicago Press.

Guervich, M. (1961). *The social structure of acquaintanceship networks.* Cambridge, MA: MIT Press.

Habegger, A. (1994). *The father, a biography of Henry James, Sr.* New York: Farrar, Straus and Giroux.

Hamilton, I. (1992). *Keepers of the flame: Literary estates and the rise of biography.* London: Hutchinson.

Hammond, N. G. L. (1980). *Alexander the Great: King, commander and statesman.* Park Ridge, NJ: Noyes Press.

Hampshire, S. (1953). Dispositions. *Analysis, 14,* 3–11.

Hampson, S. E. (1988). *The construction of personality: An introduction,* 3rd ed. London: Routledge.

Hampson, S. E., Goldberg, L. R., & John, O. P. (1987). Category-breadth and social-desirability values for 573 personality terms. *European Journal of Personality, 1,* 241–258.

Hartshorne, H., & May, M. A. (1928). *Studies in the nature of character: Vol. 1. Studies in deceit.* New York: Macmillan.

Hartshorne, H., & May, M. A. (1929). *Studies in the nature of character: Vol. 2. Studies in service and self control.* New York: Macmillan.

Hartshorne, H., May, M. A., & Shuttleworth, F. K. (1930). *Studies in the nature of character: Vol. 3. Studies in the organization of character.* New York: Macmillan.

Heinsohn, R., & Packer, C. (1995). Complex cooperative strategies in group-territorial African lions. *Science, 269,* 1260–1262.

Helmholz, R. H. (1985). *Select cases of defamation to 1600.* London: Selden Society.

Historical Figures Assessment Collaborative. (1977). Assessing historical figures: The use of observer-based personality descriptions. *Historical Methods Newsletter, 10,* 566–576.

Hogan, R. (1982). A socioanalytic theory of personality. In *Nebraska symposium on motivation* (Vol. 30). Lincoln: University of Nebraska Press, pp. 55–89.

Hogan, R. (1996). A socioanalytic perspective on the five-factor model. In J. S. Wiggins (Ed.), *The five-factor model of personality* (pp. 163–179). New York: Guilford Press.

Hogan, R., & Roberts, B. W. (2000). A socioanalytic perspective on person–environment interactions. In W. B. Walsh, K. H. Craik, & R. H. Price (Eds.), *Person–environment psychology: New directions and perspectives* (2nd ed., pp. 1–25). Mahwah, NJ: Erlbaum.

Holmes, R. (1993). *Dr. Johnson and Mr. Savage.* London: Hodder & Stoughton.

Hooper, D. (1984). *Public scandal, odium and contempt: An investigation of recent libel cases.* London: Secker & Warburg.

Hooper, D. (2000). *Reputations under fire: Winners and losers in the libel business.* New York: Little, Brown.

Hopkins, N. (2002, November 5). Detectives exhaust leads in Suzy Lamplugh inquiry. *The Guardian.* Retrieved June 18, 2008 from www.guardian.co.uk./uk/l2002/nov/05/ukcime.nickhopkins.

James, W. (1983). *The principles of psychology* (Vol. 1). Cambridge, MA: Harvard University Press. (Original work published 1890)

John, O. P. (1990). The "Big Five" factor taxonomy: Dimensions of personality in the natural language and in questionnaires. In L. A. Pervin (Ed.), *Handbook of personality: Theory and research* (pp. 66–100). New York: Guilford Press.

John, O. P., & Robins, R. W. (1993). Determinants of inter-judge agreement on personality traits: The Big Five domain, evaluativeness, observability, and the unique perspective of the self. *Journal of Personality 61,* 521–551.

John, O. P., & Srivastava, S. (1999). The Big Five trait taxonomy: History, measurement and theoretical perspectives. In L. A. Pervin & O. P. John (Eds.), *Handbook of personality theory and research* (pp. 102–138). New York: Guilford Press.

Johnson, M. (2006) *The dead beat: Lost souls, lucky stiffs, and the perverse pleasures of obituaries.* New York: HarperCollins.

Jones, E. S. (1944). Subjective evaluations of personality. In J. M. Hunt (Ed.), *Personality and the behavior disorders* (Vol. 1, pp. 139–169). New York: Ronald Press.

Joyce, J. (1961). *Ulysses.* New York: Random House. (Original work published 1922)

Kaplan, M. L. (1997). *The culture of slander in early modern England.* Cambridge, UK: Cambridge University Press.

Katz, L. (1997). *Bad acts and guilty minds: Conundrums of the criminal law.* Chicago: University of Chicago Press.

Kelso, P. (2001, December 12). Critic costs *Mirror* £170,000 for review of the worst play he'd never seen. *Guardian.* Retrieved November 13, 2007 from www.guardian.co.uk/Archive/Article/0,4273,4318090,00.html.

Kenny, D. A. (1994). *Interpersonal perception: A social relations analysis.* New York: Guilford Press.

Killworth, P. D., & Bernard, H. R. (1978). The reverse small world experiment. *Social Networks, 1,* 158–192.

Killworth, P. D., Johnsen, E. C., Bernard, H. R., Shelley, G. A., & McCarty, C. (1990). Estimating the size of personal networks. *Social Networks, 12,* 289–312.

Kinzer, S. (2002, August 1, p. 16). Mount Vernon, theme park on the Potomac. *International Herald Tribune.*

Klein, D. B. (Ed.) (1997). *Reputation: Studies in the voluntary elicitation of good conduct.* Ann Arbor, MI: University of Michigan Press.

Kleinberg, J. (2000). Navigation in a small world. *Nature, 406,* 845.

Kleinfeld, J. S. (2002). The small world problem. *Society, 39,* 61–66.

Kochen, M. (Ed.). (1989). *The small world.* Norwood, NJ: Ablex.

Korte, C., & Milgram, S. (1970). Acquaintanceship networks between racial groups: Application of the small world method. *Journal of Personality and Social Psychology, 15,* 101–108.

Kundera, M. (2006, October 9) What is a novelist? *The New Yorker, 82,* 40–45.

Lang, F. R. (2000). Endings and continuity of social relationships: Maximizing intrinsic benefits within personal networks when feeling near to death. *Journal of Social and Personal Relationships, 17,* 155–182.

Lawyer's libel damages over chocolate cake. (1988, October 22, p. 3). *Times of London.*

Lewis, R. W. B. (1991). *The Jameses: A family narrative.* New York: Farrar, Straus and Giroux.

Little, R. B., Salmela-Aro, K., & Phillips, S. D. (Eds.). (2006). *Personal project pursuits: Goals, action, and human flourishing.* Mahwah, NJ: Erlbaum.

Loewenberg, P. (1983). *Decoding the past: The psychohistorical approach.* New York: Knopf.

London, M. (1993). The "muzzled media": Constitutional crisis or product liability scam? In M. London & B. Dill (Eds.), *At what price? Libel law and freedom of the press* (pp. 1–31). New York: Twentieth Century Fund Press.

Logli, M. (2006). *Personal reputation in social groups: Content, structure and dynamics.* Unpublished PhD dissertation, University of California at Berkeley.

Longman, J. (2006, July 10). A star falters, France fades, Italy rejoices. *New York Times,* pp. D1, D7.

Longmore, P. K. (1988). *The invention of George Washington.* Berkeley: University of California Press.

Lorenz, L. (1943). *John Paul Jones: Fighter for freedom and glory.* Annapolis, MD: United States Naval Institute.

Lowenthal, D. (1985). *The past is a foreign country.* Cambridge, UK: Cambridge University Press.

Lowenthal, D. (1996). *Possessed by the past: The heritage crusade and the spoils of history.* New York: Free Press.

Lubin, A. J. (1972). *Stranger on the earth: A psychological biography of Vincent Van Gogh.* New York: Holt, Rinehart and Winston.

Lupfer, M. B., Weeks, M., & Dupuis, S. (2000). How pervasive is the negativity bias in judgments based upon character appraisals? *Personality and Social Psychology Bulletin, 26,* 1353–1366.

Lyman, S. M. (1979). *The seven deadly sins: Society and evil.* New York: St. Martin's Press.

Malloy, T. E., & Albright, L. (1990). Interpersonal perception in a social context. *Journal of Personality and Social Psychology, 58,* 419–428.

Marconi, J. (2001). *Reputation marketing: Building and sustaining your organization's greatest asset.* New York: McGraw-Hill.

Markert, L. W. (Ed.). (1990). *The Bloomsbury group: A reference guide.* Boston: G. K. Hall.

Marsden, P. V. (2005). Recent developments in network measurement. In P. J. Carrington, J. Scott, & S. Wasserman (Eds.), *Models and methods in social network analysis* (pp. 8–30). Cambridge, UK: Cambridge University Press.

Mascuch, M. (1996). *Origins of the individualist self: Autobiography and self-identity in England, 1591–1791.* Stanford, CA: Stanford University Press.

May, M. A. (1929). The adult in the community. In C. Murchinson (Ed.), *Foundation of experimental psychology* (pp. 738–785). Worcester, MA: Clark University Press.

May, M. A. (1932a). Problems in measuring character and personality. *Journal of Social Psychology, 3,* 131–143.

May, M. A. (1932b). The foundations of personality. In P. S. Achilles (Ed.), *Psychology at work* (pp. 81–101). New York: McGraw-Hill.

Mayer, J. D. (1998). A systems framework for the field of personality. *Psychological Inquiry, 9,* 118–144.

McAdams, D. P. (1993). *The stories we live by: Personal myths and the making of the self.* New York: William Morrow.

McCarty, C., Killworth, P. D., Bernard, H. R., Johnsen, E. C., & Shelley, G. A. (2001). Comparing two methods for estimating network size. *Human Organization, 60,* 28–39.

McCrae, R. R. (1994). The counterpoint of personality assessment: Self-reports and observer ratings. *Psychological Assessment, 1,* 159–172.

McCrae, R. R., & Costa, P. T., Jr. (1995). Trait explanations in personality psychology. *European Journal of Personality, 9,* 231–252.

McCrae, R. R., & Costa, P. T., Jr. (1996). Toward a new generation of personality theories: Theoretical contexts for the five-factor model. In J. S. Wiggins (Ed.), *The five-factor model of personality: Theoretical perspectives* (pp. 51–87). New York: Guilford Press.

McCrae, R. R., & Costa, P. T., Jr. (1999). A five-factor theory of personality. In L. A. Pervin & O. P. John (Eds.), *Handbook of personality: Theory and research* (pp. 139–153). New York: Guilford Press.

McCrae, R. R., & Weiss, A. (2008). Observer ratings of personality. In R. W. Robins, R. C. Fraley, & R. Kreuger (Eds.), *Handbook of research methods in personality psychology* (pp. 259–275). New York: Guilford Press.

McCue, F. (2002). Another view of the "small world." *Social Networks, 24,* 121–133.

McKinlay, A., Potter, J., & Wetherell, M. (1993). Discourse analysis and social representations. In G. M. Breakwell & D. V. Canter (Eds.), *Empirical approaches to social representations* (pp. 134–147). Oxford, UK: Clarendon Press.

Mead, G. H. (1934). *Mind, self, and society.* Chicago: University of Chicago Press.

Middlekauff, R. (1982). *The glorious cause: The American revolution,1763–1789.* New York: Oxford University Press.

Middleton, D., & Edwards, D. (Eds.). (1990). *Collective remembering.* Newbury Park, CA: Sage.

Milgram, S. (1967). The small world problem. *Psychology Today, 1,* 60–67.

Miller, D. R. (1983). Self, symptom, and social control. In T. R. Sarbin & K. E. Scheibe (Eds.), *Studies in social identity* (pp. 319–338). New York: Praeger.

Milmo, P., & Rogers, W. V. H. (1998). *Gatley on libel and slander* (9th ed.). London: Sweet & Maxwell.

Montaigne, M. (1960). On glory. In D. M. Frame (Trans.). *The essays of Montaigne* (Vol. II, pp. 323–337). New York: Doubleday. (Original work published 1578–1580)

Moore, S. M. (1993). *Act and crime: The philosophy of action and its implications for criminal law.* Oxford, UK: Clarendon Press.

Morison, S. E. (1939). *John Paul Jones: A sailor's biography.* Boston: Little, Brown.

Moscovici, S. (1984a). The myth of the lonely paradigm: A rejoinder. *Social Research, 51,* 939–967.

Moscovici, S. (1984b). The phenomenon of social representations. In R. M. Farr & S. Moscovici (Eds.), *Social representations* (pp. 3–69). Cambridge, UK: Cambridge University Press.

Mowrer, O. H., & Kluckhohn, C. (1944). Dynamic theory of personality. In J. M. Hunt (Ed.), *Personality and the behavior disorders: A handbook based on experimental and clinical research* (Vol. 1, pp. 69–135). New York: Ronald Press.

Murumba, S. K. (1986). *Commercial exploitation of personality.* London: Sweet and Maxwell.

Newman, M. E. J. (2003). Ego-centered networks and the ripple effect. *Social Networks, 25,* 83–95.

Nicolson, H. (1928). *The development of English biography.* London: Hogarth Press.

Nock, S. L. (1993). *The costs of privacy: Surveillance and reputation in America.* New York: Aldine de Gruyter.

Novick, P. (1988). *That noble dream: The "Objectivity question" and the American historical profession.* Cambridge, UK: Cambridge University Press.

Nowak, M. A., & Sigmund, K. (2005). Evolution of indirect reciprocity. *Nature, 437,* 1291–1298.

Office of Independent Counsel (1997). Report on the Death of Vicent W. Foster, Jr.: State of Mind. Retrieved September 7, 2007 from www.washingtonpost.com/wp-srv/politics/special/whitewater/docs/fosterix.htm.

O'Harrow, R., Jr. (2005). *No place to hide.* New York: Free Press.

Ohtsuki, H., & Iwasa, Y. (2004). How should we define goodness? Reputation dynamics in indirect reciprocity. *Journal of Theoretical Biology, 231,* 107–120.

Ozer, D. J. (1986). *Consistency in personality: A methodological framework.* New York: Springer-Verlag.

Peabody, D. (1984). Personality dimensions through trait inferences. *Journal of Personality and Social Psychology, 46,* 384–403.

Petersen, P. G. (1965). *Reliability of judgments of personality as a function of subjects and traits being judged.* Unpublished PhD dissertation, University of California at Berkeley.

Pollock, G. B., & Dugatkin, L. A. (1992). Reciprocity and the evolution of reputation. *Journal of Theoretical Biology, 159,* 25–37.

Pompa, L. (1990). Historical consciousness and historical knowledge. In L. Pompa (Ed.), *Human nature and historical knowledge: Hume, Hegel and Vico* (pp. 192–225). Cambridge, UK: Cambridge University Press.

Pool, I. de Sola, & Kochen, M. (1978). Contacts and influence. *Social Networks, 1,* 1–51.

Post, R. C. (1986). The social foundations of defamation law: Reputation and the Constitution. *California Law Review, 74,* 691–742.

Post, R. C. (1990). The constitutional concept of public discourse: Outrageous opinion, democratic deliberation and *Hustler Magazine* v. Falwell. *Harvard Law Review, 103,* 601–686.

Post, R. C. (1994). The legal regulation of gossip: Backyard chatter and the mass media. In R. Goodman & A. Ben-Ze'ev (Eds.), *Good gossip* (pp. 65–71). Lawrence: University Press of Kansas.

Powell, A. (1951–1975). *A dance to the music of time.* London: Heinemann.

Prince, H. (1978). Time and historical geography. In T. Carlstein, D. Parkes, & N. Thrift (Eds.), *Making sense of time* (pp. 17–37). New York: Wiley.

Rein, I., Kotler, P., & Stoller, M. (1997). *High visibility: The making and marketing of professionals into celebrities.* Chicago: NTC Business Books.

Roberts, B. (2002). *Biographical research.* Philadelphia: Open University Press.

Rojek, C. (2001). *Celebrity.* London: Reaktion Books.

Rommetveit, R. (1980). On "meanings" of acts and what is meant and made known by what is said in a pluralistic social world. In M. Brenner (Ed.), *The structure of action* (pp. 108–149). New York: St. Martin's Press.

Rosenbaum, S. P. (Ed.). (1995). *The Bloomsbury group: A collection of memoirs and commentary.* Toronto, Canada: University of Toronto Press.

Rothbart, M., & Park, B. (1986). On the confirmability and disconfirmability of trait concepts. *Journal of Personality and Social Psychology, 50,* 131–142.

Rubenzer, S. J., & Ones, D. S. (2000). Assessing the U. S. Presidents using the revised NEO Personality Inventory. *Assessment, 7,* 403–419.

Rubin, D. C. (Ed.). (1988). *Autobiographical memory.* Cambridge, UK: Cambridge University Press.

Runyan, W. M. (1981). Why did Van Gogh cut off his ear? The problem of alternative explanations in psychobiography. *Journal of Personality and Social Psychology, 40,* 1070–1077.

Runyan, W. M. (1982). *Life stories and psychobiography: Explorations in theory and method.* New York: Oxford University Press.

Runyan, W. M. (1988). Progress in psychobiography. *Journal of Personality, 56,* 295–326.

Russell, J. A., & Snodgrass, J. (1987). Emotion and the environment. In D. Stokols & I. Altman (Eds.), *Handbook of environmental psychology* (Vol. 1, pp. 245–280). New York: Wiley.

Sack, R. D., & Baron, S. S. (1994). *Libel, slander and related problems* (2nd ed.). New York: Practicing Law Institute.

Salvesen, M., & Cousineau, D. (Eds.). (2005). *Artists' estates: Reputations in trust.* New Brunswick, NJ: Rutgers University Press.

Sanford, R. N. (1963). Personality: Its place in psychology. In. S. Koch (Ed.), *Psychology: A study of a science* (Vol. 6, pp. 488–592). New York: McGraw-Hill.

Sarbin, T. R., & Scheibe, K. E. (Eds.). (1983). *Studies in social identity.* New York: Praeger.

Saucier, G., & Goldberg, L. R. (1998). What is beyond the Big Five? *Journal of Personality, 66,* 496–524.

Schickel, R. (1985). *Intimate strangers: The culture of celebrity.* Garden City, NY: Doubleday.

Schimmel, S. (1992). *The seven deadly sins: Jewish, Christian and classical reflections on human nature.* New York: Free Press.

Schwartz, B. (1987). *George Washington: The making of an American symbol.* New York: Free Press.

Semin, G. R., & Manstead, A. S. R. (1983). *The accountability of conduct: A social psychological analysis.* New York: Academic Press.

Simonton, D. K. (1991). Latent-variable models of posthumous reputation: A quest for Galton's G. *Journal of Personality and Social Psychology, 60,* 607–619.

Shopshire, M. S., & Craik, K. H. (1996). An act-based conceptual analysis of obsessive–compulsive, paranoid and histrionic personality disorders. *Journal of Personality Disorders, 10,* 203–218.

Siegel, M. (Ed.). (1997). *The last word: The* New York Times *book of obituaries and farewells, a celebration of unusual lives.* New York: William Morrow.

Skowronski, J. J., & Carlston, D. E. (1989). Negativity and extremity bias in impression formation: A review of explanations. *Psychological Bulletin, 105,* 131–142.

Skowronski, J. J., & Carlston, D. E. (1992). Caught in the act: When traits formed on the basis of highly diagnostic behaviors are resistant to contradiction. *European Journal of Social Psychology, 22,* 435–452.

Smelser, N. J., & Smelser, W. T. (1964). Analyzing personality and social systems. In N. J. Smelser & W. T. Smelser (Eds.), *Personality and social systems* (pp. 1–18). New York: Wiley.

Smith, A. (1997). Lecture on the influence of commerce on manners. In D. B. Klein (Ed.), *Reputation: Studies in the voluntary elicitation of good conduct* (pp. 17–20). Ann Arbor: University of Michigan Press. (Original work published 1766)

Solomon, D. (2007, April 1). The mind reader: Questions for Douglas Hofstadter. *New York Times Magazine,* 17.

Solove, D. J. (2007). *The future of reputation: Gossip, rumor, and privacy on the Internet.* New Haven, CT: Yale University Press.

Song, A., & V. Simonton, D. K. (2007). Personality assessment at a distance. In R. W. Robins, R. C. Fraley, & R. Krueger (Eds.), *Handbook of research methods in personality psychology* (pp. 308–321). New York: Guilford Press.

Spurling, H. (1977). *Handbook to Anthony Powell's Dance to the Music of Time.* London: Heinemann.

Stagner, R. (1937). *Psychology of personality.* New York: McGraw-Hill.

Stephen, A. (1988). *The Suzy Lamplugh story.* London: Faber and Faber.

Strouse, J. (1978). Semiprivate lives. In D. Aaron (Ed.), *Studies in biography* (pp. 113–130). Cambridge, MA: Harvard University Press.

Strouse, J. (1988a). *Alice James, a biography.* Boston: Houghton Mifflin.

Strouse, J. (1988b). Alice James: A family romance. In W. M. Runyan (Ed.), *Psychology and historical interpretation* (pp. 86–103). New York: Oxford University Press.

Suitor, J. J., Wellman, B., & Morgan, D. L. (1997). It's about time: How, why, and when networks change. *Social Networks, 19,* 1–7.

Tausch, N., Kenworthy, J. B., & Hewstone, M. (2007). The confirmability and disconfirmability of trait concepts revisited: Does content matter? *Journal of Personality and Social Psychology, 92,* 542–556.

Tellegen, A. (1991). Personality traits: Issues of definition, evidence, and assessment. In D. Cicchetti & W. Grove (Eds.), *Thinking clearly about psychology: Essays in honor of Paul Everett Meehl* (Vol. 2, pp. 10–35). Minneapolis: University of Minnesota Press.

Thomas, E. (2003). *John Paul Jones: Sailor, hero, father of the American navy.* New York: Simon & Schuster.

Travers, J., & Milgram, S. (1969). An experimental study of the small world problem. *Sociometry, 32,* 425–443.

Troxell, H. A. (1997). *Studies in the Macedonian coinage of Alexander the Great.* New York: American Numismatic Society.

Tsui, S. A. (1984). A role set analysis of reputation. *Organizational Behavior and Human Performance, 34,* 64–96.

Tucker, R. C. (1988). A Stalin biographer's memoir. In W. M. Runyan (Ed.), *Psychology and historical interpretation* (pp. 63–81). New York: Oxford University Press.

Turner, J. C., & Onorato, R. S. (1999). Social identity, personality, and the self-concept: A self-categorization perspective. In T. R. Tyler, R. M. Kramer, & O. P. John (Eds.), *The psychology of the social self* (pp. 11–46). Mahwah, NJ: Erlbaum.

Tyler, R. M. (1999). What does studying the psychology of the social self have to offer to psychologists? In T. R. Tyler, R. M. Kramer, & O. P. John (Eds.), *The psychology of the social self* (pp. 1–10). Mahwah, NJ: Erlbaum.

U.S. Senate Committee on Governmental Affairs (1985). *Federal government security clearance programs.* Washington, DC: U.S. Government Printing Office.

van der Poel, M. (1993). *Personal networks: A rational-choice explanation of their size and composition.* Lisse, Netherlands: Swets and Zeitlinger.

Vazire, S. (2006). Informant reports: A cheap, fast, and easy method for personality assessment. *Journal of Research in Personality, 40,* 472–481.

Vernon, P. E. (1933). The biosocial nature of the personality trait. *Psychological Review, 40,* 533–548.

Watts, D. J. (2003). *Six degrees: The science of a connected age.* New York: W. W. Norton.

Watts, D. J., & Strogatz, S. H. (1998). Collective dynamics of "small-world" networks. *Nature, 393,* 440–442.

Webber, M. M. (1970). Order in diversity: Community without propinquity. In R. Gutman & D. Popenoe (Eds.), *Neighborhood, city and metropolis* (pp. 792–818). New York: Random House.

Webster's New Universal Unabridged Dictionary (2nd ed.). (1983). New York: Simon and Schuster.

Weinstein, E. A., Anderson, J. W., & Link, A. S. (1978–1979). Woodrow Wilson's political personality. *Political Science Quarterly, 93,* 586–594.

Weinstein, S. (1992). *Telling the untold story: How investigative reporters are changing the craft of biography.* Columbia: University of Missouri Press.

Wellman, B., Carrington, P. J., & Hall, A. (1988). Networks as personal communities. In B. Wellman & S. D. Berkowitz (Eds.), *Social structures: A network approach* (pp. 130–184). Cambridge, UK: Cambridge University Press.

Westacott, E. (2000). The ethics of gossiping. *International Journal of Applied Philosophy, 14,* 65–90.

Westie, F. R. (1973). Academic expectations for professional immortality: A study of legitimation. *American Sociologist, 8,* 19–32.

Whitmeyer, J. M. (2000). Effects of positive reputation systems. *Social Science Research, 29,* 188–207.

Wicker, A. W. (1992). Making sense of environments. In W. B. Walsh, K. H. Craik, & R. H. Price (Eds.), *Person–environment psychology: Models and perspectives* (pp. 157–192). Hillsdale, NJ: Erlbaum.

Wickham, C. (2003). *Fama* and the law of twelfth-century Tuscany. In T. Fenster & D. L. Small (Eds.), *Fama: The politics of talk and reputation in medieval Europe* (pp. 15–27). Ithaca, NY: Cornell University Press.

Wiggins, J. S. (1997). In defense of traits. In R. Hogan, J. Johnson, & S. Briggs (Eds.), *Handbook of personality psychology* (pp. 95–115). San Diego, CA: Academic Press.

Wineburg, S. S. (1991). Historical problem solving. A study of the cognitive process used in the evaluation of documentary and historical evidence. *Journal of Educational Psychology, 83,* 73–87.

Wood, G. S. (2006). *Revolutionary characters: What made the founders different.* New York: Penguin Press.

Woolf, V. (1940). *Roger Fry, a biography.* New York: Harcourt, Brace.

Wyer, R. S., & Carlston, D. R. (1994). The cognitive representation of persons and events. In R. S. Wyer & T. K. Srull (Eds.), *Handbook of social cognition* (Vol. 1, 2nd ed., pp. 41–98). Hillsdale, NJ: Erlbaum.

Wyer, R. S., & Gordon, S. E. (1984) The cognitive representation of social information. In R. S. Wyer & T. K. Srull (Eds.), *Handbook of social cognition* (Vol. 2, pp. 73–150). Hillsdale, NJ: Erlbaum.

Wyer, R. S. & Srull, T. K. (1980). The processing of social stimulus information: A conceptual integration. In R. Hastie, T. Ostrom, E. Ebbesen, R. Wyer, Jr. D. Hamilton, & D. Carlston (Eds.). *Person memory: The cognitive basis of social perception* (pp. 227–295. Hillsdale, NJ: Earlbaum.

Young, R. C. (2001). *There is nothing idle about it: Deference and dominance in gossip as a function of role, personality and social context.* Unpublished PhD dissertation, University of California at Berkeley.

Young, S. M., & Pinsky, D. (2006). Narcissism and celebrity. *Journal of Research in Personality, 40,* 463–464.

Index